Born in Carshalton, Surrey, Kevin spent his childhood in Bath, Somerset. He attended the City of Bath Grammar School, then moved to Isleworth in Middlesex to study at Borough Road Teacher Training College. He and his wife, Lindsey, settled in Hounslow, where they brought up their two daughters, Keeley and Lucy. He taught for thirty-eight years in two local boys' secondary schools.

This book is dedicated to my mother, Brenda Annette Hall, who instilled in me the virtue of patience when completing any task. I also wish to include a dedication to the most recent family addition, Ryder Hall Stroud, a second gift of a grandson.

Kevin Michael Hall

CLASS ACT

Dear Julie,

With happy memories of our stay at your lovely guest house.

Kevin x

AUSTIN MACAULEY PUBLISHERS™
LONDON * CAMBRIDGE * NEW YORK * SHARJAH

Copyright © Kevin Michael Hall (2021)

The right of Kevin Michael Hall to be identified as author of this work has been asserted by the author in accordance with section 77 and 78 of the Copyright, Designs and Patents Act 1988.

All rights reserved. No part of this publication may be reproduced, stored in a retrieval system or transmitted in any form or by any means, electronic, mechanical, photocopying, recording or otherwise, without the prior permission of the publishers.

Any person who commits any unauthorised act in relation to this publication may be liable to criminal prosecution and civil claims for damages.

This is a work of fiction. Names, characters, businesses, places, events, locales, and incidents are either the products of the author's imagination or used in a fictitious manner. Any resemblance to actual persons, living or dead, or actual events is purely coincidental.

A CIP catalogue record for this title is available from the British Library.

ISBN 9781398402935 (Paperback)
ISBN 9781398402942 (Hardback)
ISBN 9781398401334 (ePub e-book)
ISBN 9781398402959 (Audiobook)

www.austinmacauley.com

First Published (2021)
Austin Macauley Publishers Ltd
25 Canada Square
Canary Wharf
London
E14 5LQ

Lin Evans was kind enough to read through the first draft of this book and offer invaluable support and advice. I am indebted to her for the plot development suggestions she offered, and recommendations she made for ensuring the novel's narrative flow.

Chapter 1

He was sure he couldn't teach his next class until he'd peed. Already a quarter of an hour late and unable to find a vacant staff WC anywhere in the school, he'd been forced to give up trying to find somewhere to empty his bladder and was rushing in panic through empty school corridors to get to his lesson. Motes of dust were clearly visible in the air as sunlight streamed through windows that ran the length of the corridor.

"No running in the corridors, sir!" a pupil prefect called out, as Biggsy blundered past him.

"Don't take the…" he began in reply but thought better of finishing it.

Rounding a bend at full tilt, he saw 9D lined up military style outside his classroom.

Thank God they're behaving themselves, at least, he thought, as he went to his jacket pocket for the key to Room 125.

"Ah, Mr Biggs. You've arrived."

The female voice betrayed the merest hint of gloating. It was the dreaded deputy head, Ms Toner, Mr Fingleton's enforcer. She was ten years his junior, but a few rungs ahead of him up the career ladder. He could tell she loathed him.

"There was a report of a group of boys making a noise in this corridor fifteen minutes after the start of lessons, so I came along to investigate. 9D tell me they have an English lesson with you. We've been awaiting your arrival."

"Sorry, Ms Toenail…er Toner! I was detained by a corridor incident I had to deal with," he lied.

"Really!"

The image of a huge ginger cat drooling over a dish of creamy milk flashed into his mind.

"We'd better get the boys into the classroom, don't you think, Mr Biggs?"

Why was it, he wondered, that whenever she said his surname aloud, she sounded as if she had a mouthful of meat gristle that needed to be spat out?

Fumbling with the lock, his mind raced. "This'll get back to Fingleton – more bad bloody press. Fingers'll have me in his office. She wants me out. But she's not getting rid of me. I'm ten of her. Ten! Ten! Ten!"

"Wake up, love! You've slept through the alarm. Get up! You'll be late for school!" Myra urged, trying hard to rouse herself as much as her husband.

"You're not getting me out," he mumbled dreamily.

"What are you on about? Sleep talking again. Come on – get up. It's school! A lovely INSET day," she urged, poking him in the kidney region.

"Get your hands off me!" he snarled.

His mind began to clear. He opened his eyes. Another nightmare – a great start to the day. Today of all days, the first of another year at St Saviour's.

Turning to complain at her continued prodding, her contorted face checked him and his good nature took over. He stretched out a consoling arm, but she shoved it away and pushed her legs out from under the duvet. She threw herself out of bed and made a smart dash for the door. All was not as it should be. Rolling to the edge of the bed, he lowered his feet into slippers.

A hint of sun behind the curtains encouraged him to open them. Ugly sounds from the loo suggested all was not well with his wife.

"Are you OK there in the lavvy, luvvy? Something got you on the hop?"

He poked his head around the toilet door.

"Those bloody sausages must have been on the turn. The floodgates have opened. I may be a while. Go and get Ella up," Myra bleated.

As an English teacher, he'd always been impressed by the precision and colour of his wife's expression, whatever the context.

"I don't understand my bowels," she complained. "One day I'm rock solid, the next I'm flowing."

He was late and had no time to labour the sympathy. Despite himself, his mind was working on a plot for a linked trilogy in the disaster movie genre.

Assuming his deep bass, high-testosterone, film-trailer-advertising voice, he went into full movie-promotion mode, "You marvelled at 'Constipation' and thrilled at 'Diarrhoea'. Prepare yourself for the final act of the trilogy – 'The Deluge'. Showing soon in surround-sound and glorious super-technicolour at a cinema near you!"

"You can get your own breakfast for that. I'm dying in here."

"Sorry, love. Didn't mean it. Anything I can do to help?"

"No, just wake up Ella and put the kettle on."

"Will do. But I need to get in there as well, love, before I do anything else."

He went to his daughter's bedroom and tapped on her door.

"Ella, time to get up. First day back and all that. Got to show willing."

Pushing open the door, he poked his head around and surveyed the scene. Clothes were piled on most of the surfaces – tights, underwear, blouses, jeans, jackets and T-shirts. He could still detect the smell of stale wine from the weekend sleepover. He wondered how three seventeen-year-old girls in one double bed had been able to get any sleep. Ella wasn't responding. The top of her head protruded from the duvet. Pulling the cover back gently, he tried to rouse her by brushing chestnut waves of hair from her face.

Hazel eyes appeared from behind turquoise eyelids.

"Morning, Dad. Yeah, I'm getting up," she murmured.

"Mum says to get a move on because we've overslept. You've only got to sign in for your courses this morning, then you'll have a free day after that."

"Just five more minutes and I'll be with you. OK, Dad?"

"Deal," he smiled.

Dancing his full-bladder jig as he waited outside the toilet, his nose twitched at an unwelcome odour.

"Not keen on the new air freshener," he called in.

"I'll have the last laugh if you get what I've got," Myra snapped. "You wouldn't last five minutes with this."

"You won't be laughing if I spoil this landing carpet. I need to get in there right now."

He filled the bathroom sink with hot water and picked up his razor. His mirror image seemed to be less lined after the summer break. Myra called to him from her fetid cubicle.

"You'll have to organise breakfast yourself. I'm otherwise engaged. I can't face food the way I'm feeling. I'll get myself off to work if I'm able and grab something to eat later, if and when I'm up to it. All right with you, Biggsy?"

Austin Tyrone Biggs preferred to be called 'Biggsy'. That was the name he went by in childhood on the housing estate, and he'd stuck with it. Occasionally, he heard his forename spoken aloud, as he had when Mr Fingleton had interviewed him for the post of Head of English at St Saviour's Secondary School for Boys.

"Good morning, Mr Biggs. May we call you Austin for the duration of the interview?"

I'd feel more comfortable with 'Biggsy', he'd thought.

"Certainly, Mr Fingleton."

Whenever his childhood mates had come knocking for a game of football at the park, the appellation 'Biggsy' had had a reassuring effect on his well-being. His world had Biggsy at the centre and all else rotated sequentially around it. He wasn't an arrogant, self-centred little snot, just little Biggsy, with a zest for life and a crooked grin.

"Come on, Biggsy! We need your football."

He decided against aftershave, went to the bedroom and took his trousers off the wardrobe rail. Myra rushed past him in a state of undress, tugging a hairbrush through tight, brown curls. He hurried into the little room she'd just vacated.

"I don't know if it's a good thing for me to be working at the hospital today if I've got the runs," she fussed. "Perhaps I ought to stay home."

He knew that she'd go in. She'd worked at the Middlesex County Hospital for eight years and rarely took time off. According to her, she was the mainstay of the medical office, where four of them typed up doctors' reports on patients. The department would grind to a halt if she didn't go in, resulting in a logjam of paperwork building up. He believed that his wife's medical knowledge was equal to, or better than, some of the doctors for whom she worked. She had an almost photographic memory and could reel off the correct medical terminology for any disorder or condition to which one might care to refer. If he were to fall ill with any ailment whatsoever, he had every confidence that she would know what it was and how to deal with it. She'd begun monitoring his diet recently in the certainty that his cholesterol was higher than it should be. Her conviction was that anybody with his penchant for sweet pastries couldn't survive much longer in this world.

"Are you serious? Everybody knows hospitals are full of germs. Any you've got are small fry compared with the stuff crawling the walls where you work."

"Ha ha. Very funny. On the subject of walls, you know damned well you'll be climbing them within a few days of getting back to the chalk face."

"Mmm. Hope you're wrong, but this summer's exam results did dip very slightly after last year's stratospheric success. Could have a few problems there when I front up at the results' review meeting."

"Can't be expected to be outstanding every year. That's not possible," Myra opined, adjusting the belt of her black trousers.

"Every department is expected to achieve year-on-year improvement. That means year after year after year."

"But what if the kids just aren't up to it one year? What are you supposed to do then?"

"We live in an age where every teacher is required to be adept at turning out silk purses, whatever the state of the sows' ears."

"Bloody nonsense! Look, I've got to be off. Just make sure Lady Fauntleroy is up and about by the time you leave. Bye."

She pulled on her jacket, grabbed her handbag off the dressing table, pecked her husband on the cheek, then hurried downstairs.

The front door slammed.

He listened but heard nothing from Ella's room. Picking up his mobile from the bedside cabinet, he dialled her number. Her ring tone sounded next door. He put the phone to his ear and waited.

"Thanks, Dad. I will get up this time."

******

The staff room was rocking with teachers more animated than was usually the case. Nervous and excited chatter, you-look-so-well compliments and hearty laughter assailed his ears. The PE lot were in their huddle, sprawled in easy chairs in the corner. Chris 'Doggy' Barker, the PE head, was surreptitiously eyeing two new young female members of staff. One of them was the latest English appointment, Angela Davies.

"Eyes off, Doggy," growled Biggsy under his breath.

Andy Orchard walked toward him, cradling a mug of tea and grinning broadly. He guessed exactly what was on the mind of his head of department.

"You'll have to get used to that, boss. She's going to attract plenty of attention from that quarter. Well, here we are, back for another stretch."

"We are, indeed. Had a good break?"

"Most definitely. Mags and I rediscovered each other. Played a lot of golf too. Jenna's even showing an interest in the game. She wants to be as good as her mum."

"Toner's moved up in the world," Biggsy sniffed. "Just saw the sorceress pull up in her new accessory – a Scirocco. She's parked it in 'visitors'."

Andy moved to the window to see for himself. He grimaced, as he caught sight of the car.

"Must have made a large hole in the divorce settlement."

"Wish she'd made a large hole in the school and moved on. I reckon even I'll be leaving before she does. She must have gone to half a dozen headship interviews last term and didn't crack one."

"You two look as though you need a holiday."

Sarah Clifton eased her way through the staff room press toward her colleagues. She was a welcome sight. At thirty-six years of age and married with a ten-year-old son, she was a highly regarded member of the English team with two strings to her professional bow. She not only excelled within the department, but the management team also considered her to be the best year head in the school.

"Hi, Sarah!" Andy beamed. "God, where's your lovely hair gone? Is that called a bob?"

"Sorry, Andy. You'll have to fantasise about somebody else from now on. This year, I'm changing my image. No more Mrs Nice Gal! I'm gearing up for some careering up."

"What does that mean?" Biggsy grinned, trying to conceal his anxiety.

"I'm bitching up for a shot at the head of sixth form job. Wheely's retiring, as you well know."

Wheely, Dave Wheelhouse, had been angling to retire for the past eighteen months, but the head had persuaded him to hang on. It was true his pension and lump sum would be boosted by extending his stay, but the main reason for delaying his retirement was that he was unable to resist Fingleton's powers of persuasion.

"You'll walk it, Sarah. The bad news is that you'll then be snowed under with all that UCAS shit, but at least you'll still be in the department."

"Don't get grumpy. There's a whole term at least between then and now. I'll still be yours in spirit even if Fingers gives me the job."

"We'd better get off to the staff meeting, guys. It's a quarter to," prompted Andy.

******

'Scrumpy' Bulmer, the caretaker, was finishing the job of arranging chairs in an arc of two rows in front of the lectern, where Mr Fingleton was waiting for the staff to assemble. Biggsy smiled at the caretaker as he, Andy and Sarah occupied seats in the middle of the second row. Bulmer forced the hint of a gap in his facial stubble in reply. He had made no special back-to-school effort to improve his dowdy appearance. He was still kitted out in unlaced black DMs and the emerald green fleece he wore every day of the school year in snow, rain and blistering heat.

"Scrumpy must have been on a six-week bender from the look of him," Andy whispered.

"It'll end in beers," said Sarah, with a look of doom.

The head teacher, standing erect in crumpled grey suit, put his hands together and raised them in open-fingered prayer before his mouth. He closed his eyes and inhaled deeply. Biggsy studied the unusually long digits and smiled. He must enjoy going through this routine to live up to his nickname. What a card! Mr Fingleton was old school and proud of it. He'd seen it all in the teaching game, done it all, and nothing seemed to disturb the aura of calm he projected.

To the left of the lectern sat Deputy Head Pastoral, Archie Matthews, and to the right Deputy Head Curriculum, Ms Toner, right leg crossed over her left. New shoes for the start of term? Biggsy wondered if she bought bulk consignments of black patent court shoes. They always seemed immaculate. He looked down at his black loafers. They needed a polish.

The last few members of staff arrived, hurriedly searching for empty seats. Mr Fingleton ahemed loudly, then began welcoming everyone to the start of a new school year for the twenty-third time.

"Welcome back to what I'm sure will be another highly successful year for St Saviour's. Before you all go off to spend the day on forward planning initiatives with your departments, I'd like to start our first day back on several positive notes. First, I am pleased to announce that our GCSE and A-level results once again compare favourably with the other secondary schools within the borough…"

Biggsy was looking forward to having a full day with his team, refreshed after the exceptional summer weather. He never felt a shred of guilt about the teachers' six-week break. Those who had never tried teaching couldn't begin to know the levels of mental, physical and psychological exhaustion he daily experienced. He hoped that Angela would have a rejuvenating effect on everybody, and that she would pick up on the unique ethos of his department: the commitment to children outweighing that to the onerous administrative burden. People before paper. She'd struck him as being a pocket dynamo at interview. The only drawback of the day was that he would have to spend this evening typing up a detailed report of the proceedings for Ms Toner.

He looked up from his reverie to see her nodding her appreciation at Fingleton as she stood up to take her turn at the lectern. She smiled at the ceiling, inhaled deeply and began speaking in her rapid-fire delivery.

"Welcome back, everyone. I'll get straight down to business. As Mr Fingleton has already informed you, the examination results were generally pleasing, particularly at A-level. We had forty-five per cent…"

He rummaged through his pockets to find his mobile phone and switched it to silent. He imagined the possibility of being able to switch Toner permanently to silent.

******

An hour later, he made sure he was the first to Room 125 so that he'd have time to rearrange the tables and put out biscuits. He looked at the whiteboard and saw 'Thursday, September 2, 2010' that he had written six weeks earlier, the reminder to his sixth form tutor group of their first day of the autumn term. Time had stood still in this room.

Although he had reservations about starting yet another school year at St Saviour's, he was looking forward to seeing his colleagues and students again. The bright spot would be introducing Angela.

Andy was the first to arrive.

"A pity Nick's results didn't quite do the business, mate," he murmured in an undertone to Biggsy, as he examined the food offerings. "Oh, well done – choccy biccies!"

"They were pretty good, considering some of the personalities he had to deal with. There were a few 'characters' in his group, and he didn't have the easiest of times with them."

Before he'd finished speaking, Nick Devlin and Hazel Frears arrived. Both in their late twenties, they had established themselves as capable and reliable members of staff. Hazel, exceptionally well-read and blessed with a photographic memory, was the staff liaison for the school library. Nick, burly enough to make a rugby front row, was waiting for a pastoral opportunity to come up in the school. He couldn't be faulted for his professional application. One had to respect the degree of success he'd achieved with the year eleven class, despite the behavioural issues of a minority.

Biggsy was protective of his staff, a quality that didn't always impress his line manager, Ms Toner. Fingleton had described her as 'a young and thrusting addition to the staff' when he'd appointed her six years earlier. Biggsy considered her the most ruthless careerist he'd ever come across in his twenty-eight years of teaching. 'Name and shame' was rumoured to be her favoured educational precept. He would support Nick to the hilt if the going got tough.

"He'll have no bother. I'll see to that. There are aspects of this job that I can't stand. When you take over from me, try not to let certain people get to you as much as they do me," he warned Andy.

"You reckon they'd risk me trying to do everything that you do. Bit of a long shot."

"You'll be fine, Andy. When I get the push, you'll be in."

"When hell freezes over. Nobody's ever gonna be pushing you out," Andy declared.

Sarah poked her head around the door.

"If I'm too early, have I got time to go and have a lie down in my room?" she asked coyly.

"Good idea, Sarah. We could cancel the meeting and do a spot of meditation instead," suggested Andy.

Angela arrived in company with Beth Simpson and Bridget Reynolds. The group's mood was jolly, and Biggsy wanted it to stay that way.

Blonde, tall and demure, Beth was a Cambridge graduate in her early thirties. Biggsy perceived her to be a total intellectual. He found it remarkable that he was her line manager. Single and carefree, she gave the impression of being content with her lot in life. He believed that someone of her quiet assurance and immense ability should be shunted straight into the leadership team, but she claimed to be uninterested in carving out a management career in education. Classroom teaching was all she desired. She was universally admired by male members of staff, but nobody, to date, had managed to breach her arm's length as far as developing a personal relationship was concerned.

Bridget, Beth's closest friend on the staff, was approaching her fortieth birthday. She wasn't one to pay undue attention to dressing fashionably, but she wore her heart on her sleeve. Spontaneous and extrovert, she was the secretary of the staff association and the school's NUT representative. In these twin capacities, she regularly found herself counselling and comforting those at risk of falling by the teaching wayside.

"Hi, guys! Take a seat, a biccy and relax. This is a school safe zone, but don't tell anyone else on the staff or they'll all be turning up here."

No sooner had he said these words than the school secretary arrived in a breathless state. Brushing strands of blonde hair from her eyes, Anna apologised for the interruption.

"So sorry, Mr Biggs, but Ms Toner asked if you could include this item on your meeting agenda? Sorry, it's late. Got to rush because I've five more to deliver."

He studied the sheet. Resisting the temptation to fulminate, he read aloud, "Sorry, it's last minute, but could you spend five minutes discussing the following topic with your department and report your findings to me ASAP in writing:

'Explore opportunities for introducing topics related to the world of work into the English faculty's schemes of work.'

We're expected to do this in five minutes!"

******

He pushed the Radio 4 preset on the car radio. An earnest male informed him of the need for awareness to be raised on a pressing matter of the day. He reached out and switched to Radio 3. His awareness antenna had been preternaturally raised throughout his twenties and thirties but, since hitting fifty, he'd found himself restricting its use. From his experience, those with bees in their bonnets, hectoring the public on specific matters, were just as likely to avoid as many others as possible. Much as he may once have desired to be at the forefront of the latest ecological, educational, financial, moral, philosophical, political, and social initiatives when he was a young man, his mind was now suffering from awareness overload.

He believed the phenomenon to be age-related, from two perspectives. First, the older one becomes, the less one wishes to have one's thinking constantly reshaped by 'experts' in the burgeoning list of fields that constitute every walk of human life. Second, in ages past, long before the clever people became slaves to online social networking, life had been an altogether simpler awareness-raising-free business. He occasionally felt guilty about this impulse but had come to terms with this flaw in his personality. Getting to sleep at night was difficult enough these days. There was a part of him that envied his mother's pride at being computer illiterate. Debussy's 'Girl with the Flaxen Hair' tranquillised his mind in as pleasurable a manner as he could have wished on this second day back to school.

Coming to the end of his fifteen-minute drive from Twickenham into Hounslow, he spotted half a dozen sixth formers waiting for a bus at a stop along the London Road. This wouldn't have been unusual, if it weren't for the fact that there was only one more stop on the school route, a mere three hundred yards from this one. Rather than walk that short distance, inveterate laggards were accustomed to adopting this devious strategy. It enabled them to provide the ready response 'Had to wait for the bus!' when asked to explain their lateness. They wouldn't, of course, mention that they'd been waiting twenty minutes at a stop less than a quarter of a mile from the school.

With the staggered return of students at the start of term, only sixth formers and year seven students were required to be in school on Thursday, the second day. This year, there would be the unique situation of the whole school returning on a Friday, the final day of the week. Whoever had devised this year's school calendar, he decided, needed medication.

The roads around the school were jammed with traffic. Anxious parents were treating apprehensive sons to a first-day car journey. The young lambs would soon experience a rude awakening when they found themselves jostling for positions at crowded bus stops. Easing through the congestion, he parked his old blue Golf in his favourite spot just under the window of the staff room kitchen area.

Bright new uniforms milled about at the school entrance. Groups of older boys looked on. *Back to school.* He'd seen that phrase in shop windows since the middle of July. Now the fateful day had arrived. He wouldn't describe himself as being afraid of the prospect of another year of professional baiting and back-stabbing at the hands of one particular member of the management team, but his dry cough had already returned. He'd once wondered if he'd succumbed to hay fever in middle age, but had subsequently decided that his was a terminal case of chronic cough syndrome. Myra's initial diagnosis was throat cancer and three weeks to live. However, after a more detailed examination, she concluded that he had a nervous cough induced by stress. He was forced to agree with her that his ailment was psychosomatic, and that he was something of a hypochondriac.

Most of the new boys shook off their parents outside the main gates, but a minority was happy for parents to accompany them up the drive to the main entrance. His eye was caught by one carrying an expensive briefcase, as opposed to the standard canvas rucksack. *A superb chestnut leather briefcase for a twelve-year-old,* he thought, *and I'm still making do with a PVC attaché and Tesco plastic bag.* He locked the car and made his way to the school entrance past the expensively accoutred new boy. It looked as though the bag had even been monogrammed with the youngster's name between the straps. Biggsy made out two words: Ted Baker.

He rolled his eyes at the profligacy of some of the more affluent parents. As he continued through the car park, the gleaming white Scirocco appeared out of nowhere and swept past him. It once again turned into the space reserved for visitors and gave one last roar before the engine shut down. Out jumped the slim, raven-haired deputy head in regulation matching black skirt and jacket. Dark days ahead, he mused. She smiled extravagantly in the direction of the youngsters arriving for their first day at St Saviour's, clicked her heels up the four stone steps and breezed through the main doors.

Toner – back with flash wheels and a flashing smile. Somebody's in for it.

******

He made an exception on this second day back, taking his morning coffee in the staff room. He wanted to find out if any other department heads were as peeved as he still was about the late agenda addition. However, it appeared that he was festering alone. Sitting in a quiet corner, he exchanged holiday anecdotes and curriculum notes with Kim Buttrell, Head of Science. The item had never made it to her agenda. She claimed to have jotted down a few offerings of her own in ten minutes for the deputy head and had emailed them off directly.

Self-effacing and quietly spoken, she was the consummate professional in his eyes. Her reputation for prioritising the needs of science staff and her students above all other considerations was universally acknowledged. In an age when science teachers were gold dust, she had no trouble remaining aloof from tedious management imperatives.

Before the end of break, he returned to Room 125, rearranged the tables and chairs, and awaited the arrival of his form group. He welcomed the year thirteen students as they turned up, individually and in small groups, until there were enough to make a start. Of the twenty-four in his form, twenty had managed to make it in before the buzzer had sounded for the start of the lesson. His register completed, he waited another few minutes for stragglers. None arriving, he stood up and closed the door.

"Welcome back, everyone. Hope you had a great summer. On that note, are Colley and his confederates not joining us today?" he asked the room.

"They're still in Ibiza, sir," came a reply. The spokesman was Jermaine Gibson, the strikingly handsome and newly-elected head boy. "Their flight got cancelled last night. Chris messaged me and sent you their apologies."

"Cutting it a bit fine to be back for start of term, weren't they, Jermaine?"

"They cut everything a bit fine, sir. Know what I mean?" Gibson winked.

"Yes, I *do* know what you mean, as it happens. Can't say I understand why the other three take a chance with somebody who has such a footloose attitude to his academic responsibilities," he stated in his best starchy tone.

"He's not footloose, sir. He's screwloose," confided Gibson.

General laughter erupted.

Genius brain, thought Biggsy. He could do stand-up. No wonder he made head boy. Christopher Colley, on the other hand, was a ducker and diver in danger of sacrificing academic success for a life of vulgar pleasures. Couldn't help but like him, though – one of life's charmers.

"Well, let's get on. I've got your timetables printed out, just in case you've forgotten what you're studying, and a sixth-form diary each."

He walked around the room handing out the gifts.

"Blimey, sir, somebody's splashin' out! These've got 'ard covers," laughed Aidan 'Don't-Call-Me-Cliff' Richard.

"Don't assume that just because the government intends to saddle you with tens of thousands of pounds of debt to study for a degree that St Saviour's is similarly tight-fisted, Aidan."

The laughter turned to groans of disapproval at the student debt reference.

******

The comforts of the English office were more desirable than the staff room at lunch times. He'd brought in a kettle and mug and was content to brew up and put his feet up in the seclusion of the English base, although nowhere in a boys' secondary school was strictly quiet at break times. As if to reinforce this point, a football smacked against the office window. Occasionally, a department member or two would turn up, but most preferred beavering away quietly on their laptops in their own teaching rooms. Most teachers, he believed, seized on opportunities for solitary industry. The relief from constant interaction with students in crowded classrooms was highly prized. Consequently, although there were central office bases for every department, these were often empty.

Alone in his sanctuary, he couldn't quite believe that he'd made it in teaching. He'd struggled to shake off the feeling of being an imposter. This used to be the office of Bryan Franklin, an Oxford man, in the old grammar school days. Here he was, a scruff made good from a West Country council housing estate, leading a core subject team of eight in a London secondary school. Knowledge of the social distance he'd travelled to reach this point heightened his sense of professional responsibility.

He'd discovered something important about himself recently. He'd been discussing with Myra the phenomenon of small children needing a comfort blanket, a wholly unnecessary appendage to toddlerhood in his view, he'd believed. Thinking further about his own childhood, he'd been forced to face the fact that he'd had not one, but a series of them. It had taken some time to register because his material attachment had been a variation of the norm.

He'd remembered becoming frantic when, midway through his primary school years, he'd got off a bus and realised he'd left his treasured black duffel coat with tartan lining on the back seat of the top deck. Instinctively, he'd chased after the bus as it had ground its way up toward Foxhill. His fear at being without the coat that he loved dearly was greater than the fear of being told off by his parents for losing it. The duffel enveloped him like a cosy eiderdown, making him feel totally secure when out and about in the big wide world. He could still recall the pleasure of pushing his hands into the deep and inviting pockets, where his fingers fiddled with lumps of lint nestling in the corners.

Haring after the bus, young Biggsy just about managed to keep it in view, without ever quite catching it up. Time and fatigue meant nothing to him. Breathless but determined, he eventually saw the stationary bus facing him in the distance, having turned around at the terminus. He prayed that the coat would still be where he'd left it. The conductor, sitting cross-legged on a bench adjacent to the stop and puffing luxuriously on a cigarette, gave a curious look as the little lad leapt on to the bus and rushed upstairs. There it was, awaiting him. Nobody had taken his coat. Realising what had happened, the conductor grinned at the sight of the relieved youngster jumping off the platform.

"You were lucky there, boy."

The conductor's comment had stayed with him. It was true. He was lucky, always had been.

In his early teens, with money it had taken him months to save, he'd bought himself a capacious green combat jacket at the army surplus store in town. It swamped him, just as he'd hoped. There were four huge pockets down the front, each a depository for his worldly goods. When it had worn out after daily use years later, he'd bought himself what was then called a greatcoat, an ex-military monster coat down to his ankles, from the same store. Comfort blankets all of them, taking him into adult life.

On moving up to London after A-levels, he'd become self-conscious about his regional accent. By opening his mouth less when speaking, he could soften vowel sounds and so disguise the burr that occasionally amused some of his new friends and acquaintances. Disguises and anonymity suited the insecure personality of a young man from the sticks immersed in the metropolis. Having reached mid-life, he now found that he all but felt socially confident. He believed he had his father to thank for that. Constant reinforcement from him that he was the equal of anyone had become an important component of his character.

His thoughts were interrupted by the ringing of the office phone.

"Hello, Mr Biggs. This is Ms Toner. Could I ask a great favour? Year seven boys are in for their first day today and we need another teacher to go through the school protocol programme with one of the groups. The form tutor for 7E, Miss Harper, is newly-qualified. I don't think she'd have the confidence to do the sort of thorough job one of our established teachers could manage. I see that you have a free period after lunch. If you could go to Room 226 at the beginning of fifth lesson, I'd be grateful."

"Right," was all he could manage.

"Thanks so much."

She'd done it again. Caught like a kipper. His recent nightmare came back to him.

※※※※※※

Switching off the ignition, he hauled himself out of the car, clutching his attaché to his chest. He turned the key in the Yale lock and slammed the front door behind him. He muttered his customary 'fukkem' and awaited his wife's greeting.

"This is a first. You're home before six. Has the school burned down?"

He'd first met Myra at the Hammersmith Odeon. Seated side by side, the nineteen-year-olds had exchanged occasional comments throughout the rock concert. He'd found himself concentrating less and less on the very loud act and more on the attractive girl alongside him as the evening had progressed. At the close of the show, he'd surprised himself by plucking up the courage to ask her if they might meet up for a date. The even greater surprise had been her acceptance of his offer. They'd just managed to exchange contact details before she'd been whisked away by her three girlfriends to catch their bus.

They made a good team. Compatible in so many ways, their shared sense of fun was an important factor. Myra wanted answers from life, not only on major political issues, but also on the small print of human interaction. They often found themselves laughingly investigating topics that would have been of no interest to anyone but his wife. For example, Myra had once pondered whose responsibility it was to empty pooper scoop bins. She'd never witnessed anyone doing it. Not only that, but she also wanted to know what happened to the vast amounts of canine excrement that were presumably piling up all over the country. Pursuing such investigations to their conclusions had become a matter of course in their enduring relationship. She'd also had no problem agreeing to refer to her new beau by his preferred handle of 'Biggsy'.

"Well, how was the first day with kids around, love?"

"It was smashing," he replied in a dull monotone.

"Oh, dear! Your first day back with little angels around and you've got the grumps," she soothed in her matron's voice. "Who was it this time?"

"Twice she's got me already. Toenail's after me, I know it. I'm her target for the year."

"What on earth are you on about?"

"First, she barnstormed my faculty meeting with a 'five-minute job' that will take all of two weeks, then she stitched me up to do an extra session during my first free lesson of the year."

"Could just have been a coincidence."

"No, I'm sure she's started executing the plan she's hatched to be shot of me."

"You've got to speak to her if you're not happy about something."

"No, I wouldn't give her the pleasure of my company. It'd be a waste of time. She's on a mission."

"You sure you're not over-reacting. Sometimes you're your own worst friend."

"You mean 'worst enemy'," he corrected.

"I know what I mean," countered Myra.

Chapter 2

It was lunchtime and Biggsy was on break duty. He was comforted by the fact that he'd only been back three days and there was already the welcome prospect of the weekend ahead. He counted six separate games of football taking place at once on the school field. Free space for anyone not playing football was at a premium. Knots of boys, clustered near the railings, passed the time under the tall trees on the far side of the field. The sun had brought boys in their hordes outside. Shouts and cries came from every direction. He wondered if duty staff might request ear defenders in line with education's preoccupation with health and safety considerations.

Whistle in one hand and coffee mug in the other, he threaded his way to a spot from which he could command a full view of everything going on. Taking a deep draught from his mug, he noticed a coffee drop land on his red tie. Dammit! An empty, crisp bag then had the audacity to blow at his feet. Myra had trained him up for a life of tidiness. Therefore, he was unable to resist the urge to pick up the litter. His lower back a constant consideration, he gingerly extended one leg behind him, bent the knees slowly and eased himself down. The litter safely stowed in his hand, he reversed the procedure, an operation that took a good five seconds.

"It's a long way down there, sir, innit?"

Biggsy looked around to see two year nine boys smiling at his antics.

"One day, when your bodies are as old as mine, you'll be laughing on the other sides of your faces," he glowered, making superhuman efforts to control his twitching facial muscles.

Just as he was enjoying the fresh air and relative calm, the time came to call everyone in. He put the whistle to his lips and gave three lung-bursting blasts.

"In you go!" he shouted generally to those within earshot.

"Go on, sir. Say it. Please say it, sir!" pleaded the boy who'd expressed mock sympathy.

"I can't. I'll get the sack."

"No, you won't, sir. Go on, say it."

"Right, but this is the last time," he promised.

With that, he gathered himself for an ear-splitting roar. Suddenly, the whole field came to a standstill as he bellowed the required command, "Get your asses to your classes!"

His young accomplice was bent double with laughter. For some reason, the footballers caught up in their games who'd ignored his whistle, instinctively obeyed this crude instruction.

******

Only when the last dilatory pupil had been shepherded into the school building could he make his way to his own registration group. He was late, as was always the case after a stint on lunch duty.

"Sorry, I'm late, lads. I popped into the head's office for a quick chat and he got the whisky out."

"You wish, sir," Bellchambers quipped. "You'd be lucky to get a Fanta out of him."

"That'll be enough of that, Belly. Mr Fingleton and I have a special relationship."

"Woooo!" chorused the class.

"Ah, Colley and Co! Good to have you back in dear old Blighty. Problems with your flight?"

The delayed holiday-makers entered the form room and shuffled their way to seats.

"Seven hours we 'ad to wait at Ibiffa!" Colley spluttered. "We 'ad no money and 'ad to share a can o' Coke. Takin' the piss or what!"

"That entirely convincing display of anger indicates that you're telling the truth, Chris. Sorry that your holiday ended so badly. Next year, make a booking for the beginning of August, not the end. Here are your timetables and diaries, lads."

Tim Meeks, Graham Tilley and Richard 'Banger' Dixon looked in Colley's direction, all nodding sagely. Long-limbed and already with a slight stoop, he slid himself into an entirely inadequate seat for one of his dimensions. The three acolytes seated themselves in a tight cluster in the corner of the room. Dixon was the odd one out in this ménage à quatre. Sullen and stolid, he wasn't a party animal like his pals. Although not the sharpest tack in the box in terms of intellect, he would be as hard as nails in the event of a scrap. Always useful to have some muscle on hand when in strange parts.

"Right, who's ill?" Biggsy demanded. "Anyone with a heavy cold, the sweats, diarrhoea, athlete's foot or the residual effects of malaria, I want you seated at the back of the class. I'm not starting this academic year going down with one of your highly-contagious diseases."

"Dumpy's got the love bug, sir. Should he sit at the back?" asked Bellchambers.

Ian 'Dumpy' Padfield, a fifteen-stone mountain of muscle and the star second row of the school rugby team, looked up and smirked at his form master.

"Heaven forfend, Ian! I can't believe that even you have come under the spell of the dreaded…" he intoned, pausing theatrically and narrowing his eyes, "opposite sex?"

"What do you mean, sir – even me?"

A beast of a boy on the rugby pitch, Padfield was diffident off the field, with a psyche that needed protecting. Ridiculing students publicly was anathema to Biggsy, and Padfield was someone with whom nobody should play such a dangerous game. He was a boy who lapped up all manner of compliments relating to his muscular physique and rugby prowess, but he became edgy if anyone joked about his habitually misfiring intellect or limited potential in the romance stakes.

Unlike many teaching professionals who came directly into the job after completing a degree followed by a one-year PGCE course, his form tutor was aware of the importance for teachers of psychology and sociology studies. At the West London Institute, formerly Borough Road College, he'd followed a teacher training course that had included these disciplines. Twenty-first century teacher training focused on syllabus material and the quickest and most effective methods to inculcate bodies of knowledge into students. Spoon-feeding, force feeding and the tortuous drip-drip method had all become very popular in schools but, in his opinion, were of limited educational value. He remembered attending lectures on Piaget, Vygotsky and Bruner, names with which some of his younger colleagues were unfamiliar. He was an advocate of the theory that each child's educational experience is as much about a personal search for identity as acquiring knowledge, an essential and often overlooked element of cognitive development. Consequently, he never played rough with an individual's developing sense of identity. Padfield's was a case in point. At the same time, he made every effort to include him in moments of harmless levity within the form group setting. Classroom humour must always remain within strict parameters, particularly when dealing with a personality as brittle as Padfield's.

"I assumed that a young man like you, mature beyond your years and destined for the life of a stellar sporting icon, would have exercised more caution with regard to anchoring yourself to the tedium of a *relationship*."

"You're married, sir," Padfield argued.

Biggsy was genuinely impressed by the speed and astuteness of the boy's response.

"Can't argue with you there, but that's unfair to kick a man when he's down. Back of the class with the other casualties!" he ordered, doing his best to suppress a smile. "Right, I've got information sheets about a sixth-form university conference coming up. Can you give them out, please, Ian, as you're already on your feet?"

Padfield wasn't already on his feet, but he pushed back his chair and shuffled forward for the timetables.

"Make a note of the UCAS event date of Thursday October 14th in your brand-new diaries, please. A coach will be arranged to take everyone to the venue. Details to be provided later."

He turned to face the students, but they weren't interested in their diaries. Everyone was looking in the direction of the classroom door. Looking up to see what had attracted their attention, he saw a face framed in the cut-out window at the top of the door. It belonged to Ms Toner.

******

"She just peered through the door at us all for five seconds and then disappeared," he explained to Myra.

He'd arrived home from a full teaching day and an after-school staff meeting. Huffing and puffing his way into the house and, still wearing his jacket and shoes, he collapsed full length on the sofa. This new beached-whale pose was annoying to Myra, but his latest report of professional grievance was more disconcerting. The six o'clock news was occupying her attention, but she tried to show some sympathy for her husband whilst he railed on about the deputy head's latest affront to his dignity.

"I'm a head of department with my sixth-form group, and she's checking me out," he continued, hoping to draw a condemnatory comment from his wife.

"Maybe she's been told to do more school patrols by the head, and wants everyone to witness the fact that she's doing the job," she responded, without turning away from the images of what was left of a middle-eastern city following an aerial bombardment. "Perhaps you're getting things out of proportion."

"Even if that were the case, she doesn't need to spy on my classroom. She's trying to needle me, just as she did last year. I think she's been given the word that I'm fair game for imminent removal from St Saviour's."

Myra bit her tongue. Instead of expressing exasperation at her husband's unfounded fears, she decided that comforting words of reassurance might be more advisable as far as his present state of mind was concerned. The first few days back after the summer break were often problematical.

"That's a bit extreme, love. What on earth should make you think that? If she'd come into the room and gone for your gizzard like a bull mastiff, I might agree with you. But she didn't do or say anything."

"Getting through last year with her was bad enough, but she seems to have started this year with me at the top of her hit list. You remember Dave Simpson who used to be head of the art department – went off to teach in Somerset? He said he was leaving because of her. Fancy a cup of tea?"

Relieved at Biggsy's offer of a brew, she took the opportunity to change the subject.

"That'd be lovely, thanks. By the way, I've arranged for Kevin Donovan to come around soon to do that bit of decking out the back we decided on."

He pushed himself up, went to the kitchen and picked the pair of Millennium commemoration mugs off the mug tree. A gift from Myra's parents almost a decade ago, he'd hoped to put them by for a few more years and sell them as an unmarked as-new pair. However, Myra had started using them. The dishwasher had already caused the images of the Spitfire, St Paul's and Concorde to fade.

Before he had the opportunity to discuss the proposed decking, there was a noise that sounded as though somebody had demolished a section of the stairs. Ella appeared in the kitchen doorway. She had the tight-jawed expression on her face that worried him. Clearly on a mission. But would it be Mum or Dad in the firing line? She approached her father, kissed him on the cheek, then stood before him with hands clasped behind her back and a quizzical expression fixed in place.

"Hello, Dad. I've got a Thomas Hardy essay to do on the book I had to read over the summer. I'd appreciate any useful pointers you could give me."

"What's the question, Ella?"

"It's on 'The Mayor of Casterbridge'. The question is 'Does Henchard possess a tragic flaw that leads to his downfall?'"

Biggsy smiled with lips closed, wondering when he would find time to fit in his own work that evening.

"Can you give me a bit of time to get organised, Ella? Block me in between eight and eight thirty."

"Thanks, Dad." She turned on her heel and thundered back upstairs.

******

"Why do they make us study such a depressing novel?" Ella was now in her night-time onesie, sitting cross-legged on the bed and clutching a notepad and pencil.

"Perhaps the examiners think reading Hardy is a good way to get students to think deeply about their own lives," he replied, parking himself at the end of her bed.

"How do you mean?"

He paused momentarily before answering, aware that the literary concepts he had to impart needed to be expressed clearly. The information had the potential to disturb adolescent sensibilities. And she was his daughter, not one of his students.

"Where do I start? Well, the question includes the important expression 'tragic flaw'. A Greek philosopher named Aristotle, who was around over two thousand years ago, made some important observations about the Greek plays of his day we call tragedies. One of these was that a tragic hero is a character in literature who possesses a fatal flaw – a trait or quality that leads to his downfall."

"I know that much, Dad. We did it in class. I need a bit of meat to put on the bones," interrupted Ella.

"It's handy that you know that already," smiled Biggsy. "A bit of meat, eh? Well, here we go. All human beings live with fear, in my opinion. It's a consequence of our mortality. We're all tiny specks of life in a vast terrifying universe. Do you remember how, as a child, you imagined a horrible man at the bottom of the garden whose head was covered in bees? You had a regular nightmare that he was coming to get you."

"Don't remind me of that!" she blurted out, looking aghast.

"Sorry, but that's the fear. The fear of the unknown. Scares the crap out of everybody from time to time."

"Tell me about it," she chuckled.

"People never lose it, however good they become at disguising the fact. There's always the fear. Three thousand years ago, the ancient Greeks wrote plays about it. I think they were attempts to come to terms with, or rationalise, this fear humans live with. The Greeks also built huge and imposing temples to house statues of their gods. They possibly convinced themselves these gods could protect them from life's dangers, so long as constant devotion was shown to them. The tragedies all feature one or more of these gods, looking down on high from their home on Mount Olympus on the actions of mortals. Some argue that the ancient Greeks' greatest fear was the nothingness, or abyss, that is at the heart of all human existence. Good stuff, isn't it?" he grinned. "Hope it doesn't keep you awake all night."

"Along with everything else I have to worry about, it shouldn't make much difference."

"Fair enough. Let's carry on. Fear can be a terrible thing, making people behave irrationally, sometimes in extreme ways. It's why, nowadays, some of us refuse to walk under a ladder. It was why people branded women as witches in the middle ages and burned them at stakes. It's why racism thrives everywhere in the world. Hope I'm not boring you. So, everybody wants to feel protected. But whatever cloak of apparent absolute security we choose to throw over ourselves, the sense of protection we experience is illusory."

Ella knitted her brows and sucked her pencil.

"I suppose the idea that one day we'll all die doesn't help," she said.

"Spot on. Incidentally, I've just made a connection between what I'm telling you and the need many children have for comfort blankets."

"Ah, so even children instinctively seek protection. That's an interesting one, Dad."

"Very true. So, the thing we fear most and try to turn away from is the one that awaits us all – the ultimate annihilation of the self. By the way, all of this is degree level stuff. If it doesn't make a huge amount of sense to you, don't feel bad. It's what you've got to look forward to when you go to university."

"What has this got to do with Michael Henchard?"

"Well, do you think the way he behaves is symptomatic of a deep-seated fear about his life?"

Ella's eyes bored into her father's.

"Could be," she volunteered. She pulled at her bottom lip with thumb and forefinger. "I know he's as drunk as a skunk when he sells his family, but perhaps he does it because a part of him thinks they're holding him back in some way, stopping him from making more of his life."

"An imaginative answer. Make a note of that. Besides fear, the Greek dramatists focused on another powerful impulse – pride. Their plays warn against people becoming too self-important, behaving as if they deserve more from life than everybody else. Their plays about mythical heroes focus on acts of exceptional courage, but the tales are also warnings because the gods ultimately destroy these heroes. Too much pride can be destructive. A human demonstrating excessive pride will incur the jealousy and wrath of the gods and runs the risk of being destroyed. No mortal can last long who is so proud as to strive towards the state of being a truly exceptional human being – a hero. The gods interpret that impulse as an effort to become immortal, and only the gods can be immortal."

"So, there should be no superheroes in the world," sighed Ella. "How boring!"

"Quite possibly. Have you heard the joke about how Belgium is mocked as a nation, albeit tongue in cheek, because there are, so it's believed, few famous Belgians one can think of throughout history?"

"Not heard that one," replied Ella, looking blank.

"Well, perhaps the Belgians, as a race, are wiser than anyone knows. The ancient Greeks, we're told, believed people shouldn't over-reach themselves. Perhaps that belief is built into the Belgian psyche."

He smiled to himself at the lateral direction of his thinking, but was concerned that he might be losing his daughter's interest and attention.

"Many of the famous people from history to whom statues are erected all over the world were warriors who achieved fame through bloodshed. I couldn't have been an Alexander the Great or a Duke of Wellington. There's a darkness to the concept of being a hero."

Ella was silent, then busied herself with note taking.

"Anyway, let's move on. Remember, this is all only theory – the theory of a literary art form called tragedy. The ancient Greeks, as I've said, may have placed importance on knowing their place in life and accepting their lot. That way, you wouldn't attract the attention of the gods, who could bring about your downfall for being too proud. You know the saying – pride comes before a fall. Hardy's novel is a modern tragedy, a book influenced by Greek tragedy, about a man with a fatal flaw in his personality who commits a tragic error. Is that a viewpoint you can accept?"

"So, Michael Henchard over-reaches himself because he's too proud. And Thomas Hardy is warning me not to be too proud in my own life, or I may pay for it by being punished in some way," Ella reasoned.

"Yes, you're there. It's a complex literary issue. Hardy had problems with religion, but he sensed, perhaps hoped, that there was some directing force in the universe that affected the course of people's lives, just as the Greeks of old believed in the influence of the gods over their lives. Shakespeare wrote 'The stars above us, govern our conditions', and the modern poet Ted Hughes refers to 'the clockwork of the stars'. I'm a convert because I'm a bit of a fatalist. I think there's a chance that our lives may follow a predestined course."

Biggsy looked for signs of comprehension in his daughter's expression, fearing that he may have lost her.

"Wow, you sound like a professor. How do you remember all this?" she asked.

"It's not a case of remembering anything for me. What I've tried to explain is tied in with my own search for the answer to what our lives are all about. Anyway, we're almost finished. The ancient Greeks, Shakespeare and Hardy all produced literature that deals with characters who have certain qualities that become exaggerated or over-developed. For example, Macbeth was another ambitious character who took his ambition too far. Henchard's life would probably have a run a fairly even course but, the moment he sells his wife and child, his fate is sealed."

"But it's years after Henchard sells his family that he loses his position and reputation in Casterbridge and gets punished. Surely, he should have received his punishment straight away?" Ella queried.

"Clever girl. You've hit upon another important element of tragedy. The gods delight in punishing a person for a crime, often against one of their own family, long after it has taken place, to heighten the suffering of the so-called hero. They delight in humiliating their victims before zapping them. This literature may seem depressing at first but, to me, it's exciting. It's inviting me to reflect deeply on my place in the universe and how I should behave during my three-score years and ten."

"Blimey! It's heavy stuff."

"Life's heavy, Ella, but we spend much of our time pretending it's not. Hardy's encouraging you to consider your life within the immense framework of the universe. There are powerful and unknowable forces at work. It's cosmic stuff."

"Or depressing. I don't like the idea of being a fatalist like you. You have to watch your every move. Life just seems like a rat trap that's out to get you the moment you step out of line."

"An intelligent observation. I defend myself against that argument by saying that my fatalistic outlook frees me up from worrying to excess about life's supposedly big decisions. I accept that I am, to a degree, powerless in the face of the universe. This outlook enables me to concentrate on the detail of life – the wonderful moments that other people might overlook because they're constantly wrestling with big ambitions and big decisions. Anyway, you're the ideal sort of person to analyse Hardy's writing because you sound like his opposite. You believe that you can shape your future and be in control of your own destiny."

"So, should I despise Henchard because he's an arrogant prick or feel sorry for him because he's just a tiny cog in a giant cuckoo clock?"

"What did you honestly feel when he dies?"

"I felt sorry for him, in spite of what he did."

"Good. Going back to Aristotle, he stated that the audience should feel the emotions of pity and fear at the end of a tragedy, pity for the terrible suffering of the hero and fear that what happens to the hero could happen to you. Finally, I must give you the word 'catharsis'. Write this down. The definition of this word is that feeling of cleansing or purification the audience experiences at the end of the tragedy."

"I didn't cry, but I did feel wiped out by the end of the book, Dad," she laughed.

"That'll do for me. So, in the words of every teacher devoted to the national curriculum, make a note of the following key words before starting to write your essay: tragedy, hero, pride, fear, pity, catharsis. By the way, do you think the essay question is a good question?"

"After listening to you, it seems a bit obvious."

"At first sight, it may seem that way, but look again. Do people in the novel like Henchard?"

"No, they're afraid of him, especially the rustic characters?"

"Does he deserve his 'fall'?"

"Yes. He not only sells his family, but he also bullies people. But does that mean Farfrae who takes his place will go through the same cycle as Henchard?"

"Do characters in the novel like Farfrae?"

"Yes, because he's helpful and kind."

Biggsy was impressed at the speed with which his daughter was assimilating her thoughts and forming conclusions.

"Does he deserve to 'fall' when he takes over as mayor in Casterbridge from Henchard?"

"No, because he's not too proud."

"Good again. He doesn't set out to be important. I think you've already got enough to start your essay now, Ella. If you accept the idea that it's Henchard's fate that he should 'fall', Farfrae may be interpreted as fate's agent of retribution."

"Which means what exactly?"

"Well, the gods, fate or destiny, whatever we call the force that may control our lives, use Farfrae to punish Henchard. You could see Farfrae as Henchard's nemesis. Nemesis was the ancient Greek goddess of retribution."

"Don't forget to get that idea in at some point, perhaps in your conclusion. Remember that A-Level English Literature exam questions give you plenty of latitude to be original. You can play devil's advocate and be highly imaginative – as you usually are," he reassured.

"Thanks, Dad. When I've got some ideas down, will you give them the once over?"

"Any time you like."

But he didn't feel like a professor. It was all very well spouting tragic theory and sounding like an authority on both literature and life, but he felt a fraud. The reason was that now there was a question mark over his lifelong conviction of going with the flow, the credo he'd claimed to espouse a moment ago with his daughter.

He'd adhered to the philosophy for so long, to the extent that it had become an existential comfort blanket. But its worth was now being put to the test by Ms Toner, his nemesis. In light of her perceived slights against his professionalism, he foresaw confrontation and conflict. Consequently, the notions of knowing his place and keeping a low profile might have to go out of the window.

******

He unlocked the garden shed. The familiar odours of creosote and damp wood welcomed him. He'd decided to make use of what little light remained after the early evening meal to do half an hour of tidying up in the garden. There was plenty of space to lose himself – a hundred feet with two lawns sandwiching a circular rose bed and shrub-laden borders on either side. The tall rowan ash at the bottom of the garden was the main feature, an unexpected asset for a house set in the London suburbs. An avid train spotter in his youth, he enjoyed the rattle and clunk of carriages that clanked back to memories from his early teens. The railway line beyond the tree had always been a friendly presence for the family. Aircraft, however, were a problem. They were the reason why vegetable growing had never been a consideration. He'd read that cadmium issuing from jet engines drifted down through the atmosphere and settled on all plant life within a several-mile radius of Heathrow. He didn't want to risk poisoning his family.

Recalling a visit by his sister's family to his home many years earlier, he smiled to himself, as he remembered the effect noisy London life could have on those unused to big cities. Her baby son had bawled in terror as a screaming jet had passed overhead at the same time a heavy goods train had rattled by. She'd struggled to understand how, over time, it could become possible for anyone to take such constant din in one's stride. Perhaps he did miss the comparative quiet of his childhood home, but he could never return to that parochial existence.

He mused on the notion that he'd 'repaired' to the garden and smiled at the unusual use of the word in this context. Would he be repairing himself whilst gardening? There was no doubt that he found this interest therapeutic. Spouting away incessantly to class after class often left him feeling sick of the sound of his own voice, and he enjoyed the comparative tranquillity that was immediately accessible beyond his back door. Picking up a plastic bucket and secateurs, he headed down the garden path to the rose arbour.

A rat trap. A description of human life, possibly his own, he believed he could not accept. Feeling trapped was a torment reserved for those unable to appreciate and value their own insignificance, life's great paradox.

Was fatalism his excuse for being unambitious in the workaday world? All right, he was a head of English but, by his reckoning, he'd fallen into the job, by dint of an unblemished ten-year record in the department by the time old Franklin had retired. He knew that he was good at keeping his nose clean and had a reputation for sorting departmental problems with no histrionics. Like the time a fifteen-year-old had slapped him around the face in the playground for no reason. Well, there was a reason – the boy had been as high as a kite on some class-A drug or other. Biggsy hadn't kicked off, but had left the head to resolve the matter as unfussily as possible.

He entertained the possibility of his being congenitally conditioned to resist any impulse to act decisively in life. Heroes in tragedies inevitably came to a sticky end when they 'acted'. Dramas and crises happen in life and one often does best to ride them out. Life kicks everybody in the teeth several times during a lifetime. Why complain? Why attract attention to oneself? If someone asks your opinion, why complicate matters by being honest? We've all got to get along. If there's a fence around, sit on it. This professional modus operandi had worked for him. So why did he find that the deputy head was getting under his skin in a way that nobody had ever done before in his career? He conceded that the educational landscape was being transformed into a training battleground. Not all children were academic, but he was now operating in a system that demanded he treat them as though they were. The nation's data-driven institutions were creating more childhood casualties than he'd ever known. The disaffection that blighted so many children's school lives was also taking an increasing toll on their teachers.

High staff turnover was becoming an issue at St Saviour's. Fingleton passed it off as a problem of economics: a teacher's salary was no longer enough to cover accommodation, living and travel expenses in London. Not all teachers could afford to live long term in the capital, in his view. But media talk spoke of teachers now facing acute levels of stress. The job was no longer a lifetime vocation, but a five-year stopgap before settling into something more manageable. In this number-crunching climate, a new breed of officer-class managers was taking the helm and exacerbating the difficulties of staff retention. Ms Toner subscribed to the new model. In his case, with prejudice, he believed.

He noticed the rickety larch lap fence separating his garden from that of the neighbours. One post had snapped at the base and would need replacing. That was a job for Kevin Donovan, Myra's fancy handyman, as she called him. He could add that job to his list when he came to do the decking. Biggsy searched in the shed for a length of timber which could be used as a stake, a temporary support for the post. He was good at spotting problems before they became serious.

His father had involved him in DIY jobs around the house. Learning the skills of basic household electrics, painting and decorating, and gardening had been invaluable in the early years of his marriage, when money was tight. Nowadays, he no longer had the time for major redecoration projects. These he was happy for the reasonably-priced Donovan to carry out. Biggsy still kept the garden together. This activity he continued to enjoy because, as Dad had often told him, gardening is good for the soul.

He could also save on extortionate call-out fees and avert household disaster when the washing machine packed up or there were heating or plumbing problems. A stitch in time saves financial ruin. The family home ticked over with no major alarms through rain and shine. Reliable, competent, steady. He'd believed that, with his approach to life, it was unlikely he would ever come a serious cropper. Until now.

******

He browsed the sports pages of the tabloid Myra had brought home from her Saturday morning visit to the high street. The rest of the newspaper held little interest. He looked forward to his Sunday broadsheet read for the serious stuff. He'd been a keen sportsman as a schoolboy, having particularly enjoyed his time as vice-captain of the school rugby team. In his early teens, he'd become serious about the game. An expensive pair of ultra-light rugby boots he'd bought in a sports shop in Pulteney Street had transformed his game. His teammates had admired the soles with their slim aluminium studs, a vast improvement on their own plastic-moulded monstrosities. The weightless boots had seemed to increase his speed and improve his poise on the pitch. He became a Mercury amongst mere mortals.

The team coach, Mr Pembroke, had confided to him that he had the fastest acceleration over ten yards that he'd ever seen in his age group. Flattery, of course, but that season the team lost only two matches. He never played after secondary school. University rugby players were confident young men from a different social class, regulars at the bar where they talked, laughed and drank long and hard. He'd felt awkward in this milieu that was light years away from playing the game with mates from the estate. He'd never taken to regular beer drinking and was ill at ease with the jocks' clique. His enjoyment of the game survived intact, but only as a spectator following the fortunes of Bath and the national team.

Horse racing became another of his sporting interests. At sixteen years of age, he'd been introduced to the excitement of the turf by a kitchen porter he'd worked with one summer when the only holiday work available to him was as a washer-upper at the Kingswood, a smart hotel in the city centre. Stooped and garrulous, the ancient Fred would pore over the racing pages in the hotel rest room every morning during his tea break. Out of politeness, Biggsy had questioned him about the sport. Fred had duly enlightened him. Before backing any horse, it was necessary to analyse a host of variables: bloodstock; recent form; the weight the horse carried; the trainer's and jockey's performance at a particular course; the condition of the ground; the length of the race. Countless other considerations came into any betting equation. The animated porter introduced him to a science more exciting than any he'd yet studied.

That same afternoon, he was gambling a shilling each way on a horse called Rheingold. The betting shop was a one-minute walk away in Manvers Street. He and Fred slipped out of the hotel after the lunchtime rush. The brightness of the full sun contrasted starkly with the darkness of the hotel washroom. He waited anxiously in the street, whilst Fred went in and did the business. Hovering near the entrance, he observed tourists passing by and wondered what it must be like to have enough money to travel the world. He imagined himself setting off one day from Bath Spa railway station, now bathed in sunshine at the far end of the street, on a journey of his own. Fred emerged ten minutes later from the smoky den, his aged face wrinkled in a grin. The horse had won at twenty to one, making them both rich for a few days.

Dad, not a follower of horse racing himself, had been alarmed to discover that his son was being tutored in an activity that he equated with 'going off the rails'. An apposite expression, Biggsy reflected, as he recalled the subsequent lecture on the folly of gambling. Turf accountants were tricksters and spongers who persuaded the gullible to hand over their hard-earned money, rather than deposit it in a bank.

But he had known even then that he was sensible. He would never gamble away a family fortune. He was too cautious to risk large amounts and would never be an addict, just a small-time speculator. Addictive behaviour would never threaten his well-being. Many of his peers had smoked cannabis and taken happy pills, but he'd never been tempted to indulge. You couldn't pursue the life you were intended to lead if you were perpetually away with the fairies.

His interest in small-time betting on horse racing had stayed with him. The fun now of taking the occasional punt was in trying to find the outsider that would upset the favourite. Betting on favourites was high risk, as large sums had to be laid out to secure worthwhile winnings. Well into middle age now, he was comfortably off and didn't need to gamble. The turf was an interest light years away from teaching. Horse racing was the sport of kings and, as he'd retained the ability to read form, he enjoyed taking a small share in this aristocratic pursuit. For him, it was as natural to study form as it was for others to complete the daily crossword or Sudoku.

He'd developed a scheme of selecting twenty horses each year from the lower racing divisions and following them. Horses with names that included the word 'art' had a special appeal. He had Colin, a teacher in the IT department who also enjoyed the occasional flutter, to thank for this habit. His reason was that his wife was an art teacher at a girls' secondary school nearby. It was uncanny how often horses came first past the post with the word 'art' somewhere in their name. He'd told Myra about Colin's racehorse preference. Her spontaneous response had him hooting with laughter:

"I suppose now you'll be looking out for horses with the word 'bedpan' in their name."

He'd scan the runners and riders at race meetings and occasionally back a small amount on one or more from his *stable*, if the odds were favourable and the time seemed right. Visits to nearby courses with Myra a few times a year had become an enjoyable holiday break. She shared his interest, enjoying the thrill of watching thoroughbreds thundering by at over forty miles an hour. Brighton, Fontwell and Kempton were their favourite destinations.

He perused the Ripon card. Street Art was running in the 4.30. He'd have a pound each way on that at fourteen to one. A stroll to the high street was in order.

Chapter 3

End-of-week exhaustion had set in. The year eleven essays he'd finished marking at 11.30 the previous evening had taken him three hours. A fastidious marker who corrected in detail, he provided plenty of what he hoped were constructive comments. Myra had not been pleased when he'd tumbled into bed at midnight. She regularly complained that she couldn't get off to sleep if they didn't turn in together.

The atmosphere at breakfast was strained. Myra resented the amount of 'work' time her husband had to put in at home, when he was obviously at full stretch every day. Her work at the hospital was demanding, but she could relax once at home. It seemed unfair that her husband couldn't enjoy the same arrangement. The only time they seemed to communicate seriously with each other was at weekends.

"What time do you expect to be in tonight, love? A decent hour as it's Friday? You've only been back at school a few weeks and I've seen nothing of you since term started," she protested, as she pushed a bowl of muesli in his direction along the worktop.

"No later than five thirty. I've got to hand in departmental records for checking by the management team first thing on Monday. I'm going to get them done at school before I come home tonight because I'm definitely not bringing them home over the weekend."

"Oh, good. So that means the weekend of tantric sex you promised is still on."

"Sorry, but you seem to be mistaking me for someone else," he replied in a monotone.

"Well, if that's a non-starter, can we at least get away somewhere for a few hours over the weekend? Have bit of time together?"

"What about a drive down to Brighton if the weather's fine?" he suggested, surprising even himself. "A final day at the coast before autumn closes in. Does tomorrow sound good?"

"Oooh! Sounds a bit adventurous for you, but I'm game if you are."

He kissed Myra on the cheek and spooned a huge helping of cereal into his mouth. She returned him a smile that signified a challenge.

"This had better be a bona fide offer. Now you've said it, we're going. No backing out."

"Trust me, I'm a teacher," he spluttered through his muesli. "It's a bit quiet, isn't it? Where's Ella? She in school this morning?"

"Not until ten thirty. She's laying in. You can take her up this cup of tea if you want before you go."

He went upstairs with the tea. Tapping on his daughter's bedroom door, he pushed it with his foot and looked for signs of life. The duvet had been pulled completely over her.

"Anyone at home?" he called. "Tea up. I'll be off soon so I thought I'd do the rise-and-shine bit."

"Morning, Dad," answered the duvet. He placed the mug on her Mr Clumsy coaster. There was movement under the bedding.

"How are you getting on with tragic Tommy Hardy? I haven't seen you to ask lately."

"Oh, he's a killer," Ella mumbled sardonically. "I haven't had so much fun for ages."

"I certainly wouldn't recommend him to someone with suicidal tendencies, it's true."

"I think I know more about life than is good for me after your chat about 'The Mayor of Casterbridge'."

"Think of your old dad as an antidote to 'Hello' magazine, Ella. When you feel that life's getting too frivolous, come and have a quiet chat with me," he laughed. "Seriously, though, drink this and have a sparkling day. See you later."

******

"Look at all this writing on my work, Ifty! He's written more in the margin than I have on the page," Errol said loudly to the boy sitting beside him.

Biggsy turned and looked at the aggrieved year ten student whose marked work he had just placed on the desk in front of him.

"Why has my work got loads more corrections on it than Iftikhar's?" Errol demanded.

Going into diplomatic mode, he assumed a look of chagrin that his professionalism had been called into question. Errol Wickens was a sizeable presence in the classroom, a black powerhouse of a boy a good six inches taller than his teacher. He was given to bouts of mischievous, occasionally obstreperous, behaviour that some found intimidating. Despite his erratic classroom conduct, however, Errol was a tryer who put a lot into his writing. Technical accuracy was not his strong point, whereas Iftikhar was more than competent in this area. In this instance, Biggsy reflected, the politic course of entering into a discussion on his marking technique was preferable to reminding the pupil, in no uncertain terms, to whom he was talking.

"You don't think it's any good, do you, sir? So you put red ink everywhere."

Errol had no fear when it came to challenging teachers he believed were giving him a hard time. Witnessing his father's murder in a drugs-related street attack had scarred his personality. All of his teachers were aware that he could be amenable and good-humoured one moment, and petulant the next. The room became silent. Everyone's gaze was locked on the teacher. How would he handle this one?

He looked sympathetically in Errol's direction. "I'm sorry that you're upset at the way I've marked your work, Errol. I know how much effort you put into your English and that you want to succeed. What you write is alive with imaginative ideas, but you won't achieve the GCSE grade you deserve unless you improve your knowledge of grammar. I take more time correcting your work than anybody else's because I believe you deserve my time. Remember, I'm a public servant, which means that I'm your 'servant'. By giving you constant reminders about the kind of mistakes you're making, it's my belief that you'll improve in this area. I enjoy reading your work because it has plenty of interesting detail. You just need to polish up your written accuracy, and that's what I also focus on when I mark your work."

Without taking his eyes off Errol, he inhaled deeply, breathed out slowly and awaited a response.

"So, you're saying I'm one of the privileged people in this class then, sir?" the boy grinned.

Biggsy was relieved to hear the word 'sir'. He smiled. The important thing about teaching, that he hadn't been taught at teacher training college, was the value of a genuine smile when dealing with children. It became a broad grin. Reassuring and winning over a student in this way gave him such powerful emotional feedback that he could find himself fighting back tears. At such times, he knew there was no other job that could be as rewarding as teaching. But he had become adept at concealing such displays of emotion.

"I really thought you already knew that, Errol."

******

As the boys left the room for their next lesson, sixth formers began to arrive for their English Literature class. Biggsy dug out his copy of 'Mansfield Park' and placed it in the centre of his table. It wasn't one of his Austen favourites. Some of the boys still tittered when he read sections of it aloud. In early twenty-first century England, the name 'Fanny' was unheard of. Bellchambers glanced at the book as he took his seat at the front and winced. Biggsy offered him a *What-d'you-do?* gesture with a shrug of the shoulders.

"Sorry, but it's on the syllabus and we have to study it."

When everybody else had arrived and taken their seats, his address to the class continued in a tone of dejection.

"My apologies, lads, but I've some bad news. The school has organised a formal lesson observation programme for all teachers. That means I will be observed along with everybody else on the staff by a member of the school's management team. It'll be lesson two next Wednesday morning."

"Right, sir. You're saying that the school doesn't know that you're a good teacher yet after being here since before I started over six years ago," groaned Padfield.

"Thanks for the vote of confidence, Ian, old mate. These days, teachers go through regular checks as part of the school's assessment programme. It's all about accountability. I have to prove that I'm accountable to you as one of your public servants – constantly."

"If the teachers here are all our servants, why do so many of them give us such a hard time?" queried Padfield. "You should all be asking us what we want to do, not telling us all the time."

Occasionally, students made observations that smacked of such common sense he was taken aback. This was just such a moment.

"That's a good point, and I'm serious on that one. I'll pass the comment on to the head. Now, the member of staff who'll be observing me is Ms Toner."

He held the view that absolute honesty was the preferred option in his dealings with all students. Sixth formers were far too streetwise for him to behave in any other way. He was supposed to adhere strictly to the three-part-lesson teaching format, in accordance with national and school policy, but he rarely did. The argument that children needed to know exactly how every lesson would proceed, stage by stage, had never appealed to him. Thus, he only followed the alien practice when he was formally observed.

"Does that mean you'll be going into robot-teacher mode like all the other teachers for that lesson then?" smirked Gibson.

"Absolutely and whole-heartedly, Jermaine. You won't recognise me. I'll even do up the top button of my shirt and give my hair a centre parting."

"One last question, sir. When you start the plenary session at the end and Ms Toner asks us what we've learned in the lesson, are we allowed to say the obvious?"

"What's that, Jermaine?"

"If you don't know, how do you expect us to know?"

"I don't think that would be advisable. Try to imagine, all of you, that you are robot students and that you like nothing better than to have huge amounts of data spoon-fed into your memory banks. Then, if you're good, I might let you do some group work."

"Oh no! It's not gonna be a spooning lesson, is it, sir? I 'ate them. English Lit. is s'posed to be nothin' like science lessons," complained Colley.

"Only joking, Chris. Nothing of the sort. It'll be a mind-blowing Jane Austen exposé of the repressed passions and heady ecstasies of polite society."

"Oh, I see, sir. So, will we find out what excitement happens when an amorous gentleman offers a young lady a stroll around the rose garden?" asked Gibson.

"Something like that. By the way, that's well-expressed: 'amorous gentleman'. Remember it. It's funny how times have changed. What would a young gentleman of today have to do to generate an interest in the object of his passion?"

"Best not go there, sir," cautioned Colley.

"Fair enough, Chris."

His thoughts turned to his daughter and the challenges she would have to tackle from ardent admirers.

"Anyway, best behaviour, everybody, if you want me to remain your English teacher."

"You can rely on us, sir. Just don't worry and be your normal self. No need to be nervous. We won't let you down," quipped Bellchambers.

"Why do I have the distinct feeling that I'm being set up? I should be offering the reassurances here, not you lot."

******

As he was locking the English office at the end of morning lessons, Gibson hurried toward him.

"Hi, sir. Just caught you. A few of us sixth formers fancy a kickabout this lunchtime. Can we borrow the football you keep in your office?"

"Righto. There you go," said Biggsy, fetching the ball and handing it over.

"Thanks a lot. And, sir, do you know anything about the new five-minute rule for sixth-form lessons?"

He paused, tilted his head to one side and frowned.

"Sorry. Nobody's mentioned anything to me about any new rules."

"It's just that some of the guys are a bit worried they're being treated like ten-year-olds. If you don't arrive within five minutes of the start of a lesson, the teacher's not to let you in. Like a kind of lock-in, or lock-out, I suppose." Gibson smiled weakly at his own joke.

"None of us thought it would have been Mr Wheelhouse's decision."

"Well, I certainly haven't been complaining about student lateness for my lessons, and I'm surprised that I don't know anything about this new rule."

"Don't worry about it, sir. Just thought, as you and Mr Wheelhouse are friends, you might know who we've been upsetting," Gibson pondered in a low tone, as he strode off with the football.

This was worrying. He didn't want to be stop-watching students and implementing petty zero-tolerance policies with sixth formers. He could only think of one person who might deem it good practice to institute such a measure.

******

The door to the sixth-form office was open as usual, but he tapped lightly on it out of politeness.

"Hi there, Biggsy," greeted Dave Wheelhouse, seated at his desk. He reached for the mug of coffee placed on top of a pile of exercise books. The state of general disorder in the room reassured his visitor, who had long upheld the principle that a tidy desk indicated a sanitised mind.

"Sorry to interrupt you, Dave, but I've just had a bit of a shock. The head boy, no less, just informed me that we're no longer allowed to let tardy sixth formers into our lessons."

"Welcome to Stalag Luft III. You've heard then. Toner emailed me earlier today to inform me of the new ruling. This must be her operating independently. If Fingers'd had the idea, he'd have had the decency to give us an opportunity for consultation, at least."

Dave tapped a few keys, waited for the information to appear and invited his visitor to read the text on the screen before him.

In response to widespread complaints last term about the escalating problem of sixth formers arriving late for lessons, the management team has decided to implement a new policy. All staff will reinforce to their classes the importance of punctuality and inform them that, with immediate effect, any student arriving later than five minutes after the start of a lesson will not be admitted. Subsequent absence from lessons will result in parents being informed by letter. Please ensure that all boys in Years 12 and 13 are made aware of this new protocol as soon as possible. Many thanks. ST.

"That must be her favourite word – 'protocol'. The memo's short and to the point, mate, with just a hint of '*Mein Kampf*' in the tone."

Dave's face twisted into a parody of a grin. He'd been doing this job for twelve years and had had his share of headaches in the past. This one clearly troubled him.

"This will be driving a wedge between teachers and students. It's also going to increase our admin load. Toner won't be preparing and sending out letters to parents, we will."

"I wonder if Fingleton even knows about this, despite what the email says," ventured Biggsy. "This rule seems intended to create further division within the school, as you say. It's bound to generate bad feeling between students and staff."

"Yes, the concept of divide and conquer in education is really taking off," responded Wheelhouse, scratching his thinning scalp nervously and standing up. He placed his hands on his lean hips and stretched his back.

"This is definitely going to wind up the lads. Last term, they were promised easy chairs and a coffee machine for the common room. None of that ever appeared, and now this. Punitive measures are bad news if we're trying to keep students sweet. I wish I'd been allowed to retire when I wanted. I'm not interested in any of this," he said, pointing at the screen.

"Where did all the alleged complaints come from?"

"I had only one last year from Ollie Priestley, her pet in the Technology department. In fact, he's the reason why students knew about this before any of us. He turned away a latecomer this morning and broadcast the reason why to the whole class."

"Then he seems to have been the first to know. Certainly smells fishy. How the hell does she get away with it!" Biggsy implored the ceiling. "If she thinks I'm turning students away from my lessons, she can think again. Can we do anything about this?"

"Depends how serious you want to get. Looks like I'll be public enemy number one with the students in my final months here, whatever happens. I pray they don't think I've come up with this."

"They don't. Jermaine expressed the sentiment that somebody may be plotting behind the scenes. Is there any way we can put a spanner in the works? There has to be some sort of resistance we can muster."

"It's a bit late for that if it's already common knowledge amongst the boys. She's devious, that one. It's amazing how quickly word gets around. Fingers wouldn't have the bottle to withdraw the policy a matter of days after it's been introduced. You know he thinks the sun shines out of her armpit."

"Shit! Well, I'm not participating in this wheeze. I'll be a conscientious objector on this one."

"And I thought I could fade into the sunset at the end of term with the sixth form cheering me off. Some hope."

"They will. You can rely on that. You don't deserve this, Dave, and neither do the students."

"I pity the poor bugger who takes over from me. I suppose applications for the post will be invited soon. It's likely to be a poisoned chalice for the unlucky winner."

Biggsy pitied his colleague. He also wondered whether Sarah Clifton's aspiration to occupy this office would be influenced by Toner's latest move. The last few months of Dave Wheelhouse's career were unlikely to be his most enjoyable.

******

Before making his way to the school field for another lunch duty, he stopped off at the dining hall to pick up an egg and mayonnaise sandwich for his pains. Although he'd never run the risk of being awarded a six-figure bonus for his educational efforts, he could rely on a free sandwich for every daily duty he did. There might be a howling wind and bucketing rain to contend with, but he'd have the consolation of a wholesome brown bread sandwich, albeit with no butter.

Even if rain were teeming down, there'd be a dozen or so boys playing football outside. It heartened him to think that there was still the hardy element amongst the school population that insisted on maximum lunchtime exertion, whatever the weather. The only thing that ever put a stop to football was a snowfall in excess of three inches, which was rare. He had known pupils turn up to his afternoon lessons soaked through after a midday downpour of rain, but they carried on with their studies, oblivious to any discomfort.

Then again, there were those who never spent any of their free time outside unless the rains arrived. In which case, they would throw themselves about on the sodden grass and splash through ankle-deep puddles to ensure that they became wet through. They could then report to the school nurse and spend an afternoon in the medical room, whilst she attempted to dry their outer garments as best she could. If they hit the jackpot, the mudlarks might even be sent home.

Abnormally hot weather, as was the case today in mid-September, was a difficult time for those members of staff with an aversion to the distinctive smell of adolescent perspiration. The many footballers, who raced around for an hour in the sun, returned for afternoon lessons perspiring heavily and raising a rancid stench that many members of staff found intolerable. The children never seemed aware of the problem.

On entering the dining hall, he saw Mr Fingleton supervising the dinner queue. The head felt a duty to be visible about the school out of lesson time. Alongside him, Ms Toner was bending his ear.

Wondering what she might be cooking up, he negotiated a course to the food counter that took him as far away from the pair as possible. He had no problem encountering the head, but the prospect of having to acknowledge the deputy in any way was anathema to him. As he collected his free lunch, he found himself wrestling inwardly with the irksome truth that, for the first time in his career, he might be taking himself too seriously.

He recalled his talk with Ella on Greek tragedy and wondered what change had taken place within himself to take exception to anyone in his workplace? If a teacher prioritised speedy promotion to the exclusion of all other considerations, who was he to raise objections? If Toner wanted to be attached to Fingleton's hip to get a leg up the career ladder, that was her prerogative. Perhaps he needed reminding that there were teachers, like himself, who enjoyed teaching, and there were those who enjoyed managing. His sensibilities weren't that important, after all, in the current business of teaching and learning. He'd made his educational bed and, therefore, should lie in it.

Glancing surreptitiously in the direction of his nemesis, he observed what he interpreted as a smirk of disdain directed at a member of the canteen staff who was wiping clean an empty table. Ms Toner seemed incapable of doing anything that could redeem herself in his eyes. He found it difficult to resist the idea that there was a bad smell about the place, besides the sausages, that wasn't going away.

******

The football struck him on the cheek with such force that he was momentarily stunned. It happened just as he stepped out of the door at the back of the school to take him to the rear playground and field beyond. Instinctively, he continued walking as though nothing had happened. Several boys stood stock still as they awaited mayhem. Surely, somebody would be in for a rollicking.

"Sorry, sir! I didn't see you coming. It was an accident. Really!" shouted the gangly fifteen-year-old who'd kicked the ball.

"'Course it was. Don't worry about it," he replied, without breaking stride.

This was an incident of moment. His behaviour in response to a genuinely painful, but accidental, blow from a pupil would help to cement his reputation as a reasonable man, one whom the students could respect. His cheek smarted as he walked, but he kept his hands away from his face.

One day, he was going to write a book on teaching that would concentrate all his acquired wisdom about the job for those coming after him. There was material here for his tome: Top Tip No. 1 – Never bat an eyelid in front of the kids in the event of physical discomfort, even if you're in agony.

The lunch break was uneventful until a few moments before the end of his duty. Thoughts of the Brighton trip with Myra were interrupted by shouts of 'Fight! Fight!' His heart sank. All but a handful of the boys on the field were being drawn to a point at the far corner where a scuffle had broken out.

It was his habit to take his time walking toward any playground fight in the hope that, by the time he arrived on the scene, those involved would have exhausted themselves. This one looked rather too serious, however, and he quickened his pace. As was customary, he found himself having to force a way through a crush of ravening children of all ages to get to the incident. Neither spectators nor combatants responded to the blasts of his Acme Thunderer.

Two fifteen-year-olds were wrestling on the ground, each trying to extricate himself from the other's grasp. Grunting and cursing, their white shirts grubby and dishevelled, they were locked in a violent embrace. The dark-haired and powerfully built Harry Helps was trying to sit on the chest of Mark Dignan, a short whippet of a boy renowned for his vicious tongue. But wriggling Mark was having none of it.

"Come on, you two. You know necking isn't allowed on the school premises," Biggsy joked. "And you lot had better disperse now!" he instructed, suddenly turning on the spectators and bellowing the final syllable.

Disgruntled that their fun had been brought to a premature end, the onlookers drifted away to afternoon registration. Pulling apart the pugilists, he strained to drag them to their feet, but thought better of the manoeuvre as he felt a lower back twinge. A good shaking did the trick, each boy coming to his senses in the teacher's strong grip. The adversaries stood up and began dusting themselves down, neither looking at the other.

"What was so important that you two came to blows? You've lost a button on your shirt here, Mark."

"Nothing, sir. Just a bit of fun," Mark replied with a hollow laugh, as he accepted the button.

"A bit of fun? You've got the whole school behaving like animals. You're almost men and should be setting an example to the younger boys out here. What do you think I should do with you both?"

"Dunno, sir. Detention?" replied Mark.

His heart sank. One day, he'd receive a response that went beyond the default parameters of punishments and rewards. But it was expecting too much in an environment where imagination played second fiddle to extrinsic considerations.

"Do you really think a detention would make everything fine? You're both intelligent enough to know that's not the answer I was hoping for."

"I'm not doing detention for him," Harry snarled. "He called my mum a whore."

"Is this true, Mark?"

"No, sir. I wouldn't say that. I don't even know her."

"Don't make matters worse by trying to be funny, Mark. I'll tell you what, I know Harry's mum very well and I know that she'd be mega-upset to hear that a lad from this school had said that about her. What do you say to me leaving it to her to settle the matter? I'll give her a call to come up to the school. You can repeat what you said about her to her face, and we'll leave it to her to deal with you. I don't think a detention's in order here. You see there's a lot of cowardly name-calling that goes on, particularly against women, and I think it might cure offenders if they were given the opportunity to speak their slanderous poison directly to the person concerned."

"You 'avin' a laugh, sir?" queried Mark.

"Never been more serious. It'll save me having to supervise a detention and may be the most effective way of curbing your casual cussing habit."

Curbing casual cussing. An appealing phrase.

"Are you OK with that, Harry?"

"You better not, sir. My mum'll kill 'im."

"If you can't offer me a better suggestion in ten seconds, Mark, that's what I'm doing. Well?"

Mark looked down at his feet and then at the still irate Harry.

"I'm sorry, Harry. I shouldn't have said what I did," bleated Mark.

"What's your reaction to that, Harry? Do you want him to apologise to your mother as well?"

"No way, sir," Harry replied.

"Do I take it, then, that you accept the apology?"

"Yes, sir."

"That's very decent of you, Harry, bearing in mind the seriousness of the insult. Shake hands, both of you, and tidy yourselves up before you get to registration."

He fought back an impulse to laugh aloud as an image of Harry's mother laying into Mark flashed across his mind. The boy was now showing signs of being unsettled by the situation.

The two brawlers picked up their jackets that had been used as goalposts and strolled away together. He knew that they'd be back on speaking terms by the end of the day. Giving a detention would have been the easy option, but the phenomenon of cussing required a more thoughtful approach, in his opinion. Zero tolerance didn't always work with this form of abuse. Some teachers took it lightly, one or two even joining in when they thought they were out of hearing of students. For Biggsy, the practice betokened a monolithic social problem from one end of the world to the other.

******

September was drawing to a close. The sun peeped out from between high clouds as he and Myra drove down through the outskirts of Brighton to the coast. The wide expanse of playing fields and parkland to their left was already busy with young and old out for a Saturday jaunt.

"It's strange how we never tire of coming here, isn't it, love?" Myra said opening her side window a few inches.

There was no reply.

"Biggsy, I'm talking to you!" she exclaimed. "Where are you in your head at this precise moment?"

"Sorry, I was daydreaming. What was it you said?"

"OK. Try again. I said it's strange how we keep coming back here."

"Right. It has a tawdry charm all its own. The lanes and the walk to Hove alone are the big draw for us."

"Those students across the road definitely look a bit tawdry. I'll bet they've been clubbing all night and are just going home to bed," Myra laughed.

"You're only jealous."

Turning left at last into Marine Parade, he looked for a parking space. Four hundred yards and several pound coins later, they set off on foot back in the direction of the pier.

"It's going to be warmer than I thought," said Myra, taking off her light anorak and hanging it over her handbag.

The sweet smell of dunking doughnuts, just one of Brighton's pleasures, almost had them stopping to make a guilty purchase, as they passed the entrance to the pier.

"That was a close shave," he laughed, pulling his wife by the hand sharply out of smelling range of the stall. "I almost weakened there and stopped for a bagful. What do you say we do the walk to Hove first while the sun's out? Then we can get a bus back here if we don't fancy walking any further and have lunch at Francesco's in the lanes."

"Sounds good to me."

Two hours later, leg-weary and famished, they were shown to a table at their restaurant of choice. Myra picked at the hem of the red-and-white-check tablecloth as she waited for Biggsy to make his selection from the menu.

"I'm having the carbonara," she stated firmly. "My stomach deserves it."

"Too much choice here. Think I'll have spaghetti bolognese. Never a disappointment."

Easing himself down into his plastic mock-wickerwork seat, he stretched out his legs. He watched a pot-bellied, shaven-headed man of indeterminate age set himself and his pint of beer on a bench across the square. A slim bleached blonde settled herself beside her beau. A cigarette in one hand held high and a gin and tonic in the other, she assumed a fastidious air, as she studied the other customers around her. The afternoon sun was creating good business for The Ship Inn. Biggsy waved away a fly that had settled on his forearm. He enjoyed the food at Francesco's but would have preferred to eat inside, away from the annoyance of those bugs and insects that insisted on having a share of one's meal.

"Hello, I'm here."

He turned to face Myra. She seemed put out.

"I imagined a day out to be a bit more fun than this. You've hardly spoken to me since we arrived. What's going on in that cranium of yours? School business, I imagine."

"No, I was just trying to calculate how long it would take, and how expensive it would be, to cultivate a beer gut as good as that one over the way," he joked.

"And I wonder how long it would take for me to get fed up with being ignored by my husband and look for a more sociable model?" came Myra's swift retort.

"Sorry, love. Am I that bad?"

"The older you get, the more preoccupied you become. It's like living with a middle-aged autism sufferer. I think I'd prefer it if you had Tourette's."

"Fucking hell!"

"Yes, that's more like it, you moody old Capricorn goat. Lighten up and let yourself go."

"If that's how you feel, I'm ordering a bottle of Chardonnay. What the hell! You'll have to drink most of it though 'cos I'm driving."

"Goody. I might manage a glass or two, if you insist."

A teenager in short-sleeved white shirt and neatly creased black trousers approached their table, smiled and set out cutlery, wine glasses and serviettes before them.

"What can I get you?" he asked, pen and pad ready.

******

Monday morning did not see Biggsy at his best. A tickle in his tonsils the day before had developed overnight into a sore throat and head cold. He picked up the black marker and began writing on the whiteboard. As he moved from left to right, he gradually lowered his arm so that the words went downhill for added effect.

I am very ill with a cold and sore throat. Speaking is painful. Please do not give me a hard time.

"Oh, sir! Sorry to hear that," Colley smiled. "So, you're suffering and relying on us to give you an easy ride today?"

He nodded, squinted an appeal at Colley and returned to the whiteboard.

You could put it like that, Chris. But if you're getting any ideas, remember I'm checking your university application.

"Surely you don't think I'd take advantage and make your day any worse than it's going to be, sir."

Just talk quietly amongst yourselves till the bell goes and then head off.

He scanned the expressions on the faces of his form group, sat down at his desk and lowered his head until it came to rest on the laminate surface.

"You poor old bugger, sir! You should be at home in bed with your w…with a cup of Horlicks," continued Colley.

He thought of mustering the energy to counter the boy's cheek but decided against it.

"Don't worry, sir," reassured Gibson. "If you need any help today, who you gonna call?"

"Coldbusters," he whispered.

"Hope you're OK for your observation lesson with us on Wednesday, sir," called Bellchambers over his shoulder, as he left.

"Oh, bugger! I'd forgotten about that."

******

By mid-afternoon, he was ready to take to his bed. His sinuses were well and truly blocked and he'd taken two paracetamol tablets to relieve the headache. Shouldn't have come into school. Being a 'performer', he knew that one shouldn't even try to teach when not on form. But he'd gambled on surviving the day without mishap. The free lesson just before lunch had been a godsend, giving him some respite before the final lesson of the day with 7F.

Pupils arrived and seated themselves in their favourite places. Ms Toner had required staff to provide details of seating plans for all their classes, copies of which she held in a drawer of one of her four coffee and beige metal filing cabinets. Educational experts apparently believed that one vital criterion of academic performance was based on where children sat in relation to one another. All the bad boys should sit at the front, and so on. He allowed his pupils to sit wherever they wanted but had dutifully provided fictitious seating plans.

"Afternoon, lads," he croaked, as the last to arrive found their places. "I'm not feeling my best today. Got a heavy cold, so bear with me, please. Let's just recap on our reading of the novel 'The Ghost of Thomas Kempe'. Amandeep, tell us all what's happened since James moved into his new home."

A shy and quietly-spoken boy, Amandeep sat bolt upright, pleased at being asked to speak.

"Well, James has made a new friend…"

"Simon," interjected Sam Attewell, unable to contain himself. The personification of enthusiasm, Sam was the class member who could make or destroy a lesson. Classroom interruptions were often of his making. More often, these were the result of his desire to succeed, not to disrupt.

"OK, Sam. I did ask someone else to speak, so let the class hear him. Carry on, Amandeep."

"James has a new friend…called Simon. When Thomas Kempe…the sorcerer…sets fire to the cottage of the old lady…"

"Mrs Verity!" Sam called out.

"Sam!" shouted Biggsy, turning on him. "How many times do you have to be told to shut up?"

Before he had even finished bawling out Sam, he was feeling ashamed of himself. He knew he wouldn't have reacted as he had if he weren't unwell. This was the folly of struggling in when under the weather. He was mortified to see tears welling in Sam's eyes. The classroom was suddenly silent.

"Sorry, Sam. I'm not myself today."

The apology seemed to increase Sam's distress. Tears flowed and the boy rubbed his shirtsleeve across his eyes. More annoyed with himself than Sam, he instructed the class to take out their exercise books and write the diary entry that James might produce after the fire at Mrs Verity's cottage. Sam appeared to follow the instruction along with the rest, but it was some time before he was able to put pen to paper.

He didn't speak a word for the rest of the lesson, nor did he look in the teacher's direction. At the sound of the lesson buzzer, he hurried away as quickly as possible. Wrestling with self-disgust, Biggsy gathered all he'd need to take home and did the same.

The evening would be a write-off on two counts, recovering from illness and feeling guilty for his unwarranted outburst.

Chapter 4

He struggled to put the day's shame to the back of his mind, but the evening found him agonising over the incident and its implications. He was troubled not only by the damage he'd done to his relationship with Sam, but also the possibility that the child might tell his parents about his English teacher's outburst. Relationships can be repaired, but reputations are a different matter. A teacher is in the public spotlight, subject to constant scrutiny. He had let himself down and deserved to pay some sort of price.

Wading through a pile of GCSE coursework marking would be a suitable penance to start with, he decided. The luxuries of reading yesterday's newspaper or watching television would have to be foregone. Tedious though the routine of marking often proved to be, he found the levels of concentration the task required enabled him to dismiss all other considerations from his mind. The only concession to comfort would be working in his easy chair in the lounge.

He blew his nose for the umpteenth time that day. He no longer had the sore throat, but his head and chest ached, and his nasal passages were in full flow. The only other interruptions to the silence as he worked were caused by the constant flow of planes departing from and arriving at Heathrow.

Myra was working at the PC upstairs in the box bedroom that had become the 'office'. Ella had not been at home since Saturday morning. She'd stayed for a long weekend at the home of Cath, her best friend, in Teddington. Biggsy reflected on his own time as a seventeen-year-old studying for A-levels. If he were lucky, he'd have had enough money to go to the cinema on Saturday night with a mate, then straight home to bed so that he'd be up in good time for his seven thirty washing-up stint at the Kingswood Hotel. No all-night clubbing in his day. His teenage years hadn't been easy, with little free time or money. Any luxury items, such as fashionable clothes or vinyl records, he could only have if he paid for them. Everyday life for teenagers had been magically transformed. In the new millennium, they could watch whole films on personal mobiles and no longer needed to buy music – they could steal it from the ether. He worried sometimes that, as Ella had grown up never having to earn money for herself, she might take her privileged circumstances for granted. He would never ask if she appreciated the lifestyle provided for her. It wasn't a conversation he wanted or needed to have.

The peace was shattered as the front door flew open and banged against the hall table.

"Hello! It's me," Ella sang, as the door crashed shut. "Have you missed me?"

"Hello, love," Myra called from upstairs. "Have a good weekend?"

"Brilliant! Went to Kingston on Saturday and danced the night away with the girls at Zouzou's. Yesterday afternoon, we went deer hunting in Bushy Park."

"Sounds lovely. Wish I could've come with you. There's a plate of lasagne in the fridge you can put in the microwave if you're hungry."

"Righto. Thanks, Mum. Where's Dad?"

"In here," he called.

Ella rushed into the front room, planted a kiss on her father's cheek and threw herself on the sofa. Looking at her distressed denim jacket, he was reminded that he also had one in his wardrobe, though his was not fashionably shredded. He hadn't worn it for years. There was nothing wrong with the jacket, but it somehow had connotations of youthful rebellion, an impulse he'd come to suppress.

"The weather forecast didn't mention whirlwinds today. How's everything in your universe?"

"Good, Dad. I got that Hardy essay back on Friday. Mrs Woolley thought it was the mutt's – grade A. She said I've obviously got 'well-developed critical faculties' and 'a talent for original interpretation'."

"Great news. I always said that having a teacher for a parent has two important benefits – help with school studies and as many pencils as you could ever want."

"Thanks again, Dad. Can you help me with another piece I have to do?"

"Fine. What's this one about?"

"Oh, we've just started 'King Lear'."

"That's a coincidence. I'm well into the same play with my literature class. It's wonderful. You'll love it."

"Hope so. I have to discuss the causes of Lear's anger in the first scene of the play."

"Ouch! That touches a raw nerve."

"What do you mean?"

"I haven't mentioned it to your mum, but I had a bit of a bust up with a pupil this afternoon. Only twelve years old. Nice enough boy, but I was feeling lousy with this cold and I blew my stack when he interrupted another boy I'd asked to speak. Told him to 'shut up'. I felt awful as soon as I'd said it. Shouldn't have gone into school – fatal when you're ill."

"You always say that, but you never take a day off. You can't be on form every day, Dad. You're only human. Sometimes we say things we wish we hadn't."

"True, but teachers can't afford to fall for that one. Yes, I had a touch of the King Lear's today. Only myself to blame. There are a couple of books on Shakespeare's tragedies in the office upstairs. You can have a look at those, but before you're tempted to regurgitate other people's ideas, why do you think Lear's angry?"

"Any chance that he's just a miserable old git?" Ella suggested.

"A lot of chance, I'd say. So, what particularly makes old people angry?"

"People become more impatient the older they get?"

"Bugger – that's what's happening to me and I'm only fifty. Where does this impatience start?"

"I suppose old people get angry with themselves because their bodies start falling apart. Their teeth go rotten, and they start losing their marbles."

"Is it just themselves they're angry with for those reasons?"

"I suppose it's life as well – the world. They get angry with the world. I wonder if that's what's happened to Grandad?"

Russell, Myra's father, was a grouch, one whose mercurial temperament the rest of the family had learnt to tolerate.

"Wow! Another genius in the family. Taking your grandad as a case in point, who usually ends up being on the receiving end of old people's anger?"

"Their own family. That's what always happens, isn't it?"

"Fair enough. By the way, do you remember our talk about Michael Henchard, when we considered crimes committed against blood ties? The best tragedies, according to Aristotle, are the ones where the central character, or hero, commits a crime against a member of one's own family. You could consider the idea of anger directed at one's own family as the thrust of your essay, Ella, and you're away."

"But why does he single out Cordelia? She's the youngest…and she's nice."

"Yes, the youngest," reflected Biggsy.

The image of a distressed year seven pupil came to him again. He pictured Ms Toner sitting across from him in her study, leaning forward over her desk, fingers tightly interlocked.

"I've had a complaint about you from the parents of one of our youngest pupils in the school. They say you shouted at him for no reason, telling him to 'shut up'. Is there any truth in this accusation, Mr Biggs?"

His thoughts saddened him.

"You all right, Dad?" asked Ella.

"Yes, just an old war wound."

The realisation that Archie Matthews, and not Ms Toner, would be the one dealing with any such matter gave him some relief.

"Other than what Cordelia actually says to him," he continued, "are there any other reasons that might explain why Lear flies off the handle at her?"

"Her youth. He's old and he's jealous of her for being young."

"If you think that's possible, it's an idea you could investigate. Teachers get tired of essays that don't include any original thinking – Mrs Woolley for one. You've got some good themes going already: anger, honesty, jealousy, the generation gap. You're flying. Easy, isn't it?"

"Thanks, Dad. A-levels aren't so bad really."

Ella picked up her bag, propelled herself energetically from her chair and hared off upstairs.

******

He made a swift detour away from Room 125, where a few sixth formers had already arrived for morning registration and headed for the lower school corridor. Arriving at the form room of Miss Whittaker, a young Art teacher, he tapped lightly on the door and entered. Brushing hennaed hair from her face, she smiled in his direction from her desk. The sound of thirty scraping chairs disturbed the peace, as the class stood respectfully to acknowledge his arrival.

"Well done, boys. That was very polite of you all," complimented Miss Whittaker. A single chair scraped belatedly at the back of the room.

"Well, almost everybody," she frowned. "Good morning, Mr Biggs. Can we help you?"

"Morning, Miss Whittaker. Thank you, boys. I wonder if it would be possible to speak to Sam Attewell outside for a moment?"

"Certainly. Sam, can you go along with Mr Biggs?"

More seat scraping as the class sat down again. He wondered why pupils didn't lift their chairs when they moved them, and why teachers, himself included, never asked them to do so. Sam picked up his rucksack and accompanied the visitor into the corridor.

Once in the corridor, Sam looked uncertainly into the teacher's eyes. Anxious to allay any feelings of apprehension that Sam might be experiencing, he began the apology he'd been practising over the past two days.

"Yesterday afternoon, I shouted at you in a way that was totally unacceptable. I apologise for my behaviour toward you and for what I said. I'd no reason whatsoever to talk to a good lad like you in that way. It's not an excuse, but I was feeling unwell all day. I felt even worse afterwards. I hope you'll accept my apology and we can continue to get on well together at school, as we always have done in the past."

Sam's expression relaxed. A faint smile appeared that Biggsy reciprocated.

"That's all right, sir," replied Sam. "I shouldn't have interrupted Amandeep. I felt bad too."

"Well, that's a relief. Let's shake hands and put it behind us."

They extended hands and shook, Sam looking at the floor in some embarrassment.

"None of us is perfect, Sam. Me included. I'll see you in class later then. Off you go."

Sam nodded and rejoined his form. Realising that his own group was waiting for him, he hurried away, relieved that Sam had accepted his apology and pleased that the boy had been troubled by his own conduct.

******

By break time, his energy levels were depleted, and he urgently needed coffee. He'd have to go to the staff room to fill up as he also needed to photocopy a few sheets in the AVA room nearby. Hurrying down the corridor, he decided to grab the coffee first and hope that there'd be no queue for the photocopiers.

The staff room wasn't busy yet. Josie, the tea lady, only had a few customers lining up. One of them, Chris Barker, caught his eye.

"Hello, there, Biggsy," he greeted. "And how's your little angel getting on?"

"If you mean Angela, she's brilliant. Couldn't have made a better appointment."

"You're not wrong there, mate. Looks a winner to me."

"'Ere, you keep your bleedin' eyes off her. I know you PE lot," warned Josie, as she pushed a brimming mug of coffee across the counter toward Chris.

Josie was no ordinary tea lady. Now in her late sixties, she'd been serving tea and coffee for twenty-five years at the school. She lived fifty yards away in an end terrace and did two hours' work at the school every morning. She didn't fit the shy and retiring old stager mould one bit. She was the staff room's moral guardian, always ready to put teachers right, and often with a shower of expletives to reinforce her point. It was a strange fact that she adopted the same manner with anyone, even the head, and nobody thought anything of it. It was her way, and everyone accepted it. Universally loved, she was kindness itself beneath her bluster.

"I'd know better than to do anything to upset you, Josie," joked Chris. "You might put something in my coffee."

"I know what you PE lot want in your bleedin' coffee. Half a pint of bromide."

"I'll give it a go if it improves the taste," he replied, struggling to hold back laughter.

"You cheeky sod! You can make your own tomorrow for that," she chortled chestly.

As Biggsy smiled broadly at the exchanges, he felt a sudden sting of pain. After stirring his coffee and three sugars for several minutes, Chris had removed the spoon from his mug and placed it directly on the back of Biggsy's hand. PE humour at its best. He took his own mug, nodding his gratitude.

"Thanks, Josie. Got to dash," he said, waving his sheets for photocopying and taking a hurried sip of coffee.

Manoeuvring past colleagues lining up for their mid-morning refreshment, he hoped he wouldn't be waylaid. Andy Orchard, looking apprehensive at the end of the queue, attracted his attention.

"Can I see you in the office at lunch time, mate? Something to sort out."

"I'll be in your room directly lesson four ends, Andy. See you then," he replied, immediately overcome by a sense of foreboding.

The task of negotiating a clear run to the AVA room without spilling coffee was complicated by the presence of throngs of pupils on the move.

"Can you help me with my university application, sir?"

Looking behind him, he saw Jermaine Gibson approaching.

"Straight after school tomorrow in the English office, Jermaine. Come and see me then," he called back without breaking step.

Turning into AVA, he was relieved to find that John Vernon, the technician, was the only person in the room.

"Morning, John," he smiled. "How's life in the world of reproduction?"

The technician was on his knees carrying out an inspection of the insides of the photocopier he had hoped to use.

"Don't you mean 'reprographics'?" asked John dully, as he stood upright.

"'Course I do. My mistake."

John Vernon, in his late twenties and already developing a stoop owing to his six-foot-six frame, had the saturnine temperament that reminded Biggsy of Eeyore. The IT genius, benign ruler of his reprographics kingdom, was also a master of innuendo, a trait that was exploited to the full in their many exchanges.

"Sorry to be a nuisance, old mate, but could you knock me out thirty of these – back-to-back and stapled?"

"You'll have to give me a minute because the main photocopier's broken down again. I'll have to do it with my number two machine."

"I've no objection to handing out your number twos to my GCSE class, John."

"I wouldn't advise that if you want to keep your job," came the doleful reply.

"Why does this machine keep breaking down, John? Looks like a decent enough photocopier. What's the make?" Biggsy asked, peering at the plastic plate showing the brand name. "AXOL – never heard of it. Seems more of an ASOL."

"Come to think of it," said John lugubriously, "it does knock out a strange sort of smell when I do a big run on it."

"Gotta be carcinogenic. You're working in a dangerous environment here. You should be issued with full protective clothing and special breathing apparatus."

He laughed aloud, as he imagined John clad in an outfit resembling a deep-sea diving suit.

"You could be right. Sounds like a good excuse to put in for danger money. Anyway, these are yours."

John handed over the pile of papers, assumed an expression of resignation and returned to his investigations of the internal workings of AXOL Number One.

"You're a pal, John. Many thanks as usual. Hope to see you later."

"Can't wait," replied John, at his most laconic.

******

"Check that you've all copied down the homework assignment from the whiteboard, lads," he instructed his year nine group, as the buzzer ended the lesson.

Chairs scraped and chatter erupted. The classroom soon emptied. He let out a long sigh then absorbed the silence. Two minutes of peace had elapsed before he recalled his promise to Andy. He locked up and made his way along the corridor. Biggsy found his second stacking textbooks in neat piles at the back of the room. Sunlight streamed through the windows. The smell of boys' sweat pervaded the atmosphere.

"Hi, Andy. All well?"

"I'm fine, mate, but we've got a situation," he answered with a look of resignation. "Angela's got on the wrong side of Toner. I bumped into her first thing this morning and she was a bit upset. There was a message in her pigeonhole about her failing to meet deadlines for uploading GCSE predicted grades for the assessments we completed recently."

"Not good news. Angela's unaware that delays of that sort will be jumped on. I should've warned her."

"Yes, Toner's a pain in in the backside. She does everything by the book, writing terse communications where you or I would have a quiet word in person. Angela showed me the note, and it looked more like a formal warning than a friendly reminder. She's having a hard time with her year eleven class as well. I think she needs us to rally round with a bit of moral support."

"Hasn't our esteemed deputy head picked up any pointers on emotional intelligence? If there's ever a chance to rub somebody up the wrong way, she'll take it."

He wondered once again how somebody who appeared to have such an antipathy for her colleagues could have risen so quickly up the promotion ladder. Annoyed with himself for not having been aware that Angela was struggling with her examination class, he accepted that he was guilty of a serious oversight.

"Thanks, Andy. You're usually the first to identify cracks in the edifice. I'll find her later and arrange to have a friendly chat. Do you want to be in on it? After all, you're the one Angela's confided in so far."

"You don't think she'll be intimidated by the thought of the two of us being there?"

"I don't think so. It'll give us a chance to present a united front to her. She'll be reassured to hear that we both have reservations about a certain individual's management style. I might have to confront her ladyship about this. After school tomorrow in the office OK with you, if Angela can make it?"

"Fine with me. I'll be around for an hour or so, anyway."

"Thanks. I hope that by the time you're in charge of the department, the school will no longer be haunted by the Toner spectre."

"You're going nowhere, mate," declared Andy.

As he spoke, he reached out with both hands toward his colleague's neck. Uncertain as to Andy's purpose, Biggsy smiled awkwardly and involuntarily pulled back. Andy grasped one side of his friend's shirt collar.

"Only one side of your collar buttoned down. That's sorted it."

"Thanks. Hadn't realised I'm getting to the stage where I need someone to dress me."

"You're the only member of the department to be observed by Toner. Doesn't that strike you as a bit odd?"

He'd mentioned that morning to Andy that she'd be sitting in on his A-level lesson the following day. The rest of his department needn't know that his turn to be put through the wringer had arrived.

"Not really. Rather me than anyone else. Blessing in disguise. I've covered every angle, so my lesson should go off OK. I've primed the class that I won't be in my normal teaching mode. I should qualify for a best actor award if all goes according to plan."

******

The Wednesday he'd been dreading had come around all too soon. He'd only two minutes before the start of his observation lesson. Emptying his bladder had taken him longer than anticipated. He must arrange a visit to his GP for a PSA check.

Ms Toner arrived five minutes after the start of his A-level lesson. He wondered if he should deny her entry. He'd undertaken meticulous preparation, which meant that she'd missed the entire lesson introduction. She would be writing an assessment based on an incomplete observation. This irked him. Her condemnation of a dilatory approach to deadlines, totally unacceptable in others, was clearly not something about which she needed to worry.

His problem now was maintaining his concentration with the class whilst feeling annoyed. He knew that the students would also be feeling aggrieved, their collective sense of fair play offended by the show of disrespect on her part. Colley looked in his direction, raised his eyebrows and smirked discreetly, as the deputy head sat down at a table reserved for her at the back of the room.

"So, Jermaine, could you tell the rest of the class your group's thoughts on the possible causes of Lear's descent into madness?"

"Well, sir, not everyone believed that he was completely mad," replied Gibson looking up from his notes. "Chris just thought he was really angry and depressed because he felt he'd been mistreated."

I know the feeling, thought Biggsy.

******

There was a knock on the office door. Wondering why Angela should think it necessary to knock and wait before entering, he opened it. Gibson stood before him, smiling and clutching a sheet of A4.

"You said you'd help me with my uni application after school today, sir, so here I am."

"So, I did, Jermaine. Stupid of me to forget. I've double booked. I'm so sorry. I have to discuss an important matter right now with two members of the English department. I'm free tomorrow lessons three and four. Can you make it here then?"

"OK, sir. I'm a bit worried about my student statement. I'm not very good at selling myself."

"You'll have to get used to doing that or you'll get nowhere in this world. Is that a rough draft you've got in your hand? Give it to me and I'll look over it tonight. That'll save us some time tomorrow."

"Oh, that'd be great, sir. Here you go." Gibson handed over the sheet of paper. "See you tomorrow, sir."

"Many apologies, Jermaine. See you then."

He was annoyed at himself for letting his star student down, but determined to do a thorough job on the application at home. As he was about to push the door to, Angela arrived.

Shouldering a voluminous, tightly-packed canvas holdall and carrying a set of exercise books before her, she struggled through the doorway. His only concern when appointing her had been that she was short and slight of stature. The worry was that she might have problems imposing herself when confronting class after class of bustling boys. However, her voice was her strength. Articulate and confident, her carefully modulated tone could hold a class spellbound. She also kept in reserve a decibel level that could immediately silence any unwanted outburst.

"Hi, Angela. Dump that lot on the table. Take an easy chair and I'll make you a drink. What would you like?"

"Oh, thanks. If you're brewing up, can I give you one of my special tea bags? It's green tea."

"Everyone has their favourite tea, Angela. Yorkshire's my preference. What sort of a day have you had? I've been run off my feet and I've already had to let one student down owing to a mistake on my part. Forgot all about him. Some days, I wobble a bit."

Unlike some members of staff he could mention, he believed in the importance of owning up to his own faults and mistakes.

"It's been OK, thanks. I've been kept on my toes today, but I don't mind being busy."

"That's good to hear. There's no let-up in teaching as you're discovering. Which age group do you find the easiest?"

"I'm enjoying most of my classes. Year seven are sweet, but year nine boys can be tricky. I suppose the onset of puberty is the reason for that."

"That's right. Most of us find that year group to be livelier than the others."

"The older boys are lovely, but keeping them on track with homework is more difficult than I'd imagined."

"That, you won't be surprised to hear, is a common problem across the department. Older teenagers have so many more things they'd rather be doing than studying: computer games, social networking, sporting commitments, romance, recreational drugs."

"Do you think there's much drug abuse here?" Angela asked.

"It's still a minority pastime, but the minority's getting bigger. Anyway, let's talk about our wonderful deputy head. Andy tells me she's been up to mischief again, sending poison-pen emails to members of my department."

"I hope I haven't caused you any trouble. I had all my assessment grades ready but, after marking a coursework assignment I'd set the boys, I felt I'd been a bit harsh on some of them. I had to make a few changes."

"No problem with that whatsoever. I prefer accuracy every time above all other considerations."

The office door opened, and Andy entered.

"Hi, you two. I'm bushed. But, another day, another dollar."

"Is it all right for Andy to join us, Angela, as he was good enough to let me know about the discourteous missive from the deputy head? We thought it would be a good idea for us to reassure you together that we're full square behind you on this one."

"That's great. Thanks, both of you. I'm just sorry to be a nuisance."

Andy flicked the switch on the kettle, threw a spoon of coffee into a mug and turned to face them both. He ran a hand through his wavy blond hair and adjusted the wire frame of his spectacles.

"In this situation, we both consider somebody else to be a nuisance."

"Most definitely. There are some people in the profession who get their kicks undermining and belittling workmates, and this school is saddled with one of the worst."

"She's hung up on admin. Much of her time is spent circulating pointless lists for us all to complete," lamented Biggsy.

"When she's list*less*," Andy added, stressing the last syllable, "Ms Toner is at her grumpiest. Hope I'm not speaking out of turn?"

"Hardly. We all fall foul of the deputy head at some time or another for failing to meet her paperwork deadlines, Angela, so don't feel that you're the only person she's had a go at. I'll have to talk to her about the content of the email she sent you. Ill-advised would be a polite term for it."

"I don't want to cause trouble for anyone. I've sent her everything she asked for now. I won't make the mistake of missing another deadline."

"Don't torture yourself if you can't always manage it. There's so much to keep on top of," consoled Andy.

"Enough said. I think that concludes our meeting. But before you go, Angela, can we three exchange ideas on strategies to keep GCSE classes up to speed, particularly regarding the homework issue you mentioned? We could all do with some help on that one. I'm thinking that if we have a preliminary discussion and thrash out a few ideas, it'll be the starting point for a fuller discussion at departmental level. I'll put any ideas together that we come up with here and use them as preparatory notes for a plan of action. We all prefer bottom-up campaigns to the usual top-down drivel from management that we have to wade through."

"Sounds great…Biggsy!" she responded, still a little uncertain about her head of department's preferred form of address.

"Excellent, Angela."

******

"Says here that a gin and tonic contains the equivalent of four spoons of sugar," declared Myra, looking up from her mobile phone.

"Sorry?" answered Biggsy, placing his red biro on the table beside the armchair. Staff had been instructed to mark students' work in pencil, red ink considered too intimidating for young learners. But he'd found that pencil marks tended to fade and blur. Consequently, he'd told all his classes that he'd be continuing with red ink and that nobody should feel victimised by his annotation. Red ink had been fine for twenty-seven years, and he liked it.

"I said a gin and tonic contains four spoons of sugar!"

"That can't be right in your case. You drink slimline tonic," he answered, now entirely locked into Myra's train of thought.

"True, but you can't always get slimline."

"You can, though. You know every slimline tonic outlet this side of the river."

"You've got to stop drinking white wine. It contains almost twice as much sugar as red."

"That's interesting," he said, looking again at the script perched on his knee.

"Seriously! You're only allowed seventy grams of sugar a day."

"Whoever came up with that little nugget of information?"

"I don't know what you find so funny. Women are only allowed fifty."

"I had a Mars bar this afternoon. How badly did I do there?"

"Well, that's your allowance for twelve hours. You can eat another one before you go to bed if you haven't consumed anything else with sugar in it today. But I can only eat one…and a bite of yours."

"You're really getting into this, aren't you?"

"I need to. Everyone needs to," urged Myra. "It says on this website that too much sugar makes you irritable, a side effect of the liver having to work overtime."

"That explains a lot."

"Where do you want to go this Christmas, your parents or mine?"

The sudden change of direction in the conversation momentarily flummoxed him.

"That's an important decision to make at the end of September. I haven't even had half term yet. Can we go back to talking about Mars bars?"

Myra rose noisily from her chair, picked up the television guide off the glass-topped coffee table and sat down again.

"For heaven's sake, life goes on outside the school gates. In the outside world, there are real decisions to be made. OK, let's decide something simple that I can start organising on my own. How about next summer we holiday on Kefalonia?"

"Oh God, not another Greek island! I spent two weeks last July apologising to toilet pans the length and breadth of Kos for absent-mindedly flushing bog paper down them. How is anyone accustomed to the intricacies of English latrine etiquette supposed to remember to put soiled toilet paper in a disgusting bucket every single time?"

"Oh, you're bloody impossible! I give up."

Rolling her eyes in frustration, she took herself upstairs to bed, leaving Biggsy and his red pen to their own devices. The ensuing silence discomfited him. Nonetheless, there were essays to mark, and he spent the next twenty minutes finishing them off.

Before turning in, he felt that he deserved a ten-minute telly treat. He switched on and immediately recognised scenes from the film 'JFK'. Genuine interest in the detail of Kennedy's assassination competed with misgivings about the presentation of such a gruesome historical event as entertainment. He recalled an old sixties' pop lyric: 'The news today will be the movies for tomorrow'. He experienced similar pinpricks of guilt when watching daily news reports of the world's latest accumulated tragedies. Foreign correspondents on the spot could be relied upon to adopt grave on-screen demeanours, but their careers relied upon the regular occurrence of momentous disasters and outrages. He took consolation in the fact that his job was not calamity-based.

A telly treat? He switched off and went up to bed.

******

Gibson tapped politely on the open door of the classroom and entered.

"Ah, Jermaine. Good to see you. Sorry about yesterday."

The student smiled mechanically in response to the greeting, approached the desk at which his tutor was sitting, pulled up a chair and sat facing him across a sea of textbooks, exercise books and loose-leaf A4 scripts.

He noticed Gibson surveying the clutter.

"Sorry about the mess. Things are getting on top of the teaching profession a bit these days. I went through your student statement last night, as promised, and I've done some minor tidying up."

He looked down at his desk and reached across for the statement. As he did so, a shaft of sunlight caught the frame of his glasses and the reflection flashed in Gibson's eyes, momentarily blinding him.

"This should now persuade any university vice chancellor that you're a certainty for a first in your chosen degree course."

He handed over the single sheet, pleased that he'd done such a thorough fine-tuning job.

"Thanks very much, sir. It looks great."

A tone of qualified enthusiasm was evident.

"Anything wrong? I thought you'd be a little more excited about getting closer to submitting your application."

"It's a bit difficult, sir. My parents are pushing me to apply, but I'm not so sure I want to go to university now."

"Oh. Has anything specific happened to cause you to reconsider?"

"I've been talking to friends and I'm not so sure I want thousands of pounds of debt before I've even got a job. And one of my mates said that unless you get a first or an upper second, it's a waste of three years. My parents couldn't help me with money because they haven't got any."

The logic of the arguments was sound. A middling degree pass didn't carry as much clout in the jobs market as it had done in the days when employment competition hadn't been so intense. Having come from a working-class background himself, he was pricked by feelings of guilt that he'd received a grant to study for a degree. The idea that a gifted student might deprive himself of a university place for financial reasons was a disturbing one.

"My advice to you is to go through with an application as normal and, if you still feel the same come the summer, you can withdraw then. Don't rule yourself out at this stage. You may have a change of heart."

"The deputy head said in assembly that we should all prepare applications now, whatever we eventually decide to do."

This was strange new territory: he agreed with Toner. But he needn't allow himself to become agitated by that realisation: her motivation was to bask in the reflected kudos of having overall responsibility for packing as many students off to university as possible. Dave Wheelhouse would be more concerned with ensuring that each had made the right choice for himself. Her main consideration was statistical, Dave's professional.

"If you take my advice, Jermaine, you'll keep your options open till the very last minute. I can see why you have your doubts, but I can also see that any university in the country would be pleased to give you a place."

"OK, sir. Just for you, I'll keep my options open. Thanks for sorting out my statement."

He pushed himself upright, folded the sheet into four and placed it in his inside jacket pocket.

"Gotta rush, sir. My shift at McDonald's starts in half an hour."

Biggsy produced a pantomime look of horror as the student hurried away. There were problems for the nation a few years down the line, he knew, if the life chances of increasing numbers of talented young people from less advantaged backgrounds were to be limited by economic factors.

******

"We are, therefore, very lucky that Darren has chosen to take time out of his busy schedule to visit us today."

Mr Fingleton fixed his young audience with a stern stare before seating himself to one side of the lectern at which his guest speaker was standing. Full-bearded and ruddy-faced, Darren Grant nodded toward his audience of a hundred and eighty year seven boys. Gripping the sides of the lectern and directing his gaze to the very back of the hall, he began his talk.

"As Mr Fingleton has already explained to you, I've set myself the task of completing the Three Peaks Challenge to raise funds for the charity Act Against Bullying. This challenge will involve me climbing the three highest peaks in England, Scotland and Wales within twenty-four hours. I want to raise your awareness of the national problem of bullying in schools today, in the hope that you will help me to raise money for the charity. You may not believe it, but I was bullied at school."

Biggsy sighed more noisily than he'd intended. Standing on duty to the side of the hall with five other teachers, he coughed to disguise his momentary loss of self-control. Bullying was anathema to him, but something in him resented the topic being turned into a twenty-minute sideshow. He guessed that this would be the school's token coverage of the issue for this academic year. Proof that the topic was being seriously addressed in the school would be there in black and white on the calendar, should an inquisitive Ofsted inspector be interested.

Studying boys' faces, he saw expressions ranging from indifference to brow-furrowing attentiveness. One boy, attempting to repress a mischievous grin in order to give an appearance of total engagement, was poking his partner rhythmically in the ribs with his pen. Biggsy smiled inwardly. The main issue with bullying that ardent Darren would probably dare not broach was all too obvious: bullying could be irresistible fun. You only had to tune in to Prime Minister's Question Time for a few minutes to find that out. The guilty pleasure has a fascination that many are unable to ignore, whatever their age or social background. His reflections were suddenly interrupted, as the talk moved up a gear.

"I've known people consider taking their own lives as a result of being bullied."

This time, Biggsy shifted uncomfortably from one foot to the other. He was especially sensitive to the increasing incidence of media reports dealing with children self-harming. Teenage suicides were also on the increase. Some experts in the field of children's mental health were pointing accusing fingers at online social networking. Its potential as a tool, in the wrong hands, for undermining young people's emotional and physical well-being was becoming a serious social issue.

He had the deepest reservations about broaching certain topics with large groups of children who had no choice but to sit and listen in silence. Suicide was one of them. Nobody had the right to assume that this was a subject to which every child should be introduced at twelve years of age. He bemoaned the easy assumptions made by so-called forward-thinking educationists. At the same time, he realised how out of his depth he was with the current trend of schools being 'right on', regarding all things educationally weird and wonderful. Computers were another of his concerns. They were being used as a matter of course in all subject areas. From his standpoint, technology had invaded the classroom in ways that had not been fully researched. He didn't share the excitement with which some of his colleagues embraced the development. The first lesson he'd ever managed to book in the newly-equipped computer room, he'd spent much of the time reprimanding boys for accessing online pornography. Some students had even managed to override the safety system and were teaching their peers to do likewise.

As an experienced teacher who'd formerly relied on a stick of chalk as his main teaching resource, he worried that the introduction of sophisticated electronic machinery into the learning process would encourage laziness. He had already seen it with the use of calculators in mathematics lessons. There was no need to learn times tables when a hand-held machine could do any calculation in a fraction of a second. Children needn't worry too much about thinking for themselves, if a computer could do it for them.

The internet had invaded childhood sensibilities in ways that intelligent people in all walks of life chose to overlook. Children of primary school age were playing computer games embracing sickeningly gratuitous violence – for fun. He'd read of one child in a Greater London primary who'd been ostracised by his school mates because his parents wouldn't allow him to play the latest version of 'Grand Theft Auto'. Engendering in one's charges an interest in the poetic imagination of William Blake was a tough call these days for any English teacher. For children allowed to spend several hours a day submerged in the spontaneous hedonistic depths of computer game mayhem, much of what school curricula had to offer could become an irrelevance.

Eventually, the session came to an end. He realised that he'd switched off and missed most of it. He looked around him. The expressions on the faces of several staff members on duty in the hall suggested that they had been more transfixed than most of the pupils by the force of the speaker's words.

"Our thanks for a most thought-provoking talk, Mr Grant," gushed Mr Fingleton. "You have given our boys plenty to think about, and I am sure you can rely on their support. Good luck with your challenge and thank you for giving up your time to visit us today."

Fingleton raised his hands and began clapping. Within moments, the hall resounded to enthusiastic applause. Darren beamed.

Biggsy strode out of the hall, walked the few paces across the main corridor and pushed open the adjacent staff room door. He inhaled deeply, sighed and made his way to the kitchen area. Chris Barker entered, clearly agitated after listening to Darren Grant.

"This school's got it all wrong, mate," he blurted out. "We've got to take on the bullies here and give them a taste of their own medicine."

"How do you mean, Chris?"

"We've got to take them on…zero tolerance…whatever!"

"You mean fight fire with fire?"

"Why not?"

Anxious not to alienate himself from the PE department this early in the school year, Biggsy decided to offer no further comment on the topic. He topped up the kettle, plugged it in and hovered with a tea bag and mug. Dinosaurs have little to offer on serious matters of school policy.

The kettle came to the boil, steam misting up the windows overlooking the staff car park and rose beds beyond.

"Morning, boss," chirped Andy, as he entered the staff room laden with a double armful of textbooks. "Can you tea bag a mug for me too?"

He took another mug from the shelf, grinning at Andy's balancing act.

"Did you see the latest England fiasco last night against the Danes in Copenhagen? Another dire chapter in England's football history," said Andy.

"I've given up watching England, mate. Too painful. I'd rather face an Ofsted."

"I wish I had your common-sense approach to international football. Can't help myself, though. We laboured along for an hour or so at nil nil, and then the manager tried to shake things up by bringing on that fancy midfielder – Jack somebody or other."

"Bentley?"

"No… Shit. That was it. Jack Shit. How much longer can the disaster that calls itself English football continue?"

"Fair point. You're a masochist subjecting yourself to such pain."

"Something was seriously rotten in the state of Denmark. Still, there is some consolation. Living in west London, I can now support Poland instead of England. Safer bet, don't you think?"

"Why not? They play in red and white – only a slight variation of our strip."

"You want to support your own country, pal. There are too many people only too happy to mock our national game," Chris Barker commented in a sinister tone from behind his tabloid.

"I think the England players are doing a pretty good job themselves in that respect," was Andy's smart rejoinder. Biggsy winced.

"Time we were making our way to the office. Let me help you with those books."

Chapter 5

Open Day arrived. It was early October and school would be finishing early at 1.30. Staff would then spend the afternoon putting up classroom displays for the visit of prospective parents that evening. Biggsy appreciated that parents and their sons would wish to look around the 'big schools' in their area before making their final choice. He took the business seriously. From six until eight, all members of staff were required to be on-site to welcome visitors and convince them that St Saviour's provided the best single-sex secondary education available in the borough.

He'd decided to open two of the English classrooms, his own and Sarah's. Her classroom needed no preparation, as it was already a showpiece. She'd mounted a wall display of everyday life in Victorian London to showcase samples of children's work, based on their study of 'Great Expectations'. Another wall featured GCSE coursework on 'Macbeth', with colourful illustrations focusing on the special interest that King James I was said to have had in witchcraft. His own room had the convenience of the main English storeroom at the back, making it easy to fetch and set out textbooks and learning materials.

The department was split between the two rooms. Andy and Beth would be next door with Sarah, and the rest of the department in Room 125. Prefects of all ages had been recruited to escort visitors in groups of a dozen or so around the school, visiting each subject area in turn. At 8.00 pm, at the sound of the school buzzer, all parents and their children were required to assemble in the main hall to listen to Mr Fingleton's half-hour talk. His parental address had become fine-tuned over the course of time, although he had found it necessary to make one important change from the previous year. The practice of inviting questions from the floor had been abandoned as a result of what he termed 'undesirables', possibly attached in some capacity to other secondary schools, coming along with the express intention of highlighting negative aspects of the school in an open forum. Competition between schools had stepped up a pace over the past few years to intense rivalry. He now made himself available after his talk to answer parents' questions. This wouldn't delay him too long as most were anxious to be away and first out of the school car park. This year's exodus promised to be a particularly frantic business, as there was a Champions League football match being televised.

The evening had been going well in the English area, large numbers of smiling parents arriving and departing in good spirits. With half an hour to go, Biggsy was in full flow explaining to a young professional couple the department's special needs' arrangements. He paused, as he felt someone touching his elbow. Turning around, he saw Beth waiting to speak to him. Her usual mood of calm had been disturbed.

"You're needed next door," she said in a low tone.

"I'm very sorry, but I've been called away on an important matter in another classroom. I'll take you to Mr Devlin who will answer any other questions you may have."

Having introduced the prospective parents with whom he'd been dealing to Nick, he accompanied Beth, as she led him out of the room.

"Sorry, but a lady next door is giving Sarah a hard time about her wall displays," she confided.

"Come again, Beth? Wall displays?"

"Yes. Andy tried to intervene but the woman will only speak to the department head."

As he entered Sarah's classroom, he saw her in earnest conversation with a tall, dowdily dressed, lank-haired woman who looked too old to have a child of primary school age. A heavy, black overcoat hung from her thin frame. Head held high and eyes closed, she was berating Sarah in strident tones. Her shrill voice had attracted the curiosity of a knot of parents, some of whom were finding her performance entertaining. Andy was standing to one side, looking bemused.

"I most certainly would not send my son to a school that promoted Satanism. I don't want my child being taught by you about witchcraft and the supposed instruments of darkness, thank you very much."

"I can assure you that the school does not promote witchcraft, madam, but 'Macbeth' wouldn't be 'Macbeth' without the witches," explained Sarah politely.

He hurried to Sarah's side, smiled and introduced himself to the affronted guest.

"Good evening. I'm Mr Biggs, the Head of English. Would you like to join me in the English office to discuss this matter further? I'd be very interested to hear your views."

"I cannot imagine that you have anything to say that would be of any interest to me if you condone the display of such execrable material in your department."

He was sure that she was spot on with her first opinion, but he had to get her out of the room as quickly as possible, preferably out of the school. He'd met his share of congenital malcontents in his time, but articulate ones were his least favourite variety. He doubted that attempts at humouring this woman would have any effect at all.

"These graphic posters will do untold damage to impressionable children," she continued. "My son would be dismayed at such disgusting images. I wish to inform you that I intend to take up this matter with the headmaster and governors."

Noticing that she was not accompanied by the son of whom she spoke, he asked the obvious question.

"Did your son come along with you to the school this evening, Mrs…?"

"As it happens, he did not. He is unwell, though I do not see what that has to do with the matter in question."

At that moment, his evening darkened further as he saw Ms Toner framed in the doorway. Doing her rounds of the school on this most important date in St Saviour's calendar, she'd arrived to assess the English Department's promotional work. Her expression indicated that she had overheard the conversation. She moved forward with brisk steps and introduced herself.

"Good evening, madam. I am Ms Toner, the deputy head. I couldn't help but overhear your conversation with members of our English Department. If I could ask you to allow me to deal with the matter, I shall then speak to Mr Biggs, the head of English, and Mr Fingleton, the head teacher, on your behalf."

Impressed by the sudden appearance of this apparition of professionalism, all smart black suit and appeasing smile, the parent looked down her long nose, sniffed huffily, then smiled sanctimoniously.

"That would be acceptable to me. Thank you. I shall be happy to give you my contact details and await the outcome of that discussion. Really, this sort of moral corruption has no place in an institution responsible for the welfare of young people."

"Would you, please, accompany me to my office so that I can record the details of your complaint?"

Hearing her utter the word 'please' was a novelty for Biggsy. He looked at the deputy head. Her face was impassive. He struggled to interpret her thoughts. He wondered if it were possible that she agreed with the views expressed by this harridan.

If he hadn't believed in witchcraft before this evening, he did now. As the woman was escorted out of the room, he looked at Sarah and Andy. He could see that they were also nonplussed by the bizarre interruption to their evening.

******

The open evening continued without further hysteria. The department packed everything away, rearranged the tables and chairs and managed to get away by 8.45. Toner was nowhere to be seen.

As anticipated, there was a note from her in his pigeonhole the following morning.

Mr Biggs, I should like to discuss yesterday evening's incident involving the aggrieved parent in Ms Clifton's room. Would you confirm with my secretary your availability for a meeting at 3.45 in my office today? S. Toner

Stephanie's got the bit between her teeth, he thought. Despite common sense telling him that the issue would be summarily discarded to the fruit-loop bin, the idea niggled away that some pretext would be found to hang his department out to dry.

He told himself once again that it was unnecessary to have a meeting with her at all. There was nothing to discuss. But the possibility of a back-stabbing exercise refused to disappear from the back of his mind. Such a response, surely, was inconceivable, even for the deputy head. After all, this was a ludicrous matter.

He returned to the English office and emailed Anna that he would be able to make the meeting. The practice of everything going through her secretary had amused him once, until he realised that Anna was a filter through whom Toner could significantly reduce her workload. He then thought of finding Sarah to let her know that dark deeds were afoot, but decided it would be unwise to make her feel as uneasy as he was feeling for the rest of the day.

Uncharacteristic tetchiness crept into his teaching. At one point, he found himself apologising to his A-level group for being 'out of sorts'. Whenever he was off form, he invariably fronted up to a class and came clean, as he'd done when trying to communicate with his sixth form group using only a black marker pen on the whiteboard.

On another occasion when he'd been suffering from a heavy cold, he'd tried to conduct a GCSE lesson via laptop alone, typing messages for the class to read on the illuminated screen. The challenge of getting through a lesson without speaking a single word had appealed to him. His first message had explained this strategy: *"Good morning, boys. I'm feeling very ill today and am unable to use my voice. I should be at home in bed with a hot water bottle. I hope that you will take pity and not give me a hard time."* As expected, a few students had reacted by asking an assortment of intriguing questions:

"Can we strike a deal with you here, sir?"

"Would you like me to take you to the medical room for a lie down, sir?"

"Have you thought of putting more water in it, sir?"

Once he'd started laughing aloud, it had dawned on him that his strategy was a non-starter. Laughing had been more painful than talking.

By the time the final buzzer of the day sounded, he was agitated, impatient to learn what was in the wind. He did up his top shirt button and straightened his tie. It was the one Myra had bought him in a tie shop at Gatwick airport. When he was a child, he'd been fascinated by the collection of silk ties his father had kept rolled up in a bedroom drawer. Biggs Senior, an engineering fitter by trade, had not been the most affectionate of fathers. Accustomed to keeping his son at some distance, he'd rarely abandoned himself to displays of warmth. There had been stern words for misbehaviour, compliments for good conduct, and regular tuition on sessions relating to DIY tasks around the home. The treasury of ties had seemed to provide an alternative route into his father's affection. He remembered inspecting them in turn, running their length between his curious fingers. The silky smoothness had captivated him. His favourite had been the deep claret with a pattern of small gold stars. The tie he wore today was as close a match to that as he'd ever been able to find.

He overcame his natural inclination to tap gently on the deputy head's door just off the main corridor, knocking twice firmly instead. No reply. He tried again. There came the tapping of heels on parquet and, as he turned, there she was. Being of slightly below average height, he looked at her eye to eye. There was no possibility of her failing to detect his discomfort at being this close to her.

"Sorry I'm late, Mr Biggs. Do come in and sit down," she instructed.

Lateness was her forte.

This was his first time inside her office. It was compact, tidy and characterless. He'd half expected to see a dentist's chair in the corner. Sitting with arms folded across his chest, he instinctively readjusted them when he realised the impression he was creating. He decided on one hand in his jacket pocket and the other on his knee for the time being. The polite convention of making full eye contact with his adversary across the table was, he deemed, unnecessary. He knew what she looked like. He grudgingly accepted that her almond-shaped brown eyes and high cheekbones merited the epithet 'attractive', but her thin lips spoke to him of a mean spirit.

"Open Day went well last night. Even more visitors than ever, which is all good news in respect of next year's intake."

"Very true."

"I spoke to Mrs Laidlaw, the lady who was upset with Sarah Clifton's wall display, for some time last night. As you're aware, she took exception to what she termed the 'promotion of Satanism' and, to use her words, 'the shockingly violent images' in the classroom."

She paused, as if inviting Biggsy to pass comment. He furrowed his brow and remained silent.

"Well, I'm certain that the English Department has no intention of converting our students to the minority cult to which she referred," she continued, tightening her jaw and laughing a little too loudly at her own words.

He remained impassive. She didn't sound certain of that opinion.

"However, I am inclined to agree with her to some extent. Although I wouldn't describe the wall display as 'X-Certificate', it is a little too graphic in its content for our youngest boys. As a result, I propose that Sarah remove it."

His jaw dropped slightly. He stared at her in disbelief.

"You're serious?" It was his turn to laugh too loudly now.

"I am, Mr Biggs, and I have Mr Fingleton's agreement. We must respect the views and feelings of all parents, even if we don't always agree with them. I assured the prospective parent that we would respond to her grievance."

She compressed her lips.

"I take it you're not offering members of my department the option of responding in the way they think fit to this eccentric's opinion? You're instructing us as to what we must do?"

"That may be the way you choose to interpret my resolution of this problem, Mr Biggs. I think that, under the circumstances, it is a sensible one. You may describe Mrs Laidlaw as eccentric, but she is clearly of well above average intelligence and, next year, she may be one of our parents. She was talking about contacting the local press. The school does not want to risk negative publicity over such a matter at this important time in the school year."

"I can't believe that the school is prepared to take this kind of action over a matter related to encouraging students' engagement with a recommended National Curriculum literature text. Not just any text, but Shakespeare's 'Macbeth'. This is taking parent power several steps too far."

"We must be seen to be responsive to the concerns of individual parents. Your department's display material is an issue for this parent, and one that we can manage. The criticism of the graphic illustrations is something I don't believe we should ignore," she persisted doggedly.

"But we go to great lengths in the library to encourage the enjoyment of literature – the reading habit – with any number of fiction books about ghosts, zombies, witches and wizards. What's the difference?"

He couldn't believe that he was having this discussion in a boys' secondary school in Greater London in the twenty-first century.

"True, but the boys don't *have* to read those books, and we don't have to mount grisly displays to make pupils read them."

"You'll have to excuse me, but I'm struggling to come to terms with the implications of this whole conversation," he stammered. "I'm going to wake up in a moment."

This observation had the effect of galvanising the deputy head. Pursing her lips and fixing him with a stony glare, she decided to terminate the interview.

"There is no need to discuss this matter further. As I explained, I've spoken to Mr Fingleton and he agrees with me that the display in Mrs Clifton's room will have to be taken down. I should be grateful if you would pass on that message to her."

Blowing out his cheeks and lowering his eyes, he tried to think of an argument that would make an impression on the management monster facing him. But he was dumbfounded, and nothing came to him. So, this was a sensible course of action?

"Before this meeting is concluded, I should like you to consider a few concerns of mine," he stated, looking up again directly at the deputy head.

Toner frowned and pouted in annoyance. She'd had quite enough of this awkward man.

"I do not appreciate your unnecessarily stern email sent to a newly-appointed junior member of my department. The school's management team should be looking to support young colleagues, not undermining their self-confidence. Angela found both the tone and content of your recent communication regarding her list of GCSE grades upsetting, as I did."

It was his turn to wait for a response. After a brief pause, during which she reopened the laptop she had just shut, she responded with total self-possession.

"Mr Biggs, it's essential that new teachers quickly adapt to the high standards we set at St Saviour's. It does no good to tolerate a casual attitude to deadlines."

He could have laughed aloud again but didn't.

He'd expected a reaction along these lines and was prepared. Before continuing, he reminded himself that he was fully justified in what he was about to say because he had right on his side. Unfavourable consequences of any kind would be of secondary importance.

"I recall your arriving five minutes late for the formal observation of my lesson. You missed the whole of the introduction. Would it be fair to refer to that incident as symptomatic of someone adopting a casual attitude?"

Her face flushed, Toner looked in disbelief at this insolent middle manager. Doing her best to disguise her anger, she produced the anticipated excuse.

"I was detained, despite my best efforts, owing to an altercation I was called to deal with in the playground. Senior managers have no option but to respond to emergency situations."

In for a penny, he thought, as he posed the killer query.

"I suppose an apology is out of the question?"

His expression revealed no hint whatsoever of the victory celebrations that were erupting behind his eyes. She, in turn, made a superhuman effort to retain her composure.

"I would have apologised immediately on arrival, of course, but I did not wish to interrupt the progress of your lesson. I do, of course, regret not being present at the very start."

No 'sorry' then, he reflected. *Such a difficult word to prise out of some people.*

"If we could get back to Angela, would you say that your treatment of inexperienced staff here is the same as the treatment some recommend for troublesome school miscreants – zero tolerance?"

"We appear to be on different wavelengths here. My job is to ensure the smooth running of the school in the areas of teaching and learning. The highest standards of staff accountability are, therefore, required if I am to fulfil my professional responsibilities. I should not need to be stating my position to you."

"It strikes me that damaging a young professional's morale is of little concern, then, in the world of strict adherence to school systems and protocols?"

"I don't think we can arrive at any mediation here, Mr Biggs. I fail to grasp your inability to accept the fact that schools cannot function properly if staff, however inexperienced they may be, are encouraged to adopt slipshod attitudes and practices."

My God, you're good, he thought. If this is the new face of education, you'll go straight to the top. Heaven help the likes of me!

He looked at Ms Toner's desk. Other than a telephone, her laptop and a single manila folder beneath her left hand, there were no extraneous items to be seen.

"I won't take up any more of your valuable time, Ms Toner. I have to agree with you that our conflicting educational philosophies share little common ground. Good afternoon."

He stood up, made no attempt at a cordial handshake and left without looking at her. If she needed any additional reasons for wanting him out of St Saviour's, he'd given her plenty. But, no matter, the moment had come for him to act. It was time for him to put his head above the parapet.

Chapter 6

Parking up at home, he heard a grating sound. He got out of the car and inspected his tyres. The nearside front was almost flat.

"Bugger! Deflated – must be catching." He looked up and down his road in the fading light. Early evening peace had settled over the street. *Peaceful on the surface,* he thought.

"You're late," came the greeting, as he opened the front door. "You been seeing that woman again?"

"What an irony!" he exclaimed. "You know, I'm sure you've got second sight. I did, indeed, have a meeting with her ladyship. I'm referring to Ms Toner, deputy head."

"Lucky you!" Myra exclaimed. "Did the earth move?"

"Did the earth move!" he repeated bitterly. "I can't imagine anyone being fool enough to get it on with that lipsticked automaton."

"Harsh. I've seen her. She's not bad looking."

"Her looks are the sort that kill. Medusa is alive and well and currently wreaking havoc at St Saviour's secondary school."

"What is it now? Has she closed down the English Department?"

"She's made a start. She's instructed me to tell Sarah that her 'Macbeth' wall display is too graphic and will have to be taken down."

"What brought that on?" asked Myra, the corners of her mouth twitching. She put the kettle on, took two mugs off the mug tree and put a tea bag in each.

"It's not funny," he groaned. "That lunatic I told you about last night after open evening has got Toner and Fingleton agreeing with her that younger boys may be disturbed by Sarah's wall display."

"Mmm. I've always thought some of Shakespeare's stuff was a bit sick."

He glared at his wife, as if daring her to continue.

"Only joking, love."

"I don't know how much longer I can cope with her. Perhaps I ought to jack it in and start writing pre-school zombie fiction instead. There's got to be more job satisfaction there than teaching at that place. She's taking on the whole department now to get at me."

"But you didn't put up the display. Do you really think it's something personal she's got with you? If it is, I can't see why she's picked you out. You don't represent a threat to her position."

"That's not strictly true: I'm diametrically opposed to everything she stands for in teaching. I made that clear to her just now. She's an apparatchik of the new schooling ideology. If you can't assess it, dump it. If you can dump it, dump it deep. It's people like her who will be running and ruining the schools of the future."

Myra studied her husband's face. She read anger and despair in his expression. The bigger picture that he still had at least another fifteen years in teaching was of more concern to her than this latest upset. She thought hard before commenting on his doom-laden forecast. The kettle boiled. She filled each mug, turned and smiled at her husband.

"Just try to rise above it. So long as people like you are working in schools, there's still hope."

"People like me are pissing against the anti-educational wind that's blowing through school corridors."

"You're not. The kids love you because they know their work with you is meaningful. You've always been resilient. Don't weaken just because you're being rubbed up the wrong way by a shallow-minded careerist."

"She's not just shallow-minded, she's evil."

"If that's true, why does she want posters of witches taken down?" she quipped, unable to contain her wit.

"You're not helping here, Myra. Nobody has ever been able to get under my skin in teaching, but she has."

Myra dropped the dripping tea bags into the waste bin and added a dash of milk to each mug. He smiled his thanks, took one of the drinks and eased himself on to a stool.

"She's just different from you. She's not evil."

Sipping tea, his gaze fixed on a wall tile depicting an idyllic pastoral scene. A watermill turned next to a cottage, and cows grazed beside a pond in the foreground.

"That's a matter of opinion, but she's definitely a malign influence at St Saviour's. I'm just going upstairs to get out of these clothes."

He seized the knot of his tie with one hand and yanked it loose from his collar.

"Hi, Dad. You're home late, as usual."

Ella thumped her way downstairs and joined her parents in the kitchen. She switched on the radio, tuned into a pop channel, turned down the volume for her parents' benefit and sat on the stool next to her father. He managed a smile and sipped from his mug, awaiting the offer he couldn't refuse. But all she wanted was a hot drink.

"I fancy a cuppa, Mum."

"Oh, good. Make me another one when you make yours?" Myra darted back.

"Not quite what I meant," said Ella, rising from the stool.

"It's a rat trap, Billy, but you're already caught."

He caught the line as The Boomtown Rats' hit single sounded from the radio.

"Hey, there's a pop lyric that should have a special significance for you, Ella," he informed his daughter. "You're up to speed with rat traps. Remember Michael Henchard?"

Ella looked at her father with a twinkle of recognition, as she topped up the kettle from the tap.

"A rat in a trap," he muttered to himself.

******

St Saviour's was one of the few state schools with a full programme of competitive inter-school sport. Whenever he had the time, Biggsy made a point of supporting home teams playing after school on the main pitch. On a damp and gloomy Wednesday afternoon in late October, the first fifteen was in action against local rivals, St Benedict's, in the second round of the county cup competition. He'd have time to watch the whole of the second half if he made his way outside straight after the final school buzzer.

With daylight fading earlier in the afternoon as autumn set in, the game started at two o'clock, a full hour before the end of school. Thus, two floors of teaching groups in classrooms that ran alongside the length of the pitch had free sporting entertainment during their final lesson. Teachers toiled away in the face of such distractions, in the knowledge that they would need to be on top of their own games if they were to prevent students from diverting their attention to the frenzied action outside.

The buzzer echoed through the main school building. Boys immediately began putting pens in blazer pockets and books in school bags, their teachers powerless to keep them on task for a second longer than the buzzer dictated. By sheer coincidence, Biggsy was also looking to wind up proceedings promptly.

"OK, lads, chairs under the tables as you leave, please."

It was only a two-minute walk from the English office to the pitch. As he stepped off the playground tarmac on to the muddy sports field, he took in the smell of damp earth beneath his feet. Both sets of players were in half-time huddles fifty yards apart, all mud-smeared legs, tousled hair and mouths bulging with gum shields. The vivid yellow shirts of the visiting rugby team were in stark contrast to the dark blue and claret strip of the home side.

Chris Barker smacked a fist into his open hand as he issued final instructions to his players. His counterpart, David Adams, the head of PE at St Benedict's, was addressing the tallest member of his team. The giant forward smiled, as he listened to whatever coaching advice was being imparted. He seemed to be focusing his attention on an opposition player some way from him – Dixon.

Standing on the half-way line, Aaron Aimes, the young St Saviour's PE teacher and match referee, looked at his watch then blew lightly on his whistle to call the teams together for the restart. Although of only medium height, he was powerfully built. His light tan highlighted the blond hair that almost touched his shoulders. Biggsy guessed that he was a regular at a local gym, where he must go in for sunbed treatments as well as workouts. Affecting a nonchalant air, he checked that both captains and their teams were ready for the second half.

Barker and Adams made their way back to the touchline to oversee the action. Biggsy turned as Nick Devlin approached at a run and stood alongside him. The whistle sounded again, this time loudly, and the match continued.

"It's nine-all at the moment," said Nick. "St Benny's are a big outfit. We'll do well to beat them."

"You don't play rugby yourself, Nick?"

"No. Played at school, but it would be too much of a commitment for me now. If I played, I'd want to take it seriously – regular training and that. I couldn't manage it and teach as well."

"Shame. Clubs must be desperate for big guys like you."

Three of his form were in the team. Jermaine Gibson, an elusive centre, was the team captain. Ian Padfield and Richard Dixon constituted as solid a second row as any Middlesex schoolboy team could boast.

"Dixon upset one of their forwards in the first half. He responded by throwing a punch, but Dixon just dodged it, squared up to him and laughed in his face. I wouldn't want to risk upsetting him."

"I know what you mean. He's in my form group and we have a good understanding. Got a bit of attitude, but we can't all be suave sophisticates, can we?"

They watched in silence as players probed for openings in the early stages of the second half. Much of the action took place in the muddy centre of the pitch, the two packs straining against each other for long periods. It became difficult to identify individuals from the touchline. The match was a classic of attritional schoolboy rugby. A fine drizzle started to fall. The two men did up the buttons of their jackets and turned up their collars.

A dozen or so pupils were left hanging around to watch the closing stages. The players became more vocal, shouting encouragement to each other. Barker and Adams yelled orders into the strengthening wind.

St Benedict's made twenty laborious yards upfield, then took three points from a penalty after the home team was penalised for collapsing a scrum.

"That's a bit picky of young Aaron," muttered Biggsy. "Can't imagine anything intentionally malicious going on with the scrummaging at this level."

Five minutes remained. St Saviour's ran the ball along the line. The winger received it, ran a few paces and kicked it on. His opposite number gathered the ball and walked it casually into touch to avoid taking a tackle. A lineout was formed twenty metres from the visitors' line on the far side of the pitch. Gibson had a quick word with the players either side of him then studied the opposition backs intently. The ball was launched toward the two lines of forwards and taken by Padfield, who immediately bent his back and set off toward the try line. With fifteen metres to go, St Benedict's managed to halt the advance. The referee bellowed an instruction.

"Release!"

This was the signal Gibson had been waiting for. "Now, Stuart! Get the ball out!" he called to his scrum half.

Padfield, with Dixon driving him on, still had possession of the ball. He wrenched his body around, turned toward his scrum half and presented the ball to him. In the deepening gloom, it was passed first to the fly half then to the team captain. Instead of running forward, he took a diagonal course toward the corner flag. Running across his outside centre, he appeared to deliver a pass to him as the player cut inside.

"Who's got the ball?" asked Nick. "It's too dark to see anything."

Gibson continued at speed on his diagonal course, ball still in hand. It was now the turn of the winger to cut inside him.

"Take it!"

The winger extended his arms to receive the ball, jinked inside his opposing winger and accelerated. But his hands were empty. Straightening his course, Gibson ran at full tilt, arms outstretched, the ball still held firmly in both hands. The covering full back was the only obstacle between him and the try line. Fully committed, the defender advanced at pace and threw himself at his opponent's torso. Instead of running directly into the tackle, Gibson turned deftly to his left then spun his whole body around. The tackler, unable to grasp the suddenly twisting centre, slid down his body and was left clutching at the air. Spinning away from the full back's contact, Gibson sprinted the remaining five metres to the line, launched himself theatrically into the air and touched the ball down.

Nick was ecstatic, waving his arms in the air and cheering at the top of his voice. Biggsy clapped his hands, as much to keep warm as to congratulate the try scorer. Two young pupils danced in jubilation further along the touchline. Shouts of glee came from team members who rushed to congratulate their captain and hero. Loud curses could be heard from one or two of the visiting players.

The team captain took the conversion himself, slotting the ball between the posts from the touchline. Clearly amazed at the feat, he ran shouting in delight in the direction of his teammates, to the further annoyance of their opponents.

"What a talent!" exclaimed Biggsy, glowing with pleasure.

St Benedict's desperately tried to save the match in the remaining few minutes. The ball was passed along their back line in their final attack, only for their winger to knock the ball on fifteen metres from the St Saviour's try line. At the final whistle, the victors formed a rowdy huddle, basking in the joy of the moment. They broke up to raise three cheers for the opposition, St Benedict's replying in muted imitation.

As the two English teachers stood watching the players leave the pitch, a flurry of activity broke out. Dixon fell to the ground in a heap as two boys from St Benedict's pushed him violently from behind. He was back on his feet in seconds, looking for whoever had dared to lay hands on him. Next, it was the turn of one of the St Benedict's group to be laid low, this time flattened by a roundhouse punch from Dixon. Suddenly, there was a melee around the prone youngster, a dozen or so individuals from both teams squaring up to each other and shouting blue murder.

Aaron blew his whistle and strode into the thick of the tussle. He was followed by Barker and Adams, who forced themselves between Dixon and those who were anxious to avenge the affront to their groggy comrade. An angry Barker pulled Dixon from the fray and marched him to the touchline. Biggsy had a special interest in the fate of his form member and hurried after the teacher and student. The burly sixth former, in no mood to be manhandled further, shook his arm free from Barker's grip.

"Those two big second rows were at me the whole game, sir. Calling me The Missing Link and Shrek!" he shouted. "Look at my eye. One of them gouged me with his thumb."

"Let's have a look at it, mate," instructed Barker.

He stood before the young man and inspected his face. One reddened eye seemed proof of the claim.

"I think their coach may have some involvement here," advised Biggsy. "I'm sure he was instructing one of his players to get under Richard's skin – literally."

"Even if that were the case, players can't go punching each other's lights out," argued Barker.

Realising that his teachers were taking his accusation of intimidation seriously, Dixon calmed down. Nervously, he looked around him, then at the ground. Reaching down, he began scratching at the dried mud on his knees. Nick scowled in the direction of the visiting players.

"Sorry, sir. They were needling me all the time and I just lost it."

Barker was now thoughtful, aware that his own and the school's reputations were at risk. He patted the player on the shoulder and approached Biggsy for a word.

"I hear what you're saying, but I can't condone punching. What you say about Dixon being wound up may well be true, but Adams won't have it. If I accused the opposition player, he'd deny any misconduct and Adams would back him up. He's part of the furniture at St Benedict's. I've known him for years – almost a mate."

"A mate? He's a disgrace. Just look at Dixon's eye. But I take your point."

Standing next to Barker, Dixon watched the two teams trek back to the changing rooms. Aluminium studs clattered on tarmac as the players crossed the playground.

"As your form tutor and witness to the incident, I'll speak to the head in your defence, Richard. You'll have to come with me tomorrow morning so that he can see the state of your eye. He may not excuse what you did, but he won't be happy about naked provocation. Is that OK with you?"

"Thanks, sir."

"Your boy calmed down now, has he?" inquired Adams, approaching the group. "I'll have to submit a written complaint about his conduct to your head."

Biggsy decided to remain silent. Chris Barker, his joy at defeating St Benedict's forgotten, was also taciturn, clearly wrestling with a dilemma.

"We've never had any trouble with inter-school fixtures in the past. This lad's going to need sorting out," added Adams.

"There's more to all this than meets the eye, Dave," explained Chris pointedly. "Speaking of which, show him your eye, Dixon."

"You always get plenty of knocks and scrapes in rugby matches, mate," smirked Adams, "but nobody expects to be decked."

He marched off to the changing rooms, having no contact whatsoever with any of his own team members. As he entered the back of the PE block, he called back to Chris.

"Seriously disagree with some of the referee's decisions, by the way. I'll talk about them to you later."

"Really?" Barker called back, bristling at the remark.

******

Turning into the school gates, he nosed the Golf carefully past boys dawdling through the car park toward the main entrance. There was an early morning chill, but the sun shone low in the cloudless sky. The events of the previous evening were weighing heavily on him, and he was anxious to see Mr Fingleton with Dixon before any formal complaint arrived from St Benedict's. He stopped at the head's office in the main corridor, pressed the entry button to the left of the door, and waited for the green light that would grant him admission.

"Been a naughty boy, have we?"

He turned to see the caretaker, strolling away from him, a fixed grin on his face.

"I was late for detention," came the dry reply.

The green light illuminated, to his relief, and he strode confidently into the carpeted and curtained office. Mr Fingleton, seated at his desk, turned in his swivel chair, replaced the cap on his Mont Blanc and tucked it away inside his jacket.

"What can I do for you this morning, Mr Biggs?"

"Sorry to interrupt you, Mr Fingleton, but I was hoping that I might be able to bring Richard Dixon, one of my students, to speak to you about an unfortunate incident in which he was involved at the end of last night's first fifteen rugby match?"

"Ah, yes. Dixon's been in the wars again. Mr Barker rang last evening to give me the good and bad news."

"I was watching the second half of the match and saw the incident that marred the result. There are mitigating circumstances, and I'd like to bring Richard along to you after morning registration to apologise for his misconduct. I want him to put his case before you receive St Benedict's version of events."

"Do you think he has a case?" the head queried. "Mr Barker thinks it was yet another typical Dixon outburst."

"I think he has. From where I was watching, there was clear provocation."

"Dixon continues to be a disappointment to me. He's not been the most cooperative or amiable of fellows during his time here, but we've done our best to cope with his unpredictable conduct for six years at St Saviour's. In addition, we've received complaints about his uncouth behaviour outside of school. Only last term, there was the appalling incident that resulted in him being ejected and subsequently banned from the shopping mall in the high street. He was lucky not to be expelled."

Biggsy recalled the event. Only Dixon, with his off-kilter sense of humour, could have got himself into that scrape. He couldn't imagine too many mothers pushing a pram taking kindly to being told by an over-solicitous teenager, "Eh, missus, your baby's 'aving a crap."

"Richard's certainly an unusual and sometimes challenging boy, headmaster, but this is the first time he's ever had cause to retaliate on the rugby field. As I say, he was a victim of constant provocation and deserves to be given a fair hearing."

"Whichever way you look at it," continued Fingleton, "he assaulted an opponent in a most violent manner. I can't say that I shall be sad to see the back of him next summer. By all means, bring him to me after registration, but I should advise you that this boy has tried my patience on rather too many occasions."

"Thank you, headmaster."

Deflated, Biggsy withdrew. Fingleton's 'disappointment' with Dixon was, in his opinion, petty. It didn't reflect any merit on the head as a person or his position in the school. Such casual indifference toward any student was entirely unacceptable. The boy did have a history of run-ins with members of staff for a variety of misdemeanours, but he was still a student in the school's care.

He decided that he and Dixon wouldn't be seeing Fingleton after registration. There was little point.

Most of his boys had arrived by the time he reached the form room. Dixon was the focus of attention, a fruity bruise having appeared around his eye. He was in an unusually subdued mood, showing no inclination to provide details to his questioners about the previous afternoon's events. Colley and Bellchambers were doing their best between them to tease out Dixon's alpha-male instincts, to no avail.

"Come on, mate! Give us the gen on why you flattened this St Benny's tosser," badgered Colley.

Dixon rolled his eyes and threw his head back, in no mood to discuss the matter.

"Language, Christopher," advised Biggsy.

"Maybe I should start playing rugby. Sounds like more fun than I thought."

"If you were ever allowed to represent the school at rugby, Chris, we'd be banned from all inter-school sport forthwith."

"Harsh, sir! I 'aven't got a criminal record. Never leave any traces of my handiwork in the 'hood."

"Whatever, Chris. OK, now you're all here I'll complete the register."

When the buzzer sounded, he approached Dixon for a confidential word.

"Richard, I've thought over the rugby incident and think it's better not to bother the head with the business at this stage. We'll deal with this one together later. Is that acceptable to you?"

"Whatever you say, sir," replied Dixon in a dull monotone. "Really wish I 'adn't 'it 'im, though."

"I wish you 'adn't 'it 'im too, but we all do things in the heat of the moment. Life does that to us all from time to time."

******

"Ah, Mr Biggs. Could I have a word before you go home? I was expecting a visit from you and young Dixon after morning registration, but you both failed to appear."

The head had taken him by surprise, as he'd exited the main entrance at the end of the school day. There he was, in conversation with Bulmer. As Biggsy approached the two men, the caretaker was dismissed. Scrumpy leered at him over his shoulder before making off.

"Sorry to have wasted your time, Mr Fingleton. After our conversation first thing, I reconsidered and thought it better not to bother you further with the matter," he replied, repressing an urge to ignore the man and walk away.

"When I agree to an appointment, I expect it to be kept. Out of politeness alone, I should at least have expected you to contact my secretary to inform her of your change of mind."

"Begging your pardon, Mr Fingleton, but when I brought this matter of concern for one of my students to your attention, I had been hoping for a more sympathetic response."

A few years earlier, he would have been cowed by such a criticism of his conduct. At this moment, he was seething with contempt for the man.

"I think you may be forgetting yourself, Mr Biggs. You well know that the student in question has a very chequered history at this school and is not one who would immediately qualify for one's sympathy."

"I may be mistaken in my opinion but, even though he's six foot tall, weighs sixteen stone and can be troublesome, he's still technically a child in our care," he argued, aglow with the force of truth. "I do apologise for keeping you waiting unnecessarily this morning, Mr Fingleton. I won't make such an error again."

"That may well be, but your attitude does disappoint me."

The corner of Biggsy's mouth dropped. This was a man who seemed to be in a regular state of disappointment, poor fellow.

"I should be grateful if you would take no further involvement in the matter. I shall deal personally with the student and any repercussions that may occur from the unsavoury incident. Good day to you."

"Good evening, Mr Fingleton."

There was nothing more to be said. The knowledge that he'd done something momentous energised him. He had relinquished the safety of the fence, climbed down and shown himself prepared to act. Inclining his head slightly, he turned and walked to his car. Unable to recall the last time he'd been challenged by any member of staff, the head stood motionless for a few seconds before returning to his office.

Biggsy had crossed a line that he'd never intended crossing. Perhaps he should have kept his mouth shut and continued playing the top-down game. Top Tip No. 2: Never criticise the school head to his or her face. At the same time, he bristled with indignation at Fingleton's pomposity. A student's future was at stake. As his temper cooled behind the wheel, with the help of Radio 3, he did experience some regret that the head had forced his hand. There were plenty more teaching jobs around, if the worse came to the worst. He didn't remember the twenty-minute journey home.

Sitting in the car outside the house, he considered how he would explain the day's events to Myra. He could focus on his anger at Fingleton's failure to deal professionally with a sensitive issue involving one of his students. But Myra didn't do anger in the workplace. She thought it immature, unbecoming, silly even. Had he been silly? In his current state of mind, he didn't consider it silly to stand by a professional conviction. But this was the first time he'd done so in the face of the top man.

There was a darker side to his mindset. He had a deepening despair at the direction secondary education was taking. The prospect of genuine negotiation between school managers and teaching professionals on any educational matter, at any level, was illusory. This, he judged, was the root cause of his professional dejection. He sensed a creeping inhumanity in the treatment of young people in schools. A system that perceives children as being so much data fodder has no truck with the needs of individuals. Bureaucracy had side-lined educational philosophy in the order of things. He was foolish to believe that the world of education could be guided by anything other than pragmatism, dishonesty even, like the rest of the world. Fingleton was conditioned to dismiss any opposition to the grinding tedium he was instrumental in orchestrating. It wasn't his fault. Yes, it was. Autocrats were governing education with an iron fist. Kafka came to mind.

But there was still Myra to consider. She would think that he was losing his grip on reality, that he was taking his job, teaching and himself too seriously. She would be sympathetic to a degree, but worried about him putting his job and their living at risk. Pragmatic. Was he worried about these things? Yes, his practical self was, but his intellect didn't give a damn.

He decided to play the whole thing down with her. He would explain what had happened, but make it clear that he was not worried in the least about the possible consequences for their financial security. There was a teacher shortage and would be for the foreseeable future because most sane employment hunters realised that the job was impossible. Many new appointees in schools nationally, some taken in by phony advertising campaigns on television, would leave the profession for pastures new within five years. He could get another job if necessary. He could do supply. If he didn't make an issue of his 'deepening despair', she would be fine.

But he knew that despair wasn't something one could conceal or disguise indefinitely. At some point, there would inevitably be consequences. Open hostility toward those professionals above him in the school hierarchy could well be one. He could just try to laugh off his professional misgivings. But they could soon become intolerable. He picked up his Tesco bag of exercise books off the passenger seat and got out of the car.

******

Myra was sitting on a stool at the kitchen worktop reading the newspaper. They bought a tabloid a few times a week and, to repair the resultant damage to their brainpans, a broadsheet at the weekend.

"Hi, love!" he called. "How's my favourite person in the world?"

"Better not let Ella hear you say that," she warned. "Good, yes. How about you?"

"Had a bit of a run-in with Fingers, but otherwise OK," he answered, kissing her on the cheek.

"That explains the atypical greeting. Needing some TLC?" she asked, her eyes twinkling mischievously.

"Can't get anything past you, can I? I made an appointment first thing with the head to bring one of my sixth-form students, Richard Dixon, to see him. The boy's a bit of a loose cannon, but I like him. He played rugby against St Benedict's yesterday and was goaded constantly throughout the second half of the match. He flattened the main culprit after the final whistle. I wanted to put the compassionate case to Fingleton before he receives the official letter of complaint from St Benedict's. But I stood him up – didn't bother keeping the appointment."

"Ooooh! Testosterone time," she cooed.

"Perhaps. The point is…Fingleton's reaction was so dismissive of Dixon when I spoke to him initially. I know he's not the easiest boy to get along with. So, I decided against taking him to apologise. I couldn't be bothered."

"A double diss! Bet that made the old tyrant's day. Not like you to make a fuss, though," she said, turning to the evening's television pages.

"No, I never make a fuss. Time I did."

"Ooer! I'd better watch out. My hubby's on the warpath."

"I quite like the head. Always got on well with the old bugger in the past. But today, he was just an irritant."

"Well, I don't think it does any harm now and again to rattle people's cages. Stops them getting complacent."

He suddenly surprised himself with a rare example of lateral thinking.

"Why don't we go down the road to the Italian for a meal? I know it's only Thursday, but why the hell not!"

"Where's my coat? I'm not passing up this offer."

Galvanised into action, she hopped off her stool, pushed it under the worktop and hurried upstairs. As she did so, she issued instructions over her shoulder.

"While I'm putting my face on, take the pork chops that I bought today out of the fridge and put them in the freezer. You ought to have bust-ups with the head more often. I'll be ready in ten minutes."

Doing as he'd been told, he heard a key in the front door. Ella appeared, breathless and juggling a selection of plastic bags.

"Hi, Dad. Went to the high street after school with Cath and did a spot of shopping. Where's Mum?"

"We're going out for a pasta fest down at the Italian. Mum's upstairs getting ready. I wouldn't have thought your creaking wardrobe had any capacity left for more clothes."

"Gotta pay attention to your image. You don't want people to think you're letting yourself go," she explained. "You ought to give yourself an upgrade, Dad. No offence, but I've seen more fashionable gear in Oxfam than what you wear. You want to look smart when you go out with Mum, don't you?"

"I'm not a fashionista, love. Never had the figure or the inclination to be a dedicated follower."

"Not too much wrong with your figure, Dad. A new suit would transform you. Enjoy your meal."

She took the stairs two at a time, at a speed he envied. He heard her greet her mother and then the two of them discussing Ella's purchases. A delay seemed likely before he and Myra would be able to leave the house, so he put the kettle on for a swift cup of tea.

Humming The Kinks' song that would be fixed in his head for the rest of the evening, he considered his daughter's advice. A new image might, indeed, encourage others to take him more seriously. He tried to imagine the reactions of colleagues and students, should he make an assault on menswear outlets in the high street.

Hey, it's Biggsy, the snappy dresser.

Better watch out. He means business.

Is it a bird? Is it a plane? No, it's Suitedandbootedman.

Dig those threads.

Midlife crisis! Who's he trying to kid?

Then again, did he want anyone he considered beyond the pale to take him seriously? Thinking about the persona he tried to project to the world, he itemised discrete components: quietly conscientious at all times in the workplace (a 'yes' man); a professional attitude grounded in common sense (a dinosaur); intellectually and morally principled (naïve); a safe dress sense unlikely to create a negative impression (dowdy). His approach was diametrically opposed to that of the brash educational go-getter. Such an animal was obtrusively conscientious (a poser); antipathetic to good sense ('clever'); an 'ideas' person (inconsistent); morally bankrupt (a 'visionary'); and had a sharp dress sense (a gangster).

Perhaps, however, he should sharpen himself up for his wife. Shake himself up for her benefit, as Ella had suggested. He had two jackets, a mid-blue tweed and another in beige linen. Unlike his wife, who felt duty-bound to buy a new pair of shoes every payday, he possessed only three pairs, one of which he only wore when gardening. He made a radical decision. At the weekend, he would buy a new suit. He'd make a special visit to Kingston and surprise everyone. Myra would approve. She regularly made pointed comments about the fact that his trouser bottoms only just touched his shoes, and found it hilarious that his 'best' shoes had had so many visits to the cobblers. His decision was made. The girls would be hit for six. What his colleagues and the students would think was another matter.

Chapter 7

Despite the early morning cold, the forecast promised bright sunshine later in the day. Oblivious to prevailing weather conditions, Biggsy scraped the frost off the windscreen. He was assessing the possible consequences of falling out of favour with Fingleton. In the worst case, he did not relish the thought of having to make hasty arrangements to teach elsewhere. He liked the children and most of the teachers at St Saviour's and, not being driven in career terms, he didn't welcome change for change's sake. Disinclined to the grass-is-greener philosophy of life, he saw all state schools as being of a similar breed: closed institutions, dominated by strict pedagogical systems to control the staff, with rigid testing arrangements and formalised teaching practices. It didn't really matter where one taught. Any school, in his view, was as good or as bad as any other. Ofsted might say otherwise, of course. He would move if he had to. Myra would certainly prefer him to stay put. Their lives had settled into a tidy routine that ideally suited her.

There were no alarms as he approached St Saviour's. No armed guards at the school gates barred his entry, and his favourite parking spot was available. Amused by an impulse to tiptoe past the head's office, he quietly made his way along the main corridor. Approaching the sanctuary of the staff room, his priority was to make a brew. Helen Staddon, the head of modern languages, looked up from her broadsheet and smiled in his direction as he bustled through the doorway. He wondered if the string of pearls around her neck were the real thing. She was such an elegant dresser; it wouldn't have surprised him if they were. All was peaceful. It was 7.45 am. Only a handful of teachers and a sprinkling of boys were on site. He enjoyed the fifteen-minute calm before the school burst into life.

Lost in thought as he stirred his tea, he was unaware of Angela sidling up to him.

"Morning, Biggsy."

"Morning, Angela. Hope everything with you is better than it is with me."

"Have you got a lot on your plate at the moment?"

"I'll tell you about it later. Could be a long conversation. How are those GCSE lads of yours getting on?"

"It's still proving difficult to get homework out of some of them. I'm sure it'll help listening to how everyone else copes at the department meeting after school."

"Yes, our item's at the top of the agenda. By the way, I had a word with the deputy head about the unfriendly email she sent you."

"That was brave of you. How did it go?"

"I don't think I left her in any doubt as to how annoyed I was about the matter. If you receive any more snotty messages, let me know straight away. I'm now on a crusade against unprofessional practice of that sort."

"Thanks so much. I hope I'm not making your job any more difficult than it already is."

"This is quite possibly one of the most important aspects of my job, Angela – protecting my English staff from management abuse."

"I'm really grateful to you for all this. Thanks again for everything. See you later."

"Will do. Enjoy your day."

She gathered up her holdall and went to inspect the contents of her pigeonhole. He moved to the window and studied the scene before him. Children were beginning to file through the gates, some struggling under the weight of rucksacks and kit bags.

******

"Is there something going on that I don't know about?" asked Myra, her eyes narrowing.

"Why does there have to be something going on simply because I'd like to buy a new suit this weekend?"

"You're not a suit person. I married you knowing you weren't a suit person. That suited me. And now you spring this on me."

"I thought you'd be pleased, love. You're always saying that I don't pay enough attention to my appearance."

"A new suit!" she cried. "Who's managed to get to you where I haven't?"

"I thought you'd be pleased," he repeated, aggrieved that he should be on the defensive with his wife over simply deciding to buy clothes. "Ella thinks I owe it to you to smarten up. She also said that I might be taken more seriously at school if I improved my appearance, but that's of secondary importance – excuse the pun."

"All my attempts to make you a little more fashion-conscious over the past twenty years have been a waste of time, but when Ella says one word on the subject…"

"Surely, you're pleased," he remonstrated. "Ella may have a point, too. You know the management philosophy of St Saviour's: if you look smart, you are smart. If I'm seen to be attaching more importance to my appearance, management knobheads might think twice before taking me for a prat."

He was aware that his tone of voice had become more strident on reaching his conclusion. Yawning nervously, he pushed one hand in agitation through his hair.

"Well, I'm not letting you go unaccompanied to Suits You Sir or wherever else you intend going on your own. I'm coming with you."

"I was just going to pop in and buy something off the peg. You needn't bother coming along."

"You must be joking. You'd end up coming away with some shapeless ragbag that would be a total waste of money. You're having a made-to-measure."

"Oh no. I just want something smart and not too expensive."

"Don't be silly. Menswear shops are just waiting for muppets like you who don't have a clue what to buy to walk in off the street with a pocketful of loot. They offload everything they can't get rid of on to the likes of you. No, I'll come along, hold your hand and make sure the nasty man does a good job."

"I didn't imagine it would be like this."

"Nothing is, love. Nothing ever is."

He and Myra duly made an early morning appearance the following weekend at Standish & Son, Tailors. He was allowed to plump for plain dark blue as his colour of choice, but he wasn't prepared for the selection of shimmering materials the salesman presented for his approval. He suddenly regretted the idea of attaching any importance to Ella's fashion advice. Too late, he realised, he should have been charier about taking the cue to 'move to the groove'.

******

"Got a minute, mate?"

He was back in the staff room at lunchtime, delivering agendas for the next department meeting. He turned to see Chris Barker beckoning him over with a jerk of the head to the PE area of the staff room. Ray Hollis, his second in department was sitting alongside him. He was a standard ectomorph to his department head's mesomorph. Where Barker was ruggedly muscular, thick set and dark-complexioned, Ray was tall, lean and pale. Biggsy thought Ray could do with half a dozen good meals and a visit to a tanning salon. He was Barker's irreplaceable admin expert, the PE man who did the bulk of the department's online record keeping. Good-natured and guileless, he kept a low profile and was not in the least the typical jock. Other than having a reputation for reliability, he seemed to have no obvious interest in climbing the teaching ladder.

"Thought you'd like to know the latest about your boy, Dixon."

"Oh yes?" Biggsy queried, a caution bell sounding in his head.

"Fingleton asked me at break about the skirmish the other evening. Wanted my opinion as to what sort of action the school should take against our have-a-go hero. Said he'd already seen you and wanted a second opinion."

"So, you didn't go to him after your initial phone call? He approached you?"

"Yep. I had no intention of running to him about a boy who's probably going to get kicked out, anyway. I told him it'd be best to play the whole business down and let matters take their own course."

Barker's indifference needled him.

"At first, he seemed keen to set an example, but I suggested otherwise. After all, he's the loose cannon who usually fires up the first fifteen pack when they're at risk of losing their way against the toughest opposition. Nothing like a bit of blood and thunder to inspire the troops."

Biggsy wondered if blood and thunder were qualities to be encouraged in a child. If they were condoned in a sporting context, the message could be taken that they were acceptable in other social settings.

"That was good of you, Chris."

"Fingleton seemed to see it my way, so it looks as though Dixon's safe in the short term, at least till our next match. Just hope, for your sake, he manages to see the year out."

A sardonic laugh accompanied Barker's final comment.

"I got the impression the head was considering making a meal of him."

"Yeah, could've been messy. But it's common knowledge that Fingleton hates Budgie's guts. He wouldn't enjoy being dictated to by the head of St

Benedict's. The two of them 'ave form. A couple of years ago, Fingleton got very upset when Budgie got preferential LEA treatment for their new PE block. We're still making do with our ancient gym facilities."

Geoffrey Budgen, head of St Benedict's, had a reputation for taking no prisoners in education authority dealings. His was a strident and uncompromising voice amongst secondary headteachers locally. His was one school where Biggsy would not choose to teach.

"Thanks for filling me in, Chris."

"Fingers asked me to do as much, so job done."

******

He took one of the few remaining chocolate digestives off the plate he'd placed on the table earlier. Every one of the six muffins he'd also provided had been eaten. These formed the staple diet of his department meetings.

Having decided to include only bottom-up initiatives on the agenda, he was looking forward to the next hour or so. It made a refreshing change to limit discussion to those matters his English colleagues had put forward.

"Item one then, everybody. Angela asked me if we could exchange views on strategies to encourage all GCSE students to complete homework punctually. I'm sure you'll agree that this is a thorny issue worthy of revisiting periodically. The school homework policy is rigidly enforced, so we're talking about a priority area. Any thoughts?"

"This is a really tricky one," Sarah volunteered. "If I did a thorough check, each time I set homework, that the work had been completed by every child, I'd waste half a lesson. I've got a hard core of serial non-doers in all year groups that I can't do much about. If I were to impose regular sanctions, such as detention, I'd also have to give up an hour of my time after school each day. Then there's the loss of goodwill between teacher and child that would result. Homework is probably my most insoluble problem."

Biggsy admired Sarah's honesty. He felt sure her views were shared by most of the teaching staff across all subject areas at St Saviour's, though few would admit to them.

"I'm in much the same situation," he added. "I could put individuals forward for senior staff detention taken by the head every Wednesday, but that would mean most of those present would be my students. It would be seen as a major weakness on my part if I were to take that course."

"Some of my boys simply don't come from homes where they have the right conditions to do homework," argued Andy. "The work I get from some of them makes me think they must have written it at McDonald's. I regularly have to put up with dog-eared sheets of paper smeared with grease."

"Yes, I've been there. I sometimes think I should be wearing surgical gloves when I'm marking boys' work. So, as I said, this is not a new problem. We've been dealing with this situation for some time and not found a foolproof solution. We have Angela to thank for raising the issue."

"Well, now that it's back in the frame, we've got to rethink it," added Sarah.

"Would it be a good idea to start a department homework club, where students can come along for an hour to complete their work?" asked Angela. "We might be able to encourage some of those who struggle with homework to attend."

"Sounds good," Biggsy responded. "Voluntary detention? It could catch on."

He was pleased on two counts: his junior had thought her problem through since they'd last discussed it, and there was a general nodding of heads. Beth was especially keen. Her eyes narrowed, as she wrestled with calculations before adding a comment.

"If we offered the service twice a week and we were all involved in supervision, that would only require each of us to do an after-school stint once every three weeks at most."

"I'd be happy with that arrangement. Is everyone OK about giving it a try and modifying as necessary?"

Angela's eyes widened with delight at the unanimous agreement.

******

He was wearing the new blue suit to school for the first time. This was uncharted territory. Myra had wanted the vivid apparition that her husband had become to present itself to staff and students first thing on Monday morning, but he'd put off her plan for twenty-four hours, arguing that he needed extra time to muster his mettle. His limbs seemed to have lost their flexibility once he'd put the suit on. He imagined himself a knight of old, armoured up to the gills, as he set off to battle. Myra had assured him that he'd soon get used to the sharp edges.

Her description of him that morning had been that he looked 'a dream' and taller. She'd insisted that he wear it at least once a week to work and that he should buy another soon. That way, he would find it easier to cope with the novelty of looking smart.

As he readied himself to get out of the car, he couldn't ever recall feeling so self-conscious about his appearance. He could remember the first suit he'd ever bought for his wedding. The waistcoat had seemed a wholly unnecessary addition, but Myra's word had been law even then. She'd insisted on a mid-blue three-piece, with a double-vented jacket. He'd felt uneasy about his 'loud' appearance throughout the ceremony, but had survived the proceedings. Thanks to a sudden weight gain that had required a sustained spell of gorging, that monstrosity had subsequently been consigned to a local charity shop. For the past decade, he'd had in his wardrobe one budget-priced black suit that only ever came out for funerals and weddings.

He got as far as the main corridor without incident. As he put his hand on the staff room door handle, he heard a low wolf whistle. Sarah approached him, open-mouthed.

"Love the new image, Biggsy," she gushed. "That style and colour really suit you."

"Thanks, Sarah. Thought it was time to break the mould – more for the sake of people in this place than mine."

"I see," she smiled conspiratorially. "Astute move. It really does make you look younger. Whatever you do, though, don't sit down in there. You don't want the grubby upholstery spoiling your clothes."

"Very funny."

He relaxed a little, as he entered the staff room. Helen Staddon, sitting in her usual place, looked up and raised approving eyebrows. Unable to conceal his embarrassment, he merely shrugged his shoulders.

Ten minutes later, Andy arrived, looking a little out of sorts.

"Hi, Biggsy, Sarah. Had to take the car to a mate's to be fixed. Serious engine trouble – could be costly. Nice whistle, though, mate!" he complimented, interrupting himself. "I might take a leaf out of your book and sort myself out with some new kit. I haven't bought any clothes for ages. Can't afford to at the minute, though, with the money I'm paying out on the motor."

"I reckon yours is a rogue Ford, Andy. It's always letting you down. The suit was my daughter's idea. Something along the lines that if you look smart, you may stand less chance of being routinely taken for a wally brain. I'll keep you up to speed with subsequent research, but I doubt it'll make much difference."

"I must admit seeing you in a suit takes a bit of getting used to. A bit like the pope wearing jeans. What do you think, Sarah?" he asked, catching her eye, as she looked up from a pile of exercise books she'd started marking.

"He looks lovely," she beamed. "The PE department should take note."

The staff room door opened and Ms Toner appeared, her jawline tight. She scanned the room then made a general announcement to those staff present.

"Could you let everyone know that Mr Fingleton has called a staff meeting in fifteen minutes' time at eight thirty? Thank you."

General chatter broke out as she withdrew.

"Trouble afoot," Sarah warned.

******

Despite the caretaker's best efforts to sabotage the staff meeting, it went ahead only five minutes later than scheduled. He complained under his breath to Biggsy and Andy that he'd not been given enough advanced warning to arrange seventy-five chairs in the main hall. His cursing as he eventually departed set the tone for the disturbing news to come.

Ofsted had called the school the previous afternoon with news that a team of inspectors would be paying a two-day visit that Thursday and Friday. Fingleton did his best to appear unruffled, as he delivered the news. He offered reassurance that the inspectors would only be around for two days, as opposed to the full week in days of old, and he had every confidence that the school would once again be rated outstanding. Stunned into silence, his audience exchanged troubled glances. There had been warning of an inspection at some time during the academic year, but no one would have chosen the tormentors to arrive this early.

"Over the next two days, to a greater or lesser extent, we will all have documentation to prepare for our visitors," Fingleton said, gathering his papers, as he prepared to end the address. "The school will, therefore, remain open until nine o'clock this evening and tomorrow evening. However, I urge you not to exhaust yourselves before the inspection."

As the hall emptied, Sarah nudged Biggsy in the ribs.

"I knew there must have been a reason for you buying that suit," she said. "Either somebody told you this was coming up or you're psychic."

"Quite the most unfortunate coincidence imaginable," he replied, grim-faced.

The staff room was packed, teachers choosing to voice anxieties and fears to friendly faces rather than hurry off to registration. Some struggled to control their rising panic, whilst others assumed an air of plucky bravado.

Biggsy's immediate concern was the state of the department's paperwork. The English handbook would need tidying up, but he felt that all was in order otherwise. The onerous task he and everybody else dreaded was the preparation of highly detailed plans for every lesson taught during the inspection period. In addition to explaining the focus and content of the three separate parts of each lesson, paperwork also had to include information on necessary arrangements for pupils with special needs and those considered to be 'gifted and talented'. Accountability gone mad, in his opinion. The thinking of education ministers was, he thought, seriously flawed. There was no correlation whatsoever between the production of reams of lesson notes and the delivery of an outstanding lesson. The process hadn't always been so paper-intensive. If inspectors couldn't assess someone's teaching ability without masses of forms in front of them, they were the wrong people for the job.

Dave Wheelhouse happened to be standing alongside Biggsy, as he studied the Ofsted notification sheet on the notice board.

"I could be out the door a few months earlier than I'd thought."

"Nothing for you to worry about, Dave. The sixth form's going great guns."

"I've had a few tetchy emails recently from DHM Curriculum about the sixth-form assessments. Apparently, too many of our students are coasting."

"Don't take any notice of that. You know as well as I do they always produce the grades come the summer exams."

The buzzer sounded, calling agitated staff to their charges. Every registration would be starting a little late, no doubt causing students to wonder if there were something unexpected in the wind.

******

All teachers had used much of their free time the previous day producing essential paperwork, as Fingleton had predicted. The majority had remained on the premises well beyond the afternoon buzzer, many increasing Bulmer's annoyance by sticking it out until nine o'clock. Other than comfort breaks and visits to the AVA room, the order of the day was confinement to one's classroom base. There was much to be done.

It was Wednesday break time and, out of curiosity, Biggsy decided to look in on the staff room. He counted six teachers, one of whom was Beth. She looked up at his entrance and patted the empty seat next to her.

"I'll just fetch a cuppa and be right with you, Beth."

As he approached the tea counter, Josie vented her frustration at the lack of custom.

"Where the bleedin' 'ell is everyone?" she demanded, indicating two huge pots brimming with tea and a counter of empty mugs. "I could've stayed 'ome in the warm instead of comin' 'ere an' wastin' me time. Everyone must 'ave gone to the moon."

"Could well have done, Josie. Probably the best place to be just now."

"Well, I'll do you, then I'm off 'ome. Got plenty to get on with there."

He took his tea, put twenty pence in the cash box and joined Beth.

"I should be beavering away like everyone else, Beth. I only popped in here out of curiosity. How's everything with you?"

"Oh, more or less under control," she replied, calmness itself. "Have you heard any further news about the inspection?"

"Not much, just that the registered inspector is one Helen Highwater. Apparently, she's difficult to get through to?"

"Most interesting," Beth laughed. "You almost had me there. You do need to have a sense of humour if you're to get on in teaching these days."

"I'd hardly say I've got on. Just a middle-management lackey, to be honest. On the other hand, I see you as someone who has all the potential to get to the very top in teaching, but you don't seem interested in the promotion stakes, Beth."

"Thanks for the compliment. That's me, I'm afraid. Why get yourself messy on the greasy pole? The enjoyment I seek is in the classroom, not in an office. Also, I prefer being one of those having to cope with all the shit that's thrown down on teachers from a great height, rather than the person throwing it."

He'd never heard Beth use coarse language before.

"Succinctly put. The classroom's where I get the buzz, too. But I kind of made faltering steps up the ladder in spite of myself," he all but apologised.

"There have to be people like you as line managers who can be relied upon to protect their departments from the senseless admin load. Everyone appreciates that aspect of the way you do your job."

It was his turn to smile at a compliment. It meant a great deal coming from a colleague he regarded so highly. Embarrassed, he returned to the mundane.

"I'm going to ask everyone to meet for a final pep talk straight after school in the English office. Will that be fine with you, Beth?"

"I'll be there," she nodded.

******

"I won't waste any more of your time, everyone. Good luck over the next two days. We'll laugh at all this at the weekend."

The shortest meeting he'd ever chaired lasted twenty minutes. He had no intention of keeping the department from putting the final touches to their Ofsted preparations. Andy, slumped in a chair, feigned struggling to his feet.

"That's if we come out of the two days alive. I've already got Ofsted overload and they haven't even arrived yet," he moaned.

"We're all there with you. But the good thing is we've done all the donkey work by this time. Any dodgy wall displays that need taking down before the numb nuts arrive?"

"Don't even joke about that," warned Sarah. "My sense of humour has gone on a forty-eight-hour strike."

"Sorry, Sarah, but we don't want to risk an inspector throwing up during a lesson observation as a result of catching sight of anything graphic on view. Right, I've got to contact Myra to confirm that I won't be home for evening meal again. Lots to do."

Having got themselves comfortable in the office, nobody was in a hurry to leave. Nick, arms folded and legs crossed, yawned mightily then set to extricating himself from his easy chair. Biggsy chuckled to himself, as he messaged Myra. She wasn't going to like this. Angela fumbled with the contents of her holdall, rose unsteadily from her seat, gritted her teeth and departed.

"Bulmer's really got his back up," Andy grinned. "He must have the shakes not being able to get stuck into the booze until nine o'clock two nights running. I'm keeping out of his way until I head off home."

"Poor old Bulmer. Hate to be one of the reasons for cramping his style," Nick added. His eyes glazed over. "Can't imagine what it must be like to have a serious cider session."

"Wouldn't it be funny if Fingleton had to include Bulmer as a school health and safety issue!" added Bridget.

The general laughter that followed had a hint of hysteria.

"I have heard stranger ideas," observed Biggsy.

Ten minutes later, he was alone in the office, everyone else needing to work undisturbed in the solitude of their teaching rooms. Before starting the remainder of his lesson plans, he made a point of going along to Angela's classroom. She needed a confidence boost. As he entered, he saw her searching through discarded papers in her waste bin.

"Stupid of me!" she wailed. "I've thrown away something I need."

"Don't worry, Angela. You'll find it, I'm sure. This'll be your first inspection, but there'll be many more."

"Hope I don't get one of my migraines," she said, straightening up and massaging her temple.

"There's one thing I advise you to keep to the forefront of your mind whenever you're observed. The inspector will probably be an ex-teacher who, for one reason or another, is unable to teach. But you can. Ofsted recruits many failed teachers to police the country's state schools. Pathetic, but there you are. You're the bloody good teacher the inspector would like to be. Always remember that."

"Thanks a lot. It's really kind of you to say that."

"One other thing. Another type of inspector is the sort who craves officialdom. Inspections are enjoyable to such people because they're a kind of power trip. On no account allow yourself to be intimidated or your confidence undermined by one of this breed."

"I'll try not to."

"You've probably guessed that I'm a shade antagonistic toward Ofsted and its minions." He laughed to himself, as he wondered if he might be sounding a touch paranoid. "In my experience, the inspectors let loose in schools aren't always equipped with the necessary credentials to decide what is and what isn't good teaching. We'll leave it at that. See you later."

Walking back along the empty corridor to the office, he felt a little uneasy at the force of his anti-Ofsted tirade. But he had to acknowledge the onset of a change from his usual stoic mood. His general anxiety was giving way to a growing sense of defiance. He sensed that he would be facing continued professional conflict. Against whom or for what reason, he wasn't sure. Irrational as the impulse might be, he viewed it as premonitory.

******

Having completed the typing of his fifth lesson observation sheet, he slammed down the laptop lid, stretched his legs under the table and checked the time. Fifteen minutes to go before locking up. If the photocopier were free, he'd have time to run off all the support materials his classes would need the following day.

He had been on-site for thirteen hours and would be performing for any inquisitive inspector who might turn up to his first lesson of the day in twelve hours' time. His eyes ached from staring at a screen for three solid hours after a full day's teaching. He wondered how he or any of his colleagues would manage to be on top teaching form the following day. Sarah was moving about in her classroom next door. The likelihood was that the school car park was still full.

It irked him that teachers were required to invest inordinate amounts of nervous energy and time for the Ofsted process. So much pointless effort. He thought of the hundreds of hours he'd spent writing and refining the department's handbook. An inspector would probably spend no more than five minutes perusing it. All handbooks were much the same. He'd slipped in a few spoof policy statements to see if anyone ever spotted them, but nobody had in the past eight years. His favourite was the policy on how to prevent children from sticking used chewing gum on the undersides of tables.

Secondary education had come a long way since he'd started teaching almost three decades ago. A blackboard, a stick of chalk and a smile were the tools of the trade then. No time for smiling now, or blackboards. High-tech pedagogy was the order of the day. Children conditioned to spend many hours a day staring mutely at one sort of screen or another at home could not be denied the pleasure of that habit at school. All hail the whiteboard!

His mobile phone rang.

"When the hell are you thinking of coming home?"

"I don't think I'll make it until nine thirty, love. Sorry about this, but every member of staff's in the same boat."

"Have you eaten anything since this morning?" Myra questioned, softening.

"I had a cheese sarnie from the dining hall, so I'm OK. Just feel completely drained. I'll make myself some beans on toast when I get in."

"Get the hell out of there, and try to drag as many others out as you can. People do have lives to lead. You work quite hard enough for that school as it is."

"I know, Myra, but it'll be all over in a few days' time."

"I wish it could be, but you're usually working at home at this time anyway – five nights a week – one of them Sunday."

"I know. I know. But I've just got a few small jobs to do and I'll be able to escape. See you later."

Pocketing his phone and picking up a pile of sheets to photocopy for his unsuspecting pupils, he hurried off to the AVA room. John was the only person in the room, still at work, sorting through piles of stapled sheets.

"Didn't realise you were on overtime too, John. You must have been knocking out duplicated dross all evening judging by the chemical smell in here. Is the photocopier free for the next ten minutes or should I go away and slash my wrists in the gents?"

"Help yourself," came the terse reply.

He inserted the papers into the tray on the top of ASOL Number 1, set the programmer and pressed the start button.

"Who's all this stuff for?" he asked, observing the piles of printouts that were occupying the washed-out technician.

"Management materials. Deputy Head wants them first thing tomorrow."

"Must be a right ripping read. Let's have a look at one to see what insomnia-inducing treats the inspectors have to look forward to."

He picked up a stapled selection randomly off the top of one pile. The heading read 'St Saviour's Self-Evaluation Form'. The section of the document that caught his interest was that which provided performance data, department by department. Aware that the inspection team's judgements would be guided by the gradings the school management team provided, namely DHM Curriculum, he searched for information on his subject area. He found the relevant section and discovered that English had been graded as outstanding for its examination results. However, leadership of English had been adjudged good. Not so bad, he thought. However, his spirits sank when he read on and discovered that the leadership of both Mathematics and Science was deemed to be outstanding.

"The bastards! Taking the piss!"

"What's up? Have you found some typos?" asked John, feigning concern.

"I've been stitched up," seethed Biggsy.

Chapter 8

The national rugby stadium towered over him as he turned towards Twickenham town centre. He'd been to several international matches over twenty years ago but, despite his love of the sport, he no longer applied for tickets. He wouldn't entertain the idea of paying the inflated prices for a game that, in his view, had gone corporate. One amusing Twickenham recollection, from way back in his early twenties, however, always came to mind when he looked back on times when his pocket could afford a place on the South Stand. Just as Dusty Hare had been kicking the penalty that secured a narrow England victory over Ireland, he'd felt a steady flow of urine spattering against the back of his coat. It was hardly worth complaining under the circumstances, bearing in mind that a constant stream of pee had been flowing since midway through the second half from the top level of the stand to the lower level where he was tightly enclosed next to his father-in-law. A soggy parka was a small price to pay for victory. The Irish fans loved their beer, particularly when they were engrossed in a rugby clash with the old enemy.

He drove through empty streets, over the bridge past the railway station and turned right toward the terraced house that he and Myra had bought twenty years earlier. Although lacking in space, the property was now worth several times more than they'd paid for it. Beside the network of transport links, the proximity of the rugby stadium was possibly one of the factors for high property values in the area. Should they ever have the inclination to move out of London, they'd be well set. He was thinking that such a move now might be a good idea. He'd have to broach the subject with Myra and Ella soon to try to win them over. They'd have to be happy with the idea first. He couldn't sell his wife and daughter short.

The feeling of bitterness consuming him, on discovering that his leadership was considered merely 'good', as opposed to the 'outstanding' qualities of the two other core subject leaders, would stay with him for the rest of his time at St Saviour's. He knew that he would never be able to take this perceived slight on the chin and carry on as usual. It occurred to him that he was turning into the person he'd never intended to become.

He switched off the ignition and slumped forward over the steering wheel. When he had summoned the energy, he need only walk eleven paces to the front door. Getting out of the car, he looked up and down the street, wondering how he'd feel should they choose to move away. The desirable postcode was a major plus, but there were deeper connections with the house. This was where his daughter had been born. He'd also put a lot of himself into the home, including the installation of electrical ring mains in a time before the nanny state decided that only certificated professionals could carry out such hazardous work. He'd picked the brains of an acquaintance, a qualified electrician, and rewired the whole house for less than a hundred and fifty pounds. None of the flush-mounted wall sockets had worked themselves loose as friends had warned and, to his knowledge, nobody had yet suffered fatal electrocution on his premises.

"Fukkem!" he whispered, as he pushed the front door to behind him.

Myra was already in her dressing gown, curled up in a corner of the sofa with the newspaper. The television was on for the ten o'clock news. Framed in the lounge doorway, he dropped his bag where he stood and kicked off his shoes.

"Made it home again, then," she smiled. "Just about to file a missing person's report. I don't know how the hell you, or anyone else at that place for that matter, will be able to perform to the required ludicrously unrealistic levels tomorrow after the two days you've just had. You've also been away from home for almost fourteen hours without a proper meal."

He shuffled across the carpet and dropped himself next to her.

"I don't really have an appetite now. I'll just have some bread and cheese when I've got my breath back. Ofsted's bad enough, but there was worse news as I was about to leave school."

"I couldn't imagine anything worse for a teacher than Ofsted."

"I felt the same until half an hour ago. I was in the AVA room and spotted some photocopies John had been asked to run off by the management team for the inspectors. The school's self-evaluation summary, masterminded and executed by Toenail, rates my leadership as good, whereas maths and science have outstanding leaders."

"The bastards!" erupted Myra.

"Funny, but that was my reaction too."

"Is Toner responsible for putting the summary together?"

"How did you guess?" he replied, leaning over to kiss his wife on the cheek.

He decided to play the discovery of this latest affront low key. Myra had listened to too many of his complaints about the job recently. The time to investigate the matter fully would be after the inspection.

"There's no excuse for that. You've sweated blood for the school and more. How petty-minded can some people get!"

"So, you think there may be something in what I've been saying about her since the start of term after all?"

Myra gave him a sympathetic look, raised her eyebrows and shook her head. He wouldn't say another word on the subject because he didn't want her getting into a state before they turned in. Although all manner of school tedium could interfere with his own sleep pattern, there was no point in them both having a restless night.

"I can't be getting into even more of a state about it. Gotta keep myself together for the inspection game – the big match kicks off tomorrow at 8.00 am."

There was also the English Department to consider before his own preoccupations. His main responsibility the following day would be to his colleagues: his support and reassurance could be vital to securing a favourable outcome. He had to be on top form with his own teaching if he were to negotiate successfully the three-part lesson regime for two whole days. He hoped that none of his students would give the game away to visiting inspectors that their teacher had been replaced by a machine.

"Poor you, having to go through this pantomime every couple of years!"

"That's brilliant," he brightened. "You've given me an idea. I think I might audition for the part of Wishee Washee in Richmond's Christmas panto. Could be a more sensible option than teaching."

He made his way to the kitchen to dig out some cheese from the fridge.

******

His head was full of Hendrix's 'Are You Experienced?' backward guitar solo – the genius of chaos issuing from the CD stereo within the confines of his car on the journey in... Just get your mind together.

This morning, he needed an emotional boost, one that Radio 3 was unable to provide. He needed to be energised for the day facing him at St Saviour's. This was no time for faint hearts. He would not allow himself or his department to be cowed by the system.

Schools were now run rigidly according to the Apollonian impulses of uptight, upright, up-their-arses education ministers. Ofsted inspections drove the illusion of educational success. There was no place today for the outasight Dionysian.

He battled daily against the fashionable falsehood that every activity taking place within a school must be measurable and assessment-criteria related. This trendy establishment mantra promoted genuine professional anger within himself. Perhaps he should take a lesson from Hendrix and reverse the order of his lesson plans, beginning with plenaries on any topics that took his fancy, engaging students in group work, and finishing with starter activities. That would shake the inspectors up.

He took comfort from the fact that he was able, so readily, to convert anger into humour. Used intelligently, anger could be a great motivator. In his book, negative emotions were given too much bad press. Take hatred, for example. As an O-level schoolboy, he'd had a loathsome chemistry teacher who'd habitually humiliated him during lessons. Mr Dawson had ignored his struggles with the subject, once angrily tearing homework pages from his exercise book whilst the rest of the class looked on in amusement.

The revenge he'd exacted had been original in its conception and thrilling in its execution. A few months before the public examination in chemistry, he decided to steal, on a temporary basis, one of the huge textbooks handed out at the beginning of each lesson. It had been a straightforward matter of intentionally leaving his rucksack in the classroom when the end-of-lesson bell sounded and returning to the science block during lunch hour to retrieve it. With nobody around, it had been easy for him to take a book off the top of a pile, stuff it in his bag and make a hasty exit. The next stage was the difficult part. Having decided to read the book through, not once but twice, he'd only two months to complete the task. On top of his revision in other subjects, this had been a tall order, but he'd stuck to his mission.

Instead of failing the exam abysmally, as per Mr Dawson's confident prediction, he'd passed with a high grade. A creditable result born of hatred. Returning to sign up for sixth-form courses in September, he'd been a member of a select group sitting once again in Mr Dawson's laboratory. As the head of science, the detested teacher was encouraging anyone with the minimum required grades to pursue his subject to A-level. Biggsy had achieved the required chemistry grade, and then some.

He enjoyed replaying the incident that followed in his mind in moments of crisis throughout his teaching career. Standing up and seething with contempt, he'd approached the teacher's desk, placed the book in front of him and delivered a brief speech.

"No thank you, sir. I won't be studying chemistry again. I found this book. I think it's one of yours."

He'd smiled a smile of triumph as he'd looked into the eyes of the adult adversary who'd believed that he was worthless. Ecstasy.

"Fukkem!"

Top Tip No. 3: It is possible to be despised as a teacher, yet be successful.

The car park was full at seven thirty. His spot had already been taken. No time for a staffroom cuppa today – straight to the English office. Voices clamouring for John's favours could be heard as he passed the AVA room. The panic had started.

"Got you a tea here, boss!" called Andy, hurrying from the staff room toward his line manager.

"Thanks a million! I wasn't going to bother trying to get to the kettle this morning."

He desperately wanted to be alone in his classroom, setting out the reams of documentation in strict order that he'd need for the day. He also had to see every member of his department before the start of school to encourage and fortify.

Andy caught up with his boss, followed him into Room 125 and placed the mug of tea on his table.

"Whatever time did you get in, Andy? I thought I was early."

"Been here since just after seven. Bulmer was unlocking the place when I arrived."

"What a stalwart! I'm referring to you, of course, not Bulmer. Are any of the others in yet?"

"I think Beth and Nick are in. Not sure about the others."

"Right. I'll quickly set my crap out so that I'm as organised as I can be, then I'll pop in on everyone to wish them good luck. How are you fixed for today?"

"Couldn't be any more prepared. Now it's in the lap of the gods. I'll catch up with you later."

He turned on his heel and hurried away up the corridor.

"Thanks, again for the tea. You're a saint."

******

Angela and Bridget were in good spirits, laughing together in the corridor about the arrival of the 'teaching police'. Bridget wondered if they'd be carrying truncheons or Tasers in their briefcases as standard issue. She speculated that tremulous Ofsted personnel might require the reassurance of such equipment for their personal defence in the face of the screaming pupil hordes they were too afraid to teach.

Nick, at the far end of the English corridor, was sitting stony-faced in his classroom, sorting through a pile of A4 sheets.

"You look as though you've got everything under control, Nick."

"Didn't get to bed till two o'clock. I couldn't teach for much longer if I had to go through this amount of preparation on a regular basis."

"Well, you don't. This is just a ridiculous sham we have to put on once every three years or so to keep everyone happy. You've done bloody well at St Saviour's. Nobody could fault your commitment. Just remember, throughout the two days, that you're excellent at doing a job that very few people could manage. Trust me, you'll probably find yourself experiencing a sense of mild exultation by tomorrow when this is behind you. Anything I can do for you before the off?"

"Thanks for that. If you could get the caretaker to install a lavatory in the corner of the classroom, it might help. Ofsted does wonders for sorting out constipation."

Nick managed a thin smile. Biggsy grinned in return at the teacher who, he thought, reminded him of himself almost three decades ago – a perfectionist struggling to establish himself in the most challenging of careers.

"I'll send Bulmer straight down. But, even if he manages to sort something out for you, he's bound to do a shitty job."

******

Every member of his tutor group had assembled within five minutes of the first buzzer sounding. After completing the online register on his laptop, he turned to the whiteboard and began writing out the lesson aim and learning expectations for his first class. Ordinarily, he never did this, but duty called.

"Hey, sir!" Colley called out. "You been on a teacher-training course? You've never put this guff on the board before."

Colley's query prompted a ripple of laughter. Biggsy smiled to himself, as he carried on scrawling away with his brand-new felt-tip board marker.

"As you've made a point of questioning me on my INSET credentials, Chris, you could say I've seen the light. I went to a staff meeting recently, which had the effect of transforming me from a mild-mannered and underpaid boys' secondary school teacher into Robot Teacher. I'm now going to do everything by the book to ensure that my students are never in any doubt as to what they are supposed to be learning."

"If that's true, where's the fancy superhero costume?" asked Gibson. "You might be impressed with that new suit of yours, sir, but it still spells M&S to us."

"I may only have to go into my office for a few seconds to pull off this suit, shirt and tie in order to reveal myself in my new superhero guise."

"Bit late in the day for you to change into Robot Teacher, though, sir. You'll be retiring soon, won't you?" queried Bellchambers.

"I'm insulted. I've only just passed my half century. I've another six months left in me at least before the pressures of baby-minding you lot see me off."

"We'll give you a good send off, sir. We'll 'ave a whip round and buy a bunch o' daffs for the top o' the coffin," added Colley, baring his teeth in a mockery of amiability.

"Anyway, my impending demise apart, the inspectors are in school today. So, please be at your mature best in the classroom and around the school. Remember, you're expected to set the very best example to younger pupils."

"You know you can rely on us, sir. We'll even say 'thank you' when we nick their dinner money," smirked Colley.

"Sometimes, I'm not sure whether you're joking, lads. Well, there's the buzzer – off you go and wish me luck."

"The best of British, sir. If you're not here on Monday, we'll assume you got the sack," Bellchambers concluded, as the form members slouched off for their first lesson.

He sighed, momentarily content. Repartee with sixth formers was a joy.

******

Morning break offered much-needed relief. He'd had no HMI visitors so far. But this meant that hours of microscopic lesson preparation the previous day had been a complete waste of time.

On the one hand, he didn't want an inspector to come near his classroom, invading his personal territory. On the other, if nobody observed him teaching, he'd wasted twenty hours of his life.

His first two lessons sped by. The year seven pupils leaving his classroom had been model students. Checking that his materials were set out in order on his desk for the third of his five lessons, he readied himself to do another colleague check. A straggler, slowly collecting his possessions, delayed him.

"Come on, Noah. You won't have any of your break time left if you don't get a move on."

"Sorry, sir. I can't find my new pen. It was on the table in front of me all lesson, but now it's gone."

A short, tubby boy, slow of movement and habitually anxious, Noah was an only child. His nervous disposition was symptomatic of an innocent caught up in the torment of a violent domestic situation leading to marital break-up. Biggsy had special sympathy for children from such backgrounds. Noah's peers were as patient with his slowness of thought and movement as was his teacher.

"That's strange. What sort of pen was it?"

"It was a special ink pen. My dad only just got it for me. I see him on Sunday, and he'll ask me if it works all right."

A little light-fingered activity no doubt, but Biggsy didn't have time to deal with the matter at this very moment. Noah nervously brushed a wave of dark hair off his forehead. He was doing a good job of holding back the tears.

"I can see how important your pen is to you, Noah. I promise you'll have it back by the end of the day at the latest. Deal?"

"OK, sir. Thank you, sir," Noah replied, looking up hopefully, as he shuffled out of the room.

Invading the clutter of his mind, he made the finding of the pen a priority. He could not, on any account, overlook the theft. Whatever extraneous demands were being made of him by the presence of school inspectors, he knew that the worm of Noah's pen would niggle away at him until he'd acted. He decided he'd visit form 7B during afternoon registration to carry out preliminary investigations. In the meantime, he had to catch up with his department.

Bridget was returning to her classroom, a mug of something hot and herbal clutched in both hands before her. He interpreted the smile she returned him as a good sign.

"Any visitors yet, Bridget?" he asked.

"Yes, first thing with my year ten GCSE group. A very officious older gentleman came in at the start and sat himself at the back of the room. He stayed for twenty minutes, didn't say a word, then stood up, nodded in my direction and left us in peace. The boys were fabulous – totally ignored his presence and were on their best behaviour."

"Just what we need, Bridget. Good for you!"

"Don't thank me, thank my lovely class."

Sarah and Andy, in earnest conversation, ambled toward them. They'd also managed to get themselves drinks, protecting them as best they could as boys hurried past in either direction.

"You two are looking pleased about something," Sarah said.

"Bridget was just telling me how she's successfully seen one off already. Have either of you been observed?"

"No sign of the enemy yet," Andy replied, "All quiet so far with Beth and Hazel too, but Angela's been seen. Saw her in the staff room and she was buzzing. Loved it!"

"She's a trooper. What a great bit of news. I'll just go and see Nick before next lesson."

He knocked and found Nick carrying out a last-minute check on the line-feed connection between his laptop and the whiteboard.

"Anybody seen you yet, Nick?"

"No, but I hope someone makes my next lesson with year nine as I've prepared a sequence of language materials for the kids that I'm really excited about."

"Well, I wouldn't wish an inspector on anybody, but I'm prepared to make an exception for you at this minute. See you later."

The buzzer sounded. Chattering boys were already lining up as he reappeared in the corridor. His progress was halted, as he stopped and turned in response to hearing his name being called behind him.

"It's Mr Biggs, isn't it?" said the visitor who had to be the gentleman Bridget had described. He looked to be well into his sixties, but his trim physique and penetrating gaze suggested a younger man. He bent slightly at the waist as he looked down at the head of English.

"Yes, just off to my next lesson."

"I won't delay you now, but would it be possible to have a word at lunch time? I'm Seymour, one of the inspection team, and I'd appreciate a few moments of your time."

"Certainly, Mr Seymour," Biggsy replied, trying his best to mask the concern he felt at this unexpected request. "The English office will be available."

"Most grateful, but I'd prefer a quieter location where we could speak privately."

This qualification marked a shift from unexpected to strange, from concern to unease.

"Oh, well, in that case, there should be a quiet spot in the library."

"Excellent. I'll wait for you in the staff room if that suits?"

"Right, I'll come and meet you as soon as I can make it after my lesson, Mr Seymour."

"Thank you, Mr Biggs."

There could be all manner of innocent reasons for the request, but he could only guess sinister ones.

******

"Make sure you've all written up the homework details in your diaries, lads, or I'll be for the chop if Ms Toner discovers somebody hasn't done so when she does her next diary check."

He'd been able to deliver the pointed reminder because there was no inspector present. None of his classes had been observed so far on this first day, and there was only the single lesson to go after lunch.

Several students laughed at what they perceived to be their teacher's joke, but he couldn't have been more serious. Seated at his desk, he formed a gun with his right hand, pointed two fingers at his temple, jerked his hand backwards with the recoil and dropped his head on the table top. His performance prompted further chuckling.

"If they gave you the chop, sir, we'd all go on strike," reassured Adrian Welby, one of the brightest prospects in his year eleven class. He stared levelly at his teacher, indicating that he genuinely meant business. Several boys concurred.

"I appreciate your faith in me, Adrian, but the long knives are out for failing teachers. I'd appreciate you being a character witness for me, however, if I'm ever in the dock. Right, I need to lock up pretty smartish. There's an important gentleman in the staff room waiting to interview me. I shall, of course, pass on all details to you if I don't make the grade."

The class left quickly, as requested. He straightened his tie and fished in his jacket pocket for keys, perturbed that he'd have to delay doing catch up with his team. That would have to wait. Locking the door, he set off for the staff room.

******

The corridors were at their bustling best. Boys hurried past him in the direction of the dining hall, as he hastened to his appointment. Entering the staff room, he immediately became aware of the subdued tone of conversations. There was little of the usual banter or laughter. The only important issue was how well individuals had performed under the closest scrutiny. Nick and Angela, seated at one end of the room, looked up at his approach.

"Can't stop, I'm afraid," he apologised. "Hope you've both had a good morning. I've a meeting with an inspector right now. You haven't been aware of anyone looking for me, have you?"

"Sorry I'm late, Mr Biggs," came a voice behind him. "I've just been observing Mr Orchard, one of your colleagues teaching 'Macbeth'. Fascinating!"

The inspector's piercing blue eyes opened wide, as he uttered the glowing epithet.

"Not a problem, Mr Seymour. I've only just arrived myself."

"Oh, good."

"See you later, you two," Biggsy called over his shoulder as he departed with his new friend.

He had no difficulty finding a quiet spot in the vast library at the start of lunch hour. The inspector seated himself and briskly pulled out a sheaf of papers from his antique leather briefcase. No supermarket plastic bags there. An expert hand had carved the word 'BORED' on the table. He moved his elbow to cover the engraving.

"Thank you for taking time out to have a word with me, Mr Biggs. I particularly wanted to talk to you regarding an anomaly in the school's self-evaluation report that I wanted to investigate."

Alarm bells started ringing. Was he the source of a monumental clanger in his department's record-keeping? He watched as Seymour adjusted his glasses, held before him the relevant document, and turned to a page he'd earmarked with an adhesive red marker. Red for danger? He could feel the blood draining from his face, as he awaited the verdict on his unfitness for office.

"I've looked at the information provided by the school on the examination performance of all subject areas within the school. On the basis of what I've read and what I've seen so far this morning, I'm surprised that your leadership has not been considered on a par with your core-subject colleagues who were adjudged to be outstanding. Have you any thoughts?"

He paused a moment before answering to replay to himself the words he'd just heard. He felt his anal muscles relax. Leaning toward Mr Seymour, he attempted a quizzical expression.

"I'm unable to say anything on that point, Mr Seymour. I'm not party to judgements made by the management team."

Containing jubilation had never been a problem for him. He could maintain professional reserve under the most trying of circumstances. Vindication! He felt the beginnings of a warm glow at the back of his neck. It moved down his back, round to his chest and filled his abdomen. He sighed gently, unfolded his arms and looked at Seymour. Could it be possible that he'd found an ally amongst one of the enemy? An Ofsted inspector, of all people, was questioning the school management's decision to do him down.

"Well, by every inspection standard, the English Department more than matches achievements in science and mathematics within the school. In my opinion, your department's performance must, in no small measure, reflect exemplary leadership qualities. From what I've seen so far, I have no doubt that this is the case. I shall, therefore, be recommending your leadership be upgraded."

Suppressing an urge to jump on the tabletop and attempt a hornpipe, he nodded at Seymour and offered a tight-lipped smile in thanks.

"That's very generous of you, Mr Seymour. As you may imagine, I very much appreciate such a decision."

"Think nothing of it, Mr Biggs. It's important that we recognise strengths in schools, especially when they're staring us in the face. If there's nothing further you'd like to add, then our business is finished for the time being."

He stood up, returned the sheaf of papers to his briefcase and extended his hand. They shook, the strength of the inspector's grip stopping just short of crushing a few of the bones in Biggsy's right hand.

"I'm glad I've sorted that out. I might also mention that I intend to watch you with your year eleven class tomorrow after lunch. That'll be my observations finished then."

"You've been very kind, Mr Seymour."

"I'll make my own way back to the staff room then. See you tomorrow."

Before leaving the library, the inspector winked at him. A wink of confidentiality.

It was unheard of for an inspector to give advance notice of an observation. He found himself being doubly grateful. Not only had he been upgraded, he'd also been told exactly when Seymour would be visiting his classroom.

Remembering Noah's missing pen brought him back down to earth. He had half an hour to fetch a cheese sandwich from the dining hall and sort himself some refreshment in the staff room.

######

Sitting in his form room, laptop at the ready, he awaited the afternoon registration buzzer. His students, displaying their best behaviour, arrived punctually. Using the intranet register, he signed them in, then excused himself for having to rush off on an important mission.

"Got a date, sir?" asked Colley, slumped in his seat and with legs outstretched.

"Indeed, Chris. A date with destiny. I've got to find a young lad's pen. It mysteriously went missing during one of my lessons this morning. My credibility as an upholder of all things honest is on the line here."

"I know the feeling, sir. I find it difficult sometimes being one of the only honest Johns around this place myself."

Delicious sense of irony, thought Biggsy. He'll go far.

Assuming a stern expression, he pointed a finger at the head boy.

"Jermaine, you are now in charge of the classroom in my absence. If any member of staff comes looking for me, explain that I've been called away on an urgent matter and that I'll be returning shortly. Hopefully, you won't be troubled by any inspectors."

"But I've already decided I don't want to be a teacher."

"Stop griping, man. For that, you can come and sit at my desk while I'm away. Come on. Get yourself up here."

"This is a set up," groaned Gibson, pushing back his seat.

"I'll be back very soon."

He folded his laptop, tucked it under his arm, smiled mechanically at his form group and hurried off to 7B's form room.

As he approached, he heard Aaron Aimes calling his class to order. He knocked and strode into the junior boys' classroom. His sudden appearance silenced the class. Aaron looked up from his seat, his pen suspended in the air.

"Sorry to interrupt you all, Mr Aimes, but may I talk to your class about an urgent matter?"

"Quiet now, everyone," Aaron instructed unnecessarily. "Mr Biggs needs to speak to you."

Rows of wide-eyed twelve-year-olds looked up at their visitor.

"After my lesson with you all this morning, Noah stayed behind because he was upset after discovering that his brand-new pen had gone missing. It was an expensive gift from his father. My guess is that somebody was in such a rush to get off to break that he picked it up by mistake, as he cleared away. He probably doesn't even know that the pen is in his pencil case. Could I ask you all to do a quick check of your belongings now? Look in your pockets, too. You never know where it might turn up. If we can quickly get Noah his pen back, we can all get on with the rest of what is a very busy day."

School bags and pockets were emptied with as much fuss as possible on tables.

"Make sure that when you put everything away again that you don't leave anything lying around. It's very easy to mislay things. I do it myself all the time. Sorry to be creating such a disturbance, Mr Aimes, but I wanted to deal with the matter as quickly as possible."

"No problem at all," Aaron replied.

Noah, downcast, searched his belongings again with the rest of the boys. Finding nothing, he began collecting up his few pencils and crayons. As he did so, the boy next to him raised his arm smartly. He held a blue silver-topped cartridge pen in his hand.

"Sir, I've found Noah's pen in my pencil case, just where you said it'd be."

"Very well done, Tony! You're a star," Biggsy grinned.

I had a feeling you might be involved; he was thinking.

Tony Tranter returned the pen to his 'friend' and patted him on the back. Relieved and delighted, Noah smiled and thanked him. Biggsy was aware that Tony was developing a reputation for being light-fingered. Petty theft could be a symptom of an unhappy childhood. Tony wasn't the best turned-out pupil in the class, reflecting the fact that his home life, like Noah's, was difficult. Pilfering from one's peers could too easily become an ingrained habit. Top Tip No. 4: Exercise caution before labelling a child a thief.

"Thanks, lads. Good result. It is important not to be in such a hurry to pack away in future. Thank you for your time, everyone, and thank you, Mr Aimes."

Turning to leave, he almost bumped into Ms Toner entering the room. She acknowledged him by raising her eyebrows a fraction. Focusing her attention on Aaron, her expression changed to one of genuine warmth. He hurried away, keen to put as much distance between himself and the deputy head as possible.

It was difficult deciding which of his two recent successes had given him more satisfaction. He could never be found guilty of indulging in self-adulation, but he was suddenly buoyed by a renewed sense of equality amongst his peers. He couldn't be sure of the cause, but throughout his life he'd been prone to feelings of social and intellectual inferiority. Recognition from an inspector, of all people, had given him an inner professional glow he'd not experienced for some time. This triumphal moment even trumped his victory over Mr Dawson all those years ago. In an educational world where professional jealousy, contempt and backstabbing were increasingly the weapons of choice for the ambitious, any opportunity to affirm his own self-belief had to be seized. Similarly, the restoration to Noah of his missing pen might, hopefully, have unquantifiable emotional benefits for the fragile young boy. Biggsy's sensitivity to the promotion of well-being amongst his students made him keenly aware of the potential long-term damage that could result from acts of casual heartlessness. He would have to maintain a protective watch over the year seven boy from now on. Tony Tranter would also need sympathetic handling.

******

Relieved to get back to his classroom, he was pleased to have a few spare minutes before the end of registration. Gibson wasted no time in vacating his form tutor's seat.

"You won't be catching me sitting there again, sir. Once is enough."

The members of his form group, dutifully waiting for the buzzer, watched with amused expressions as their tutor set out several neat piles of paperwork for his next lesson. He comforted himself with the knowledge that he was unlikely to be observed for this last lesson of the day. It was possible, however, that an inspector other than Seymour could decide to put in an appearance.

"What you smilin' about, sir?" asked Bellchambers. "Can't imagine having the school crawling with inspectors is much to smile about."

"You know what, there are still some things in life that are worth celebrating. There'll be plenty of unexpected surprises in your life, you'll see. Always keep your eye on life's small details and you shouldn't be disappointed."

"Thanks for that, sir. Can I get off the couch now?"

"Bet you'll be glad when today's over, though, sir," commiserated Gibson. "Definitely no way I'm ever going to be a teacher."

"You've made that clear enough, Jermaine. It's a demanding job, especially on days like today. But teaching's nothing like any other line of work. Nobody can imagine, unless they try it, how fulfilling the job can be on its best days."

"I'll take your word for it on that one, sir."

The sound of scraping chairs immediately followed the buzzer.

"Good luck, sir," encouraged Dixon. "Got everything crossed for you."

He was taken aback at this sincere expression of support and nodded his gratitude. No sooner had the room emptied, than he became aware of his raised heartbeat as year ten boys started lining up outside.

"Come in, boys, and prepare yourselves for action," he instructed. "Take your seats as quickly as possible. We've a lot to get through this afternoon."

******

The second day of the inspection passed without incident. Biggsy's final lesson, with Seymour observing, had gone well. Within a few minutes, the whole school would return to normal.

As the last pupil filed out of the classroom, he sighed expansively. Myra regularly told him that he had to get out of this old-man habit. The inspector stowed his papers away, stood up and massaged the small of his back.

"Most enjoyable, Mr Biggs. Hope you didn't mind me staying for the full lesson, but I wanted to see if the students appreciated your efforts as much as I did. I found some of their contributions to the plenary very insightful."

"I'm glad you saw them at their best, Mr Seymour. My thanks to you once again."

The lesson couldn't have gone better. The switch to inspection-mode pedagogy had made one or two of his year eleven pupils smile, but the enforced modifications to his teaching style had more than passed muster with the inspector. Tired, but relieved, he decided to put away his teaching materials much later, at some unspecified time. He picked up his laptop, went into the English office and switched on the kettle. Bridget was the first to arrive.

"It's over. We survived."

"Hopefully, everybody will be as pleased as you are with the way things went, Bridget. Seymour visited my classroom last thing. First impressions are deceiving. I think he's one of HMI's good guys. Despite my fears, there must be a few of them around. My lesson went pretty well as planned, but I suddenly feel exhausted."

Angela, Beth and Sarah arrived in good spirits.

"We've come seeking solace and sanctuary," joked Sarah, throwing herself into an easy chair. "The corridors are awash with weeping and wailing teachers."

"Quick! Come in and bolt the door, for God's sake!" urged Biggsy.

He switched off the kettle and busied himself with preparations for tea and coffee.

"Just as I thought I'd escaped, someone came in to watch my last class of the day," groaned Sarah. "Po-faced, she was, throughout the observation. The kids didn't like her, I could tell. Still, she's gone now."

"I feel guilty," admitted Beth, pressing her lips together and raising her eyebrows. "Nobody bothered me yesterday or today."

"The sun shines on the righteous," confided Sarah, putting an arm around Beth's shoulder.

Andy arrived, flustered and perplexed.

"Hi, gang. Hope none of you've had any situations as zany as the one I've just had. I finished my lesson with year ten and the lay inspector had a quick word with me afterwards. He wondered why I hadn't focused on the religious context in our plenary discussion when we talked about Billy Casper's interest in falconry in 'A Kestrel for a Knave'."

"Sounds like a check-list pedant to me, Andy," Biggsy replied, pouring boiling water into half a dozen mugs. "Glad I didn't have that one checking me out. Tea's ready, everybody. Help yourselves."

"I wanted to tell him that I'd not introduced the theme because it had never entered my tiny mind, but I kept my cool and agreed that it might have been a good idea. No problems with him otherwise, though."

"That's set me thinking, Andy," said Bridget. "I suppose you could argue that Billy Casper's experience with the kestrel is quasi-religious. And remember, he did take the hawk from a nest in the wall of a ruined monastery?"

"That's a really interesting line of thought, Bridget," agreed Beth. "I do like that interpretation."

"Makes you realise how impossible it is to teach the perfect lesson, especially with an inspector looking on," opined Sarah. "There are just so many elements that constitute the assessment of a teacher's performance."

"I tend to focus exclusively on whether or not the boys are listening to me," joked Bridget, "but that's not nearly enough."

"Best not to dwell on how well or badly we may be thinking we did. It's behind us now, so let's put it to bed," suggested Biggsy.

The door swung open. Nick stood stock still, staring blankly ahead of him. Then a smile appeared on his face as he made an important announcement.

"I can teach. It's official. The registered inspector, no less, said she enjoyed my lesson."

"Blow me, Nick! For a minute I thought you were preparing to hand in your resignation," laughed Andy. "So, all that time we told you how good you were, you never believed any of us."

"Nick's got a point," reflected Sarah. "The profession gets so much stick day in day out – from politicians, parents, pupils and the media – that it's small wonder we doubt ourselves. Teaching's a hell of a job."

"Very true, Sarah, but it's reassuring to know that this department can showboat with the best of them," enthused the delighted English head.

"Everybody's going to The Crown this evening for a post-inspection piss-up. Solidarity, brothers and sisters. What do you say we join them?" Andy asked.

"I'm only going if you can promise me there'll be no assessment record kept of the units of alcohol I imbibe," Bridget responded warily.

"It's the least we deserve," said Biggsy. "The first round's on me."

Chapter 9

His prostate was causing him increasing concern. The morning after the staff post-Ofsted celebrations, his flow had been a problem. Consuming large amounts of alcohol must now be off limits. *One of the advantages of having few genuine friends,* he thought, *is that habitual drinking becomes less of an issue.* The occasional drink or two was manageable, but no more.

Even during his school days, he recalled, he'd had many acquaintances but only one friend. His relationship with Dave Wall had ended abruptly the moment he'd moved up to London to study for a teaching qualification. Playing school rugby alongside each other and listening to Bob Dylan LPs together were happy times. Celebrating his seventeenth birthday with Dave was the first time he'd been drunk. Out together in Bath's city centre, the evening had ended with them running away from a policeman. Two youths larking about noisily at the bus stop outside the Empire Hotel had attracted his keen eye. Fortunately, even in a drunken stupor, the two young rugby backs had managed to outpace their pursuer.

He'd got into the habit of counting in his head how many seconds it took him to evacuate his bladder first thing each morning. What had taken twenty seconds a few years ago now took him thirty-five. He knew he'd never drunk enough fluid throughout his career. Drinking causes urination, and teachers can't leave classrooms as and when.

As he stood over the bowl, he found himself composing an alternative folk lyric.

"Where does all the wee come from, long time passing?"

Myra poked her head around the bathroom door, interrupting his concentration on the urinary tract musical composition.

"I've just had an idea, love. Why not give yourself a break? After the week you've had, you need a change of air. Go and visit your family in Bath tomorrow.

I can't make it because I've got so much to get done this weekend, but there's no reason why you shouldn't go. You'll have the day to yourself."

She was adamant. He could see the sense of what she was saying, not having visited his mother for almost two months. She'd miss not seeing Myra and Ella, but he would, indeed, appreciate a day away from London. He agreed that it would be a treat after the horrors he'd endured.

******

The traffic out of town was lighter than he'd anticipated, as he accelerated along the slip road on to the M4. He lowered the sun visor and fumbled for his sunglasses in the glove compartment as the glare hit him. Windsor, Slough and Reading were soon behind him, and he began to pay more attention to the welcome views of open countryside. Myra was right: the further away from London he travelled, the more relaxed he began to feel. Perhaps he'd become allergic to the big city. His joke with Myra that it was life itself to which he was becoming allergic no longer amused her. He felt certain his sighing habit and tendency to hyper-ventilate had been getting worse recently.

With time on his side, he decided to take a comfort break at Membury services. The sunshine, the promise of coffee and the illusion of freedom lifted his spirits. He parked beside a VW campervan, sporting a stunning lemon and white paint job. The perfect vehicle to appreciate the freedom of the road. Sauntering through the services entrance, he registered the fact that all visitors were required to walk past every single retail outlet before reaching the WCs.

He joined the queue for fresh coffee rather than use a vending machine. As he enjoyed the rich aroma, he ruminated on the rebirth of the cult of coffee. Looking about him, however, there was no evidence of coffee-house society discussing important issues of the day. Of the dozen or so customers seated at tables, only two were not focused intently on a mobile phone. Then again, he supposed, virtual conversations were, perhaps, better than none at all.

******

Rapping heavily on his mother's doorknocker to make sure she heard, he noticed that the porch he'd painted for her a few years earlier needed another coat. He'd done the job in a rush just before winter had set in and had only managed a single coat of white gloss. The end terrace was on what had once been a quiet and tidy council housing estate. She and his father had managed to buy it thanks to Margaret Thatcher. Despite her socialist tendency, Mum always acknowledged that the first female prime minister had done her a great favour.

"Coming, son. Coming," he heard, as arthritic fingers fumbled with the Yale lock.

"Lovely to see you, son," his mother sang, as the door opened. "Hope you've got an appetite because I've a nice lasagne for you from Sainsbury's."

"Hello, Mum. How did you know it was me?"

Leaning forward, he gently clasped his mother's frail shoulders, kissing her on each cheek. She beckoned him into the kitchen where she took his meal from the oven and served it up on the plain wooden tray he remembered from his childhood.

"Mum, you know I wanted to take you out somewhere to eat," he complained meekly.

"I don't want you wasting your money in restaurants with their fancy prices. Sandra went shopping for me yesterday and bought it for you specially. Only took half an hour in the oven."

He knew that he'd be eating alone. Whilst he sat with the tray on his knees at the end of the sofa in the lounge, she sat opposite him in her aged easy chair, clasping a glass of water in her lap.

"I want to hear all your news. How's that lovely wife and beautiful daughter of yours?"

He enjoyed talking to his mother. Everyday life was becoming a struggle for her, but she battled on against infirmity. There was no doubting her ability to rage against the dying of the light. She was one of life's fighters. He prided himself that he'd inherited her survival gene.

"They're both as busy as ever and keeping well. Ella's enjoying her A-levels. They send you all their love and hope you're still getting out and about as much as ever."

"I'm frightened to go out on my own now. Everywhere you look, there are these pit-pony dogs and hoodies about. Sandra takes me to the supermarket once a week now. I'm getting so clumsy these days, I'm not safe on my own. I used the ladies in Tesco and guess what? I dropped my loyalty card down the pan."

He shook his head in mirth. Her body might be failing, but her spirit fought on. Defeating bowel cancer five years earlier and living with angina had taken its toll. Her face was heavily lined, but her eyes shone with bravado. As she gazed upon him, he read the mingled emotions of warmth, love, fatigue and apprehension. Turning away, he gazed out at the garden.

"Sandra's done a good job keeping your lawn under control, Mum. It looks very tidy out there."

"She's good at DIY too. She changed a fuse in a plug for me last week."

Life, for her, was a passive waiting game, waiting for visits from family and friends, for the six o'clock news each evening and for sleep. But the waiting was not a hardship, more the opposite. She had striven throughout adult life to do right by herself and her family and was now in the privileged position of being one of the growing army of life's non-combatants, having served her time with distinction. He hoped that in thirty years, despite being withered and arthritic, he would face the inevitable with the same equanimity. She was proof, for him, that life in old age remained as sweet a gift as in youth. Unencumbered by the cares of the world, she lived a life of detachment and grace.

"You're coping OK then, Mum? Still managing on your own with everything, I mean?"

"You ever known me not to, love? I'm fine. Can't do a lot more, but there's always somebody popping in or at the end of the phone to keep me on my toes."

He smiled, as he imagined his aged mother trying to support herself on her toes. Being an English teacher, the reflex of everyday language analysis was a constant indulgence.

After his hot meal, they sat together sipping the tea she'd allowed him to prepare, sunlight warming them as it streamed through the bay window. Hunched in the armchair, his fingers picked at the brittle-worn upholstery of the armrests.

"Had a busy time last week, Mum. The school had the inspectors in, and they had a good look at my department."

"Not surprised with somebody as special as you in charge."

"We did OK, so I think I'll keep my job for a couple more years."

"These inspectors can't be up to much. Schools are in a terrible state from what I see on the news – roofs blowing off and asbestos everywhere. Children are being poisoned. What on earth are these people supposed to be inspecting?"

"Just the teachers. Nobody bothers so much about the school buildings. Glad you're on my side, Mum."

The midday sun soothed mother and son into a peaceful lethargy.

The spell of calm was broken by the sound of the door knocker. Putting his empty mug to one side amongst the clutter of framed family photographs on the table beside his chair and standing up, he anticipated the magic words from his mother.

"Wonder who that can be?" she obliged.

Opening the door, he was greeted by his sister, Sandra, wide-eyed and open-mouthed. She gave a squeal of excitement, hugged him tightly and planted a kiss on his cheek.

"Hello, Austin. This is a nice surprise. You and Mum having a good chat together?"

Only family members referred to him by his first name. Sandra had once expressed amazement that her brother encouraged everyone else to call him 'Biggsy'.

"We're just taking it easy over a cuppa, Sandra. Thanks so much for getting the lasagne, by the way. Life looks to be treating you well."

He looked his sister up and down. Well into her forties, she was still trim and youthful. Taking care of a young teenager on her own and working full-time as a secretary in an accountancy firm hadn't dimmed her zest for life.

"Jogging along quietly as usual. I can stay an hour then I have to go and prepare a meal. Come back with me for a while to see Mark. Anyway, how's the big-city teacher getting on these days?"

Sandra's hero worship of her brother made him uncomfortable. The fact that he'd been the first member of the family to go into higher education, in London of all places, and had then remained in the capital, made him exceptional in her eyes. His single-minded pursuit of a teaching career caused him pangs of guilt. She'd also shown academic potential and could have followed in his footsteps, but family loyalties had kept her close to home. Their father had died suddenly of a heart attack soon after her A-levels, and she'd remained in Bath to support her mother. Biggsy's life had opened out, whereas hers had been confined. She and her son, Mark, lived in a terrace on a neighbouring housing estate a mile away from his mother.

"Doing OK, Sandra, thanks. The girls are both well and send their love. Although Myra couldn't make it this weekend, she insisted that I come down. She's looking forward to seeing you all next time."

"Good. We're fine and Mum's well, as you can see. Nice to see our boy again, isn't it, Mum?"

Sandra hugged and kissed her mother with such force that he raised concerned eyebrows. His sister had always been the more passionate of the two children.

He helped her out of her puffer jacket, and she immediately began tidying away the lunch things.

"I'll just do a bit of tidying up, whilst you two carry on talking. Then I'll make another cup of tea for us all."

Running Mum's home, as well as her own, was second nature to her.

"Don't know how I'd get by if it weren't for Sandra popping in and out. Lucky to have her so close by."

Biggsy realised he was lucky, too.

Sandra's presence emboldened him to raise the old chestnut again with his mother.

"Do you ever fancy moving to a smaller place, Mum? We'd all help you if that's what you'd like."

"That's considerate of you, son," she replied with an arch look, "but I've no intention of moving anywhere. Your father and I moved here fifty-eight years ago and were very happy with the house. He was carried out in a box when he left, bless him, and I'll be carried out in a box when it's my time to leave."

He was unable to check an involuntary chuckle. Sandra, bustling about in the room, paused mid-step and looked at her mother in alarm.

"Mum, you shouldn't speak like that. It's tempting fate," she protested.

"Nonsense, love. I've got years left in me yet. Nothing's going to take me off in a hurry."

There was some relief to be had from not having to get involved in the evils of conveyancing on his mother's behalf, but images of her corpse being tossed into a box and carried out to a waiting van by a few strangers disturbed him. Ultimately, he surmised, our physical selves are just so much rubbish that somebody else must deal with. Shelley's 'Ozymandias' came to mind. The words 'the decay of that colossal Wreck' spoke to him of the folly of getting hung up on personal vanity, whoever one might be.

Suppressing unwelcome thoughts, he reasserted his belief in the existence of the soul. He accepted that the breath of life can be extinguished, but his belief in the enduring force of the human psyche, in some unknowable form, remained fixed. Irrational, clearly. But happily accepting the inevitability of one's own annihilation at the end of three score years and ten was also illogical. What value rational thinking? His mother's stance on changing her domestic arrangements was irrational, and he fully supported her decision.

"Sandra's invited me round to hers to see Mark, Mum. You don't mind me popping off for an hour, do you? I'll come back here afterwards to see you before I head back to London. Is that all right with you?"

"You do that, son. It'll be nice for young Mark to see his uncle. Mind you, you'll see a change in him. He doesn't look so young any more. He'll soon be a man, and one to be proud of."

"Right, all done," said Sandra. "I'll go and put that kettle back on."

******

She turned the key, swung open her front door, stepped into the hallway and kicked off her shoes. Biggsy followed and did likewise, though less vigorously than his sister. He'd not been here for at least six months. The booming bass of rock music from upstairs was a welcome contrast to the silence of his mother's home.

"Mark!" yelled Sandra to the empty landing. "Your uncle's come to see you. Come down and make him a cup of tea."

The hallway was cluttered with items that Mark had deposited just inside the door. Myra wouldn't have tolerated the trainers, hoody, kit bag and rucksack being left there for one second. Taking off his shoes and putting them in a free space on the beige carpet, he followed Sandra into the living room. The quickfire thump of heels down the stairs brought Ella to mind.

"Hi, Uncle Austin. How ya doin'?"

Mark had, indeed, changed. Taller now, lean of physique and with shoulder-length black hair, he resembled a young George Best. Mark's father, Don, a heavy drinker who'd been habitually inflamed to fits of temper, had left the family home when his son was ten years old. He'd visited Mark a few times a month for the first three or four years after the divorce, but he rarely appeared these days. The only regular contact with his son was by letter, with money gifts on birthdays and at Christmas. Working as a warehouseman and living in Bristol, his time was spent running around after a new partner who, according to Sandra, gave him the dog's life he deserved.

Far from being distressed by the split, Sandra had expressed relief at being able to raise her child in a peaceful household. Biggsy's first-hand contact with so many boys from single-parent families concerned him. The risk of teenagers going off the rails was significantly increased, in his opinion. His sister had a more unconventional point of view. She put the case that, with so many children nowadays having just the one parent to look after them, those with both could just as easily experience taunts, and even bullying, as a result of the jealousy of their single-parent peers.

"Oh, you know, struggling along like everyone else. You're looking fit. Still playing rugby for the school?"

"Yeah, I'm captain this year – fly half. We won our first two games but lost the third thanks to West Hill School's biased ref."

"Teachers! You can't trust them, Mark."

"You should know, uncle."

"He wants to be a jockey," Sandra said. "His father put the idea into his head and Mark won't let it go. I've told him to stay at school and apply for uni, but he's dead set against it. Tell him he should forget the daft idea and study, Austin."

The belief that children should be given the chance to develop special interests and pursue personal ambitions caused him to hesitate. Who was he to dash the dreams of a future Grand National winner? He knew that spending years to acquire academic qualifications wasn't the right option for every child. Exam passes at whatever grade are no guarantee of happiness, fulfilment or security in life.

"I'd say that if Mark has already investigated a future in horse racing, then he should be given encouragement. Many of those I teach have no idea what they want to do with their lives, even after A-levels."

"I go to Bath racecourse and do voluntary work with the father of a mate at school," Mark offered, his face animated. "He says he's going to speak to a trainer he knows to see if I can get weekend work at a local stable."

"That sounds really promising. I'm a fan of horse racing myself. Stick with your GCSE courses and then reassess how you feel after you've taken your exams next summer. Best to keep both irons in the fire at this stage."

"That's what I'd planned on doing. I'll just see how it goes."

Biggsy snatched a glance at his sister who looked as though she needed more convincing.

******

Back at his mother's, he readied himself to take his leave. She smiled at him over her cup and saucer. Drinking tea from her Aynsley bone china was one of her greatest pleasures.

"Sandra's a bit worried about Mark's ambition to be a horse-racing jockey, Mum."

"I know, son. A jockey! Wild horses wouldn't get me on a horse, but if that's what his heart's set on, that's his decision. He's a sensible boy, just like you were. He'll be fine."

"I agree. He convinced me that he's serious about the whole thing. Mum, before I go, can I ask you again to think about something? Supposing Myra and I moved out of London and came down this way, or somewhere on the south coast, would you fancy moving in with us? We could afford a place big enough for you to have your own space. We'd all love you to be with us."

"Fancy bringing that up again just as you're about to get off home. I love this house and I couldn't imagine being anywhere else. Have you mentioned this idea to Sandra?"

"Not yet. It's only recently I've been thinking seriously about a change of air. Give it some thought over the coming months. It's still just an idea in my head."

"Well, it's thoughtful of you, son. I'll say that. But I'm happy enough to see my time out here. And there's Sandra and Mark to think of."

"It's a lot to take on board, I know. As I say, I'm not even sure yet that we'd be up for a move. But just mull the idea over."

"I honestly don't see myself leaving this house except for what I said before."

"I'm not one for big changes myself, but the idea could grow on all of us."

"We'll see. Nobody knows what the future will bring, least of all me."

Deciding that this was the moment to depart, he leaned toward his mother and gave her a gentle hug.

"I'd better make my way home then. Don't want to be late back and worrying Myra."

"Right. You get on. Be sure to give all my love to Ella and your gorgeous wife. She's a class act, that one."

******

Biggsy's mobile phone sounded, as he hung his jacket on the coat stand.

"Hi, Andy. Just walked through the front door. This is a late social call."

"Not a social call, I'm afraid, mate. Bad news. One of your lads has been stabbed. Gibson – head boy. It happened early this evening."

"Jermaine stabbed? What do you mean – attacked?"

"Stabbed in the street. He's in intensive care at St Mary's. Critical condition. A member of the public found him in a bloodied heap near Hounslow bus station. I can't believe it. Sorry to be the one having to tell you this."

Myra, emerging from the back room to welcome her husband home, hesitated at his shocked expression. He looked at her and shook his head. Keeping his eyes fixed on hers, he spoke into the phone.

"Who could stab Jermaine? He's a star. He wouldn't harm a fly."

Myra's mouth opened in alarm, her eyes widening.

"I know. One of Jenna's friends just messaged her. I don't know anything other than those details at the minute. So sorry, mate."

"This doesn't make any sense. What the hell's going on? Look, can I get back to you later, Andy? I'm a bit shaken up – like you."

"Of course. We'll keep in touch, in case either of us hears anything further."

Biggsy ended the call and stared down at his shoes.

"Madness. Madness."

"I'll put the kettle on, love. Go and sit yourself down."

"I can't. I've got to do something. I'm going to the hospital."

"You can't do that, Biggsy. What will you do there? You can't impose on family grief."

"I won't be. I've got to go. I'll call you. Don't worry. I'll keep in touch."

******

He pulled off the London road into the hospital entrance. Fine rain began covering the lenses of his glasses, as he wound down his window and reached for a parking ticket. The usually packed car park was almost empty. He locked the car, checked the door lock, then pulled his jacket tight around him as he hurried toward the main hospital complex. His mind ran apace and threw up an image of Gibson inert on a hospital bed. A voice nearby took him unawares.

"Got change of a pound, mate? I need a fifty pence piece."

He turned and faced a squat, balding, middle-aged man proffering some coins.

"You'd think they'd let you off paying for parking at weekends, wouldn't you, especially when your old mum's on her last legs in a hospital bed."

The hospital visitor smiled awkwardly and shuffled his feet. Awkwardness, Biggsy thought, was the default response to human suffering. He reached into the pocket of his jeans, pulled out some loose change and handed over a fifty pence coin.

"Take this. I'm sorry about your mother."

"Thanks, mate. She won't want to be hanging about much longer. She's 'ad enough of this lot."

He threw his head back, leaving his new 'mate' to reflect on the meaning of 'this lot'.

Despite the lateness of the hour, there was a queue at the reception booth. He took his place behind a young mother in grey hoody and black leggings. She balanced a dummy-sucking baby on one arm and carried a plastic bag of clothing in the other. Adjusting the baby, she advanced to face the receptionist, protected behind a pane of reinforced glass. A few moments later, after a brief conversation via microphone, the mother was on her way. Biggsy moved forward and asked for directions.

"Jermaine Gibson. He's in ICU. Take the lift to the fifth floor. Ward B. No visitors are allowed, I'm afraid, unless you're related."

"Thank you very much. I'm here to meet his family," he lied.

Moving off, he fought a reflex to tremble. He pushed cold hands into jacket pockets. As he waited for the lift, he now asked himself how he'd explain his presence to the family. It struck him for the first time that he was making wholly unacceptable assumptions in this situation. He replayed Myra's warning. She was right, of course. There was every probability that his appearance would be perceived as an intrusion. Gibson wasn't his son, however protective he felt about the student for whom he had such admiration.

Exiting the lift, he heard urgent exchanges to his left. Looking along the corridor, he recognised the head boy's parents, the father with one comforting arm around his tearful wife's shoulder, and the other touching the elbow of a young man in a white coat. The Asian doctor, nodding his head repeatedly, was trying to extricate himself from the situation. He was urgently needed elsewhere. Biggsy shuddered. He felt nauseous. He would see no more. Nobody had seen him. He made a smart step back into the lift. As it began its descent, he searched for a tissue in his pocket to wipe the perspiration from his brow. Within ten minutes of leaving his car, he was back behind the wheel.

******

"Thank goodness you came to your senses. I can't imagine what got into you, rushing off like that."

Myra stood in the middle of the hallway, arms tightly folded. He shook his head, hung up his jacket once more and wrestled his shoes off.

"Is Jermaine OK?" called Ella, rushing down the stairs.

"Don't know, love," answered her father, struggling to throw off his embarrassment. "I decided Mum was right. The family wouldn't want anyone else around, least of all me."

"On his way home, he was attacked by a gang at the bus station," Ella added, making her way downstairs.

"How do you know that?"

"It's all over social media. Looks to me as though the boys who did it knew him."

"Look at you, love," said Myra. "You're as white as a sheet. You're in shock. I'll make you a cup of tea. Or do you want something stronger? You need something."

"Thanks. Tea might calm me down. Don't understand what made me hare off like that."

"Shock can do strange things to you. I know how highly you think of that boy."

"I just caught sight of his parents at the hospital. They didn't see me. His mother was out of it. If anything happens to him… I couldn't have done anything there."

"That's right. Come and sit down. All we can do is wait and pray."

Chapter 10

When he entered the staff room on Monday morning, half a dozen teachers were gathered around the head teacher's noticeboard, Dave Wheelhouse amongst them. Fingleton had posted a message explaining that the head boy was in a critical condition in hospital as a result of a knife attack. His final sentence was a plea to all staff members to pray for Jermaine's full recovery.

Wheelhouse met Biggsy's gaze and shook his head.

"How could anybody do such a thing to a boy? Can't imagine what state his parents are in. My grandson's the same age as Jermaine—"

"I'm sorry to interrupt, but may I have a word with you in my office, Mr Biggs?"

Mr Fingleton touched Biggsy's elbow and inclined his head toward the door.

He was shown once again into the snug office. The head extended an arm, opened his palm in the direction of an easy chair, then eased himself into his swivel chair. He rested his elbows on his sturdy desk and steepled his fingers.

"What happened to Jermaine has sent shock waves through the school, Mr Biggs. I can't begin to imagine how his family are coping. I know that, as his form tutor, you will also be acutely distressed. I am informed that his condition is critical but stable. The school now has a responsibility to protect the poor boy and his family from the inevitable curiosity of the media. I will call a staff meeting at lunch time and inform all staff members that, on no account, should they speak to the press."

"I understand."

"May I ask exactly when you heard about last evening's terrible developments?"

"Andy Orchard phoned me with the news just as I'd returned from a day trip to Bath. My daughter also picked up information on social media."

"Ah, the insidious *anti-social* networking. I see it as a curse, causing so much more damage to young lives than good."

Biggsy had long had serious reservations about the worldwide and 'dark' webs in which many youngsters became ensnared. He hoped that Ella would always have the good sense to stay in the light. The sight of Jermaine's desperate mother clutching at her husband's arm in the hospital corridor forced itself into his mind.

"I don't think I'd want to argue with you there, headmaster."

"Was your daughter able to provide you with any details of the horrific attack?"

"Only that he was the victim of, what seemed to be, a premeditated assault by a group of youngsters. She found out no more than that."

"That seems to be correct. The police have already asked me if Jermaine had been involved in any conflict situations with students at this school or any other in the borough. Has anything of that nature come to your attention?"

He paused. The head boy was unique, talented academically, a gifted sportsman, self-assured, but one who liked to keep his own company. He'd never heard him speak ill of anyone, nor had he ever attracted hostility of any sort at school.

"There's nothing I can report of that sort, Mr Fingleton. I can't see anyone at St Saviour's being responsible for what happened last night."

"That is some small consolation. If anything comes to mind, however unimportant it may seem to you, Mr Biggs, would you please be sure to tell me?"

"Certainly, headmaster."

******

The atmosphere at morning registration was sombre as he stood in front of his form group. He'd never spoken to a class before on a matter such as this.

"You all know what happened over the weekend to Jermaine. Like you, I'm struggling to understand why anyone should do such a thing. The idea that a group of boys could feel they have reason to attack, and do serious injury, to any individual is beyond belief to me. That a person such as Jermaine should be targeted is totally incomprehensible. I know that you will all be feeling as distraught as I am."

He paused to look at the faces of each member of his form. Padfield appeared to be looking intently in his direction, but his focus was on the wall, as though he'd like to do some serious damage to the brickwork. Colley pushed his chair back from the table, rested his chin on his chest and fixed a gaze on the patch of floor between his feet.

"He's holding his own just now. The next twenty-four hours will be important – for him, his family and for us. Mr Fingleton has reminded me that the press will be pestering both staff and students for information. Please don't speak to them. If anything comes to mind that may help to identify the attackers, please speak to me or the head before you consider talking to anyone else. I do mean *anyone*. And those of you who have religious convictions, would you offer up a prayer for Jermaine's full recovery? Thank you, lads."

He hadn't expected there to be much conversation following his words, but he was surprised that there was none. Shock, distress and anger showed on the faces before him. There was, of course, one other consideration of which he was sensible – fear for oneself. Careless talk in school could be dangerous, in whatever company. The buzzer broke the silence. As the boys dispersed, he wondered if any of them were keeping quiet, for reasons of personal safety, about details that could identify the attackers. From his experience, the schoolboy commandment of 'never snitch' was as powerful an influence over children's behaviour as ever.

******

A full day of teaching nowadays left Biggsy with an aching fatigue, that lasted an hour or so after each school day. Listening to occasional footfalls in the corridor outside his classroom, he sat motionless at his desk, registering the achievement of struggling through one of the most difficult days of his career. Gibson had never been far from his thoughts. When the soft hiss in his head had stopped, he would summon the energy to tidy the classroom, gather his evening's work in his bag and go home.

He remained motionless, locked in a torpor. Not for the first time in recent months, he admitted to himself the increasing levels of both physical and mental weariness he experienced in the job. At that moment, this thought outweighed whatever degree of satisfaction he felt about his day's teaching. Interaction with the students continued to be enjoyable, but the content of much of what he had to impart to them was nonsense, he knew. In an age when data hounds were roaming ravenously through the forests of educational prescription, the demands of simply training children in 'skill' areas were making his teaching increasingly sterile and lifeless. Spoon feeding children had given way to force feeding. Government ministers had taken education so far into the assessment wilderness that it had become expedient for them to carry on along that course. His time as a teacher, surely, was coming to an end. But who, or what, would children be left with if teachers like himself hung up their boots? In all likelihood, computer screens. He envisaged schools of the future with learning as an entirely mechanised process, adults on hand as maintenance and service support for the all-powerful electronic teaching gadgetry.

A knock on the door roused him. Christopher Colley entered, pursed lips reflecting a troubled mind.

"Hello, Chris. A bit late for you to be still here. Can I help you with anything?"

"Can we go into your office, sir?" he asked, already walking in that direction.

This was a Colley he'd not seen before. Relieved to find that the English office was empty, he motioned to the student to sit down, fixed a quizzical look on his face and waited. The young man's easy manner and dismissive air were no longer evident. He kicked agitatedly at his instep with one toe of his trainer.

"I know what 'appened to Jermaine, sir."

Biggsy offered a sympathetic expression and waited.

"Quite a few people know, but they're scared. I could be in some serious shit for telling anyone what I know."

"Are you sure it's me you want to talk to, Chris?"

"I don't really want to tell anyone, but I know I have to tell someone. So, I came to you." He looked away, rubbing his temple with his index finger.

"Jermaine never really has anything to do with kids on the street. He stays out of trouble by keeping to himself. But there's a gang of dudes, black guys, who think he rates himself as being better than them. Lonnie's the one behind it. He's got a younger sister, Leanne, who fancies Jermaine, but Jermaine doesn't want to know. Lonnie got the hump when he found out. He said Jermaine had dissed his sister and—"

"Sorry to butt in, Chris, but you appear to know an awful lot that nobody else knows. Where did you get this information?"

"My sister's in the same year as Leanne at Highview Girls. She overheard Leanne telling a friend about it at lunchtime today and then messaged me."

He shifted in his chair and scowled.

"My mate got knifed because he didn't want a girlfriend."

Colley paused in his narrative. His face drained, he wrung his hands in frustration. Biggsy realised how difficult it had been for the young man to confide this information. He'd forced himself to overcome two powerful behavioural controls: adherence to the principle of never 'grassing', and fear.

"I know how tough it's been for you to tell me all this, Chris, and I'm very grateful that someone in the school has the courage you've just demonstrated. There are many others I can think of who will also feel that way. I've got to think very carefully about what to do next, as I now have to consider the safety of both you and your sister. Tell nobody else about this and advise your sister likewise."

Colley's taut jaw relaxed. He became circumspect.

"Will you tell the police what I've told you?"

"The police will have to be given this information at some point, but we will put the case of confidentiality to them for your protection. They may be able to obtain a confession without your ever being further involved."

"I'm not a coward," insisted Colley. "Lonnie and his mates can't knife everyone who knows what 'appened."

"That's true enough. But, as I said, do make sure that you and your sister keep all of this to yourself. I'll get back to you as soon as I can after I've had another word with the head."

Colley nodded and offered a half-smile of reassurance.

Biggsy was filled with admiration for his student, whose conduct, in this instance, had nothing to do with bravado. Few would have come forward with such dangerous evidence. Colley was desperate for justice.

******

He looked at his watch. Six fifteen. He'd lost track of time. There was a message on his mobile from Myra: *'Have you decided to do an overnighter at school?'* Colley's story weighed on his mind. Before going home, he had to decide what was to be done. He pushed the pile of exercise books he'd been marking to one side and stood up. The responsibility to protect the student and his sister was uppermost in his mind. He'd speak to Fingleton first thing in the morning, urging him to use any argument whatsoever with the police to keep the information source anonymous. But he was troubled by the possibility that this request would cut no ice.

The school was silent, all students and staff long gone. He often found himself the last person on the site these days. At such times, there was an odd sense of comfort in being alone in the building. He enjoyed imagining generations of boys past, long dead, populating the busy corridors. A myriad individual destinies had taken boys off to all parts of the globe from this centre. He was part of the rich history of St Saviour's, an integral cog in the clockwork of students' fates. Comprehension of the nature of this responsibility usually buoyed him up with no little pride. Today he feared that the future of one of its best students would be cut short.

Darkness had fallen over an hour ago, and only the main corridor was lit. Determined to shake off the spell that seemed to be holding him here against his will, he snatched up his attaché and stuffed a few papers inside it. He flexed his shoulders, pulled on his jacket and set off. As he'd had to park the Golf in the rear car park that morning, he would have to exit via the back of the school. Passing along the corridor, he turned into the dark passageway that took him in the direction of the gym outbuildings. As he walked along the path to the car park, a sound came from within the old gym changing rooms, as if someone were moving a piece of furniture. With a light tread, he approached the outbuilding and peered through one of the frosted windows. Although no lights had been switched on, he could just distinguish moving shadows in the darkness, adults engaged in furtive activity. He approached the door and silently opened it an inch. Looking through the gap, he saw a male and a female, encouraging each other with ardent whispers. He was able to identify Ms Toner and Aaron Aimes engaged in advanced horseplay. The ancient pommel horse that was being temporarily stabled in the changing room, stuffing issuing from a tear in the suede leather, was being used as an accompaniment to their amours. Shocked at the sights and sounds of two colleagues abandoning themselves to immodest pleasures in the unseemly surroundings of a sweaty children's changing room, he withdrew with some urgency.

******

His disbelief at what he'd witnessed was so great that he began wondering if his imagination might have been playing tricks on him. As he pulled out of the car park, he decided to drive slightly out of his way back round to the front of the school to check that Ms Toner's car was still in its usual spot.

There it was, the Scirocco, the only car left on the site, confirmation that he was not losing the plot.

He initially recoiled at the images that were indelibly imprinted on his retinas, then the thought occurred that he might be turning into *Disgusted of Tunbridge Wells*. She was a good ten years older than young Aimes. Did that matter? New to the profession, Aaron was already putting his career at risk. Neither of the pommel-horse participants was married. No problem there. Only he had observed the coupling. No major damage done. But, clandestine sex on the school site? Surely not! Another thought, more powerful than any other, came to the fore. These two professionals had behaved in a grossly undignified manner on the day that the rest of the school was coming to terms with the fact that one its students was fighting for his life in intensive care. Bad deputy-head timing.

It was none of his business. He must forget what he'd seen. He could not use such a discovery to his advantage and subject Toner to humiliation. There was also Aaron to consider, against whom he had no grievance. However odious he considered her to be, vindictiveness was not in his nature. He should tell no one. But should he tell Myra?

He became aware that he'd not been giving his full concentration to the road ahead when a cyclist pulled out of a side road, causing him to brake abruptly. He swore at himself under his breath. *Concentrate on the road, you idiot!* he urged himself. He alone had been privy to the after-school antics, and it was imperative he tell no one. Who would believe him anyway? He decided to keep his discovery from Myra. Knowing how much he detested the senior teacher, might she even have doubts about the story he'd tell her? His school focus at this moment was Gibson's health.

******

Interesting as the television documentary on the Mayan civilisation was, he couldn't concentrate. He looked at his phone, hoping for good news from Ella about the head boy. Young people are always the first to know anything. She was revising at a friend's for the evening. She'd contact him immediately if there were anything to report. The fact that he remained in a stable condition offered hope. The following day's meeting with Fingleton wouldn't be easy.

Myra hadn't known her husband to be this preoccupied since he'd started teaching. He had a natural tendency towards introspection, and this inclination could become exaggerated at times of stress. She was worried about him. It was as though he were grieving for his own son. She decided to leave him alone in the living room, whilst she replied to a few emails on the PC tower in the office upstairs.

******

He went to Fingleton's office first thing to communicate Christopher Colley's account. The head assured him he would inform the police that the details had to be treated as coming from an anonymous source for the time being. However, he was unsure how long it would be before they insisted on the identity of the informant being revealed.

The moment Colley arrived for registration, Biggsy took him to one side and explained the situation. Reassured by the news that the form tutor had, as promised, insisted on his identity remaining secret, Colley nodded and went to his seat. Dixon and Padfield engaged him in conversation as the register was called.

No early morning banter with their form tutor today. The latest news on their form mate was that he was still holding his own. The development everyone awaited was that Gibson was no longer in intensive care. Colley took his mobile phone from his pocket and began using it out of view under the table. Biggsy realised what he was doing, but decided that he wouldn't enforce the school rule on phone use in the classroom on this occasion.

At that moment, Ms Toner knocked on the door and strode into the classroom. Chris looked up from his phone, hurriedly replaced it in his trouser pocket and smiled feebly in the direction of the deputy head. Alert as was her custom, she was in no doubt about the reason for his furtive movements.

"Morning, Mr Biggs. I hope you don't choose to turn a blind eye to your students using mobile phones in the classroom. Some of our older students think that the special privileges they have in the school allow them to do whatever they like. I've had to speak to Mr Wheelhouse recently about some unruly elements in the sixth form."

She threw a false smile in Colley's direction. She was pleased with herself. As pleased as lyricist Sammy Cahn must have been on discovering that 'carriage' rhymed with 'marriage'.

"Morning, Ms Toner. No unruly elements here, as you can see. I see to it that none of my students ever abuses the privilege of his position in the school."

He spoke with such force that the deputy head switched her attention from the student to the teacher.

"I was just asking Christopher if he could give me the head boy's phone number. I never allow horseplay in my room, as all members of my form will confirm."

He continued to look directly at her. No reaction whatsoever to his choice of words. *Impressive self-possession,* he thought, *or amnesia.* She approached his desk. He thought it a good idea to stand up.

"You may remember, Mr Biggs, I asked you a few weeks ago if you could discuss a curricular matter with your department and email me a report summarising your colleagues' views."

His mind went blank but, on this occasion, he was unconcerned. Perhaps he was the amnesiac. He thought he'd cleared the administrative backlog that she'd put his way over the past month or so. However much he tried to rummage through redundant information stacked up in the various channels of his cortex, a provocative image from the previous evening imposed itself in his mind. Attempting to stifle a smile, he raised his hand to his mouth and cleared his throat.

"I'm sorry, but could you refresh my memory?"

Her steely composure was unsettled. Her ace-serve deliveries were being returned with confident backhands. She found herself thinking it would be advisable to continue the conversation in an undertone.

"You may remember that I'm trying to put together a school policy document that shows links between each curricular area in the school and the world of work. You were asked to make this initiative the first item on the agenda of your faculty meeting several weeks ago at the start of term. Yours is the only curricular area from which I have received nothing."

The lively conversation with colleagues immediately came to mind. He'd felt a little guilty at not having delivered the information she'd demanded, particularly as she had been responsible for providing the English Department with such an entertaining session. They had split their sides at Bridget's first suggestion: career advice on running either a betting shop or chippy from the reading of 'A Kestrel for a Knave'. By the time they'd got to Andy's offering, establishing links between the activities of the three witches on the heath in 'Macbeth' and the pharmaceutical industry, tears were flowing, stomachs aching and chair legs creaking. He'd submitted no report because nobody had been able to take the topic seriously. His attempts, once at home, to cobble together an acceptable document had come to nothing. It was a rare case, for him, of one of those jobs that had never got done.

"Ah, yes. Now I do seem to remember that late request. My apologies. The information will be with you first thing in the morning."

There is absolutely no possibility of that happening, he thought as he nodded slightly in her direction.

"Thank you very much, Mr Biggs. I shall look forward to it."

Poor you! If that's what floats your professional boat, you're in a bad way.

Toner waited for him to offer further apologies. None forthcoming, she left with a puzzle to piece together.

"Ooh, sir. Didn't you do your homework?" chipped in Colley, suddenly animated. "Thanks for that one, by the way, sir. I was actually looking at a message about Jermaine on my phone just then. He's regained consciousness."

A cheer erupted from the students, and Biggsy joined in.

******

He was explaining to Andy his conviction that small is good, as they sat with the rest of the staff awaiting the appearance of Mr Fingleton. He'd called an impromptu meeting in the main hall to update everyone with the latest news on the head boy's condition.

"Take secondary education, the fashion's been for schools to become larger and larger since the 1960s. The bigger the organisation, the more impersonal it becomes. That goes for students as well as staff. The sense of belonging, that many kids need, can go out of the window. It happens to teachers as well."

"I agree with you in principle, but don't you think it's unrealistic to expect our huge secondary schools to downsize overnight. Unfortunately, small just isn't a practical or financial option these days."

"I take your argument, but I can't do huge any longer. It offers too much scope for professional indiscretion, malpractice and a reduced duty of care.

Ideally, I'd like to get out of London tomorrow and teach in a small secondary. The urge to get away is becoming an obsession with me."

"Are you serious, mate?" Andy asked, concerned at the change in direction of their conversation.

"People can get away with murder in big institutions these days. Teaching's becoming too cut-throat. There has to be greater transparency in a smaller establishment. And there are too many knives on the streets up here, too."

The head arrived and stood before his staff. He resisted the impulse to look pleased, aware of the continuing media focus on the school and the fact that Gibson was not yet out of the woods. His arms hung loosely at his sides.

"Good morning, everyone. I'm sorry to be taking up your valuable time, but I wanted us to share an important moment together. I've received some heartening news about the condition of Jermaine Gibson. Despite the serious injuries he sustained when he was attacked, St Mary's hospital has informed the school that he is now out of danger. Yesterday, he regained consciousness and late last night he was moved out of the intensive care unit. I'm sure you will all be feeling as relieved as I am at this time. We must be grateful to the medical team that may manage to deliver Jermaine back to his family and to us."

A part of Biggsy wanted to rejoice, but he could only offer a diffident smile. One or two teachers began clapping their hands, and the rest joined in the celebratory mood.

"I won't keep you any longer, everyone. Thank you for your time."

As staff filed out of the hall, the headmaster approached him.

"I'd like a quick word. This will only take a few seconds. You'll be relieved to hear, as I was, news I received from the police about the evening of the attack. They were able to access CCTV footage from a camera positioned at the bus station. Images of what happened are apparently clear enough to indicate the identity of at least one of Jermaine's assailants. He's already known to the police, and it's their intention to issue arresting orders. I'm optimistic that, once this suspect has been questioned and admitted his offence, it may not be necessary for them to follow up the information provided by Christopher Colley."

Biggsy's eyes widened in delight at the fortuitous developments.

"That'll be good news for Chris and, of course, for Jermaine, Mr Fingleton."

"Indeed. I did think it best not to pass on these facts to all staff at this time. I should be grateful if you would treat these details as highly confidential. Not a word to anyone, including Colley. I hope the boy has had the good sense to tell no one other than you what he discovered."

"I did stress to him the importance of strict confidentiality. Thank you very much for passing on the information, Mr Fingleton."

******

Myra had convinced her husband to wear his new suit for the occasion. He'd put up token resistance but had eventually relented. He preferred smart casual for eating out.

"Fifty-five years of married life together is unusual these days, so let's make it special for Mum and Dad."

"I'll do my best, Myra, but a lot depends on the mood your dad's in."

"I can tell you what mood he's going to be in – grouchy."

"It's a strong Jackson family trait, as you know only too well, but I'll do my best."

"Hey, don't even think of taking a pop at me. I'm not in his league."

Myra was devoted to her mother, Annie, a retired schoolteacher who'd made it to deputy head in a nearby primary. She'd been ideally qualified for that position and no further because she preferred being the person who got everything done behind the scenes. Her head, Frances McKay, an efficient administrator but nothing more, had relied on her to ensure the completion of one initiative after another for over a decade. Myra's father, Russell, had always said, "Fanny did all the fannying around, and Annie did the donkey work." He did not intend this remark to reflect well on his wife, believing that she had been a fool to allow herself to become the feckless head's doormat.

An abrasive individual, Russell Jackson was a 'character' who didn't suffer fools gladly. At least, this was the euphemism Myra regularly used when describing his tetchy personality. Biggsy's appraisal of the man was a little more blunt. He had an unfortunate congenital disposition: he thought everybody but himself was an idiot. Despite his antipathy for his father-in-law, he kept his own counsel whenever they were together. Difficult as it was, this had proved to be the best approach for keeping the family peace. How such an exasperating individual had managed to attain a middle-management position in the civil service was incomprehensible to him.

Myra's childhood had been a difficult one. Her explanation for her father's constantly finding fault with her was jealousy. He wanted exclusive control over his wife's doings and affections, and Myra got in the way. Annie had had to put her husband first in all things, or her life would have been made even more unbearable than it had proved to be. She knew that she'd made a mistake marrying the man, but she believed that she must keep her wedding vows for better or worse, even if he didn't.

Myra had managed to get Ella to join them for the meal at Bellini's.

"Just humour him, like you always do, and he'll be fine," she reminded Ella, who needed no reminding. "Switch on the charm and he'll be like putty in your hands."

"I know how to deal with him, Mum. I just hope he doesn't say anything embarrassing in the restaurant. He's so hard of hearing and he speaks so loudly. Do you remember that time we were with him in the supermarket queue and he said…?"

"I don't know how anyone could let their son get that fat," interrupted Myra. "How could I ever forget?"

"That's right," laughed Ella. "When the boy's mum turned around, I thought she was going to slosh Grandad with her handbag. She was certainly big enough to have done it, and I wouldn't have blamed her."

"With everyone constantly tiptoeing around Russell, even he must realise that he's being patronised by us all," added her father. "Anyway, changing the subject slightly, I still haven't worked out why your parents got married in November. Late November at that!"

"If you're implying that's got anything to do with me, just watch out, matey," warned Myra. "People got married whenever they could fifty years ago."

"I'm just saying it's a strange time to get spliced. But then, everything about your dad is strange."

"I've had enough of this conversation. He's always been a sod. He's not going to change, so let's just get the evening over as quietly as possible, for Mum's sake. Eyes and teeth, everyone, and that's an order."

Biggsy was beginning to feel a little awkward about his gender. He wondered what proportion of the country's older male population was able to get away with ingrained boorish behaviour, whatever the company or setting. He'd long ago formed the opinion that those of advancing years who were most strident in their ritual condemnation of others' failings, particularly with respect to the younger generation, simply enjoyed indulging in crass insensitivity. Habitual ill-temper directed toward others was also, in his opinion, an inverted form of self-disgust.

******

"Oh, here they are. Late again," chimed Russell, opening his door to the family.

They presented practiced smiles in unison, each wondering who was going to speak first. They were five minutes later than the time agreed to pick up the anniversary couple. Russell had made a point of answering the door in order to get his barb in directly. The preoccupation with punctuality, one of his most ingrained fixations, offered him the regular satisfaction of being able to condemn humanity.

"Hello, Dad. Ready for the off?" Myra asked.

"Well, I am, as you can see, but your mother's also late. She's still upstairs powdering her nose. She'll be late for her own funeral like the rest of you. Come on in and see if you can prise her away from her dressing table."

A keen club cricketer in his youth, Russell had once been lean and supple of frame, a model of athleticism. He cut a different figure in old age. Well above average height, his girth had expanded alarmingly in recent years, a consequence of his taste for homemade wine, dairy produce and pastries. From humble beginnings as the son of a village railway signalman in Hampshire, he'd penny-pinched his way into middle-class society. He'd had the good fortune to meet Annie when she was training to be a teacher. From her, he had learnt how to disguise the rough edges of his character with a veneer of respectability. She'd always done her best to make him feel important, whereas he had worked toward achieving the opposite for her. Myra ached at this systematic undermining of her mother's self-confidence.

"As I live and breathe, she's ready at last."

Annie made her way downstairs, choosing to ignore her husband's sarcasm. Myra couldn't imagine many women well into their seventies being able to look as elegant as her mother. She appeared in the hallway, immaculate in grey skirt, white blouse and dark red jacket. She prided herself on keeping trim and looked a good ten years younger than her husband. Genuinely pleased to see her family members gathered in the hallway, she embraced each one in turn. Russell, by contrast, showed no interest in outward signs of affection.

"You look fabulous, Mum," praised Myra. "Love the outfit. Where did you get it?"

"Oh, don't be silly. You know I get everything from M&S."

"Let's get going then, for God's sake," Russell instructed, irritated by praise of his wife. If he couldn't be bothered to compliment her, nobody should.

******

"Well, all things considered, I thought that went rather well. Mum loved it."

It was ten thirty and the Biggses were back home, basking in the heat of the gas coal-effect fire and sipping mugs of tea. The anniversary celebrations had passed off without incident, and Myra was relieved.

"Ella should take a lot of the credit for that. Getting your mum and dad to reminisce about their childhood experiences was a master stroke."

"Yes, being evacuated took its toll on both of them, but it was particularly bad for Dad."

"You always get that part wrong, love. Your dad was evicted when he was nine, not evacuated. His parents had had enough of him."

"Not funny. I often wonder at the damage that was done to all the kids who were ripped from their parents during the war."

"Oh, come on, love. He and his mates, Leakey and Sulley, had the time of their lives when they were let loose in the New Forest."

"Grandad has so many funny stories about those times," said Ella. "Once he started on them, it was as though he were reliving every moment. I've never known him talk to me like that before. I can't imagine how awful it must have been for him living with that weird old couple in the middle of nowhere."

"If he'd had a normal childhood, he wouldn't have turned into such a misery, I'm sure of it," affirmed her mother. "His parents became strangers to him over the years he was away."

"But not every evacuated child was transformed into the monster from the black lagoon, love."

"You can poke fun, but I know different. Life is a wonderful thing, but it damages people, some more than others."

"I think Mum's right, Dad. I saw Granddad in a different light tonight. I don't think he enjoys being the way he is with people."

"You may be right, both of you, but spare a thought for your grandmother. She's the heroine who's put up with him for the past half century. What a woman!"

"Good old mum," Myra concluded. "You're right. She is a wonderful woman."

She waited a few moments for a compliment to come her way, but nobody obliged.

"Right, I'm off to bed, you two."

******

The school Christmas tree had been erected in the entrance lobby, its cheery lights illuminating the aged honours boards. It was early December and staff and students alike were becoming impatient for the end of term. The promise of a two-week festive break after almost four gruelling months was within sight.

Biggsy escorted his students to the sixth-form common room immediately after he'd registered them. The other groups were also filing in, and a mood of expectation was growing. Boys talked quietly amongst themselves, anticipating the approaching moment of celebration. A banner reading 'Welcome back, Jermaine' stretched from one side of the common room to the other.

The head boy was making his way gingerly along the corridor, his parents either side of him. He'd lost weight and his features were drawn. It would be some time before he regained the easy confidence that he'd formerly shown to the world. His father smiled as he pushed open the common-room door for his son. The assembly erupted. Jermaine's face relaxed as he took in the scene of whooping and cheering boys. They parted before him, as he made his entrance. The cheers only subsided when Dave Wheelhouse stepped forward and raised his arms to quell the din.

"Welcome back, Jermaine! I hope you'll find that nothing's changed in your absence, although you'll notice that some of your fellow students couldn't help but become a little louder and, of course, uglier over the past few weeks."

Gibson's mouth tightened, as he shook Dave's hand. Struggling to muster his old self-control, he began a brief unrehearsed response to the outpouring of warmth.

"It's good to be here again, guys. I never imagined this sort of welcome back. Thanks for all your emails and texts. It'll take me hours to delete them on my phone. I haven't been able to do much schoolwork for the past few weeks, so I've got to start trying to catch up with you lot straight away."

"Never mind that. You've got to get back to rugby training," interrupted Dixon, stepping forward and giving him a hug.

The force of the embrace caused his team captain to start and clutch his side.

"Oops. Sorry, mate. Forgot!"

As the strains of 'For He's a Jolly Good Fellow' rang out, Dave went to Gibson's rescue, smiling at the students surrounding their hero.

"That's all for now, folks," advised Dave as he ushered his overwhelmed guest into the sixth-form office for refuge.

Biggsy approached the parents who stood recovering themselves for a moment, as the students drifted off to class. The difference between the Gibsons' mood now and how they'd appeared to him the last time he'd observed them was dramatic. Proud and statuesque, the tall and slender Mrs Gibson's eyes were aflame in admiration of her son. Her husband, the same height but double her size, chuckled to himself.

"Hello, Mr and Mrs Gibson. It's so good to see Jermaine almost back to his old self again."

"Thank you, Mr Biggs. Our prayers have been answered. The family's been through a terrible time. All his relatives back in Jamaica are so relieved. Our boy is back," enthused Mrs Gibson, patting her eyes with a tissue.

"Jermaine is lucky to have such devoted parents. I shall do everything I can to make sure he's able to get back on track with his studies. Can I ask you, by the way, if he's decided whether or not he wishes to apply for university?"

"Of course he's going to university, Mr Biggs. Why should you be asking such a question?"

"Oh, no particular reason. Just checking. One of my first tasks, now that Jermaine is back, will be to arrange a meeting with him to finalise his application."

******

"But, it's not what I want," the head boy objected.

Biggsy had had a full teaching day after a busy weekend preparing GCSE mock examination papers. Myra had been patient whilst he'd spent most of the previous day closeted in the family office. She'd finally insisted after Sunday lunch that he take an hour off to drive to Bushy Park for a stroll. He had to admit to being grateful that his wife insisted on 'sanity breaks' at regular intervals in their lives. She saw him as being unable to resist the slavish devotion to nonsensical drudgery. Habitually immersed in supplementary school chores whilst at home, he periodically found himself being forced by Myra to come up for air.

"But it looks as though the matter's out of your hands, Jermaine."

Gibson leaned forward, his slender fingers splayed over his knees as he sat to the side of his form master's desk in the English office. He was gaining in strength daily. Just at this moment, his self-assurance and determination were strongly in evidence.

"I'm fine now – completely recovered. I can't see why Lonnie should face any charges if I don't want him to."

"What exactly is your reason for wanting him to escape any punishment for what he did to you?"

"I don't want someone going to prison because of me. That's all. My mum and dad think I'm stupid, but I can't help how I feel. Somebody told Lonnie I'd dissed his sister, which I hadn't, and he just reacted stupidly. He was somebody else's victim, and I was his."

This logic was worrying to a teacher concerned at the growing problem of knife crime amongst young people. Gibson could easily have been killed as a result of somebody peddling false information online. He feared for Ella one day becoming a social networking gossip target.

"I appreciate where your arguments are coming from, Jermaine, but there are two considerations that take precedence over them. First, you might easily have lost your life. Second, now that the police have identified your attacker on CCTV, they will prosecute him on behalf of society, not you. Your feelings about not wanting charges to be taken up are irrelevant. The only chance of a prosecution not being pursued would be if the footage did not provide conclusive evidence of your attacker's identity."

The student cradled the back of his head in his linked hands, looked up and studied the ceiling. Biggsy sympathised with the boy's wishes, but felt the responsibility to explain the legal complications of the adult world awaiting every young person. He changed course, deciding that now would be a good time to turn the conversation to the delicate matter of university application.

"I'm truly sorry that I can't be more helpful to you in this matter, Jermaine, but there are other forces at work here. To add insult to injury, could we spend a few minutes talking about your university application?"

Chapter 11

"I seriously thought you lot might have given a bit more thought to Mufti Day."

To a man, the students had conformed to the default attire of hoody, denim jeans and trainers that most of the other pupils in the school had adopted that day. For a one-pound donation to the Children in Need charity the school supported, the boys had the privilege of coming to school in civvies. However, for most, this involved replacing one uniform with another. Sixth formers were no longer required to wear the blazer and tie they'd worn for five years, but they did have to conform to the smart-casual dress code. To the disgust of many of the senior boys at St Saviour's, the school didn't recognise jeans as acceptable clothing, however smart they were. Mufti Day for sixth formers became Payback Day.

"One day a sixth former will cock a snook at his scruffy peers and turn up on Mufti Day in a sharp suit," continued Biggsy. "You're all young men now, but you continue to give way to peer pressure and dress as down as possible when given a free choice."

"What you talkin' about, sir? Scruffy? These strides set me back an 'undred and twenty-five," piped up Colley, placing one leg on his table and caressing his beloved denims.

"You were robbed there, Chris. They're out at the knee – full of holes."

"God, sir. That's what you're paying for. These are distressed jeans."

"Yes, very distressing from where I'm looking. You're paying good money for holes. And you're still wearing the same damned hoodies!"

"Hold up, sir. These may look like the same damned hoodies to you, but I also paid big money for this designer label last week," declared a peeved Padfield.

Once again, his young scholars were playing into his hands.

"Oh, I see. Paying an extra fifty quid for a label makes all the difference, of course. Thanks for reminding me."

"Ah, come on, sir. It's the modern world. Labels don't come cheap," protested Padfield.

He smiled in gratitude: the door had been opened for him to deliver his diatribe against all things designer.

"You may have noticed, guys, that nothing I wear has a company name or logo scrawled across my chest. I can't understand why your designer gear costs more than the clothes I buy. It should be cheaper. If someone from a clothing company paid me a large sum of money to wear an item displaying its logo, I'd consider accepting such an offer. But I wouldn't shell out several additional pounds of my own money for the privilege of advertising that brand. It would be a case of exploitation, with me as the exploited party. Advertising something for nothing makes no economic sense. Don't you object to being ripped off?"

"It's just the way things are, sir. Everybody's being ripped off these days," Colley concluded sagely.

World-weary at eighteen. Biggsy sighed. This conversation was no longer fun.

"Can't argue with that, lads," he admitted. "I suppose we all get hooked one way or another. I'll come around and collect your pounds."

He approached the table at which Colley and Dixon were in earnest conversation. They handed over their donations begrudgingly. Then Dixon looked up.

"Sir, do you do social networking?"

"Why do you ask, Richard?"

"Chris and I were just looking at Facebook last night. Couldn't find you, sir. Some of the other teachers are on it."

"No need for me to use it. I haven't got any friends. I don't even waste time online trying to kid myself that there are people interested in me."

This observation elicited the anticipated reaction. Colley assumed an expression of mock concern.

"That's so sad, sir. I'm wellin' up."

"Don't waste your false sympathy on me, Chris. The great advantage of being a Billy No Mates is that I'm not tempted to waste fifty hours a week talking nonsense to people attempting to create virtual existences for themselves because they don't have real ones."

"What, sir?" queried Colley. "Can you give us all a few minutes to work out what you just said?"

"It's simple. Most social networkers are into self-promotion. Don't kid yourself that there are masses of people out there who are genuinely interested in you and your life. It's all about me, me, me. As far as I'm concerned, my life is not complicated by the uncontrollable urge to be going online constantly to check if my imaginary friends have messaged me."

"What do you do with all the free time you have then?" laughed Padfield.

"Tonight, I shall be mostly marking books. The way I see it, though, social networking is becoming more social bullying from what I read in the papers. I'm better off out of it."

He scrutinised the faces before him. Would anybody attempt to contradict his heresy?

"You could 'ave a point there, sir. My sister gets loads of flak from girls she thought were her mates. Lethal stuff. She's always unfriending them," admitted Padfield.

"You're not implying that girls are more acerbic in their messaging than boys, I hope."

"All depends, sir."

"On what?"

"What 'acerbic' means, sir."

******

Myra was having a Saturday lie in. He slid out of the bed and made straight for the wash bin to put on yesterday's socks. Just a temporary measure: it was very cold. He pulled on his dressing gown. The 'World's Best Dad' badge Ella had given him on Fathers' Day a decade ago was still attached to it. He headed for the bathroom to sort out his complaining bladder. As he approached the end of his third decade in teaching, it concerned him that he'd not drunk enough fluid to keep himself regularly hydrated. If he left a class to relieve himself, there would be a riot going on when he returned. He counted thirty-eight seconds of urinating. It was taking him even longer. Male colleagues had warned him to watch out for the onset of 'dribbly dick'. He told himself, yet again, he must get a PSA blood test sorted out.

Once downstairs, he flicked on the central heating, turning the thermostat up a few notches, filled the kettle, plugged it in and switched on the radio.

"Society seems to have lost the plot…"

Myra had been listening to talk radio again. Not to his taste. He pressed the Radio 3 pre-set and the aching strings of Mahler's Fifth filled the galley kitchen. The image of feeble Aschenbach fading away on the beach of the Venice Lido occupied his thoughts as he prepared two mugs of tea. Strange, he thought, that a piece of music composed to convey a sense of wonderment at the birth of one's child should double up as a funerary dirge. As he made his way upstairs with the tea tray, another of his classical favourites began. He was transported to Wagner's world, 'Siegfried's Funeral March' following him up the stairs. He wondered what might comprise a manic depressive's list of top ten classical hits.

Hope this musical theme isn't a herald of bad luck, he brooded. He must sort out a GP appointment.

Myra was stirring in the semi-darkness of the bedroom. He placed one mug on her bedside cabinet and climbed back into bed clutching his tea, spilling a few drops on the cream duvet cover as he did so.

"Shit!"

"Thought you'd just done that," came a voice from the other side of the bed.

"No, just a pee for now. Plenty of time for that later. Drink your tea before it gets cold."

"What plans have you got for us today then, love?"

"What are you on about?"

"People don't believe me when I tell them what it's like being married to a teacher," she ruminated, hauling herself up from the depths of their king size. She plumped her pillow up against the headboard and began sipping her decaffeinated tea. "What are your plans for today then?" she asked again, with heavy emphasis on the word 'your'.

"No plans as yet, although I'll have to put the finishing touches to the year eleven English mock exam papers."

"I was thinking of things that might be connected to the real world – our world – not your assessment mountain."

Choosing to avoid the possibility of being drawn into an argument that he could only lose, it occurred to him that this might be an opportune time to revisit the subject of upping sticks.

"What would you say to moving out of London to somewhere with a bit more open space, possibly the coast?"

Myra looked up from her mug, her dreamy eyes narrowing.

"Have you got somewhere in mind?"

Relieved that she hadn't used the 'why' word, he offered a few likely locations.

"South, say, to Chichester, Brighton, Portsmouth, Bournemouth…?"

"You know I'm not ready for such a dramatic lifestyle change. I like it here. What about all the friends we have? Or should I say, 'I have'. And what about Ella? She wouldn't want to move."

"She'll be heading off to university soon. She wouldn't worry where we were living. And we'd still keep in touch with friends."

"I don't really want to be put out to pasture yet, love. Perhaps in a few years' time. What's got you thinking about moving?"

He wanted to present the idea as an entirely positive step forward in their lives, an exciting enterprise offering new life-affirming opportunities. Unfortunately, he was unable to conceal the motivation of anxiety, even fear. Professional anxieties and disillusionment wouldn't be convincing arguments for his wife to uproot her life. He couldn't look her in the eyes, glowing with excitement at the prospect of a new challenge and whatever dreams may come.

"I feel that London's over-heating. It's not a place where I feel as at ease as I used to."

He couldn't admit to more.

"Is anyone completely at ease with living in London? Or anywhere else for that matter? There are disadvantages living here, but the benefits are enormous."

Myra didn't want to spoil her Saturday morning by considering this matter further, but she didn't want to appear entirely unsympathetic by rejecting the idea out of hand.

"I'll think it through. If it's something you're keen on, I'll consider all the angles. Don't rush me, though."

"Deal."

Anxious to keep in his wife's good books after broaching the topic of moving out of the capital, he ran his colours up the flagpole with, what he considered, a masterstroke of an offer.

"Look, what do you say to skipping breakfast here and having a brunch at The Grill in the high street?"

Myra's lethargy forgotten, she hauled herself out of bed, hurried into the bathroom and slammed the door behind her.

Urgent instructions were issued from within.

"Finish your tea and get your trousers on. I'll be five minutes."

******

"Flies are buzzin' 'round my head…"

A serenade greeted him, as he arrived early for his sixth-form lesson after morning break. Richard Dixon was the only student present. He was sitting at a table, eyes closed, singing along to something on headphones attached to his mobile phone. Nodding his head rhythmically, he was totally preoccupied with whatever music was in his head. It wasn't until Biggsy moved the chair back from under his table that the student returned to the everyday world with a jolt. He looked up and smiled disarmingly at his tutor.

"Good stuff?"

"The best."

"The lyrics sound a bit morbid to me, Richard."

"No, it's 'Optimistic', sir."

"I'll take your word for it."

"It's Radiohead."

"Oh. Fair enough."

"Do you like the band, sir?"

"Not heard that much by them."

"You should, sir."

"I may take up that recommendation. Losing yourself in music and dance is beneficial for a healthy mind," said Biggsy, stating aloud principles he recalled from his studies of ancient Greek drama.

He recalled the third element contributing to the ecstasy Greeks of that period enjoyed in their celebrations – alcohol. A cautionary word of qualification seemed advisable.

"But best to avoid alcoholic excess as you enjoy the vibe," he smiled.

"Of course, sir," Dixon grinned.

Padfield's huge frame suddenly filled the doorway.

"You'd better come out 'ere, sir. The caretaker's gone ballistic."

He launched himself from his desk. Dixon, engrossed in his music, looked up and followed the teacher's frantic progress, a look of bafflement on his face.

A large crowd of children was concentrated in the centre of the playground. Whatever was going on was different from the standard confrontation between two pupils because there was no chanting of 'Fight! Fight! Fight!' This crowd was silent. As he forced himself through to the centre of the throng, he was appalled at the sight before him. Scrumpy Bulmer, in the grip of two older pupils pinioning his arms, was mouthing curses in the direction of a junior schoolboy. The caretaker was clearly in an alcoholic stupor, judging by his heightened ruddy complexion and slurred speech. As he struggled to wrench himself free from the two boys who were doing a sterling job of restraining him, he bellowed gruffly in the direction of the youngster.

"Let me get my 'ands on the little bleeder. I'll bloody murder 'im!"

The focus of Bulmer's wrath, a cowering lower school pupil, wore an expression of utter amazement.

Biggsy pulled his trusty whistle from his pocket and blew a long blast, as much to shock Bulmer back to whatever senses he could still control as to address the stunned onlookers.

"Everybody inside now!" he bawled, straining his larynx to the limit. "Anyone hanging around and making himself intentionally late for his next lesson will be placed in detention. Inside! Now!"

The power of the Acme Thunderer began to work its wonder. He stood before Bulmer, placed his face directly in front of him and reduced his tone to little more than a whisper.

"If you wish to avoid criminal prosecution, pull yourself together. Go indoors and make yourself a cup of strong black coffee."

Bulmer stopped struggling and the two students relaxed their hold, now concentrating more on keeping the inebriate upright. He shook himself free, wobbled a little and then did his best to stand unaided.

"Little perisher shouldn't 'ave taken liberties."

Biggsy took a closer look at the little perisher, a wiry year eight boy he didn't know by name.

"I only went and got me ball back from 'is garden, sir. He came running after me and then went off on one."

The caretaker's house was adjacent to the school. As the gate from the rear garden to the playground was often left open, owing to Bulmer's forgetfulness, boys had become accustomed to retrieving stray footballs without asking permission.

"Well, no serious harm done to you, thank goodness. Can I ask you to go straight to your form room and explain what happened to your tutor? Who is that, by the way?"

"Miss Andrews, sir."

"And your name is?"

"Bevan Francis, sir."

"Right. She'll know what to do, so off you go."

"Yes, sir."

The older boys, who'd prevented the caretaker from being in even greater trouble than he already was, stood watching the young boy as he hurried away.

"You two did a good job preventing what could have turned out to be a most unfortunate incident. Come to my classroom after school so that I can thank you properly."

They nodded and sauntered off. Bulmer trudged away in the opposite direction, still cursing under his breath. The playground had almost emptied, but for a few stragglers dragging their feet. Chris Barker appeared around a corner.

"Heard there was something going on. What happened?"

"Scrumpy lost it with one of the younger pupils. Blind drunk he looked to me. Took offence at a boy who was in his garden looking for a football and went for him out here. I think we may have seen the last of Bulmer."

"Bloody hell!" guffawed Chris. "I knew he liked a drop, but I'd have thought it was a bit early even for him."

"He's in such a state; he must have started drinking straight after breakfast. Wonder what tipped him over the edge?"

******

"Fingleton had no choice this time, mate. He had to go."

"I think his wife walking out on him was the clincher," added Biggsy.

He and Andy were sharing two minutes of quality time in the staff room. The administration backlog of every member of staff was mounting daily, as the Christmas holiday approached. Coincidentally, both teachers had opted to take their coffee with like-minded colleagues who'd decided that morning break, for once, really should be a morning break. Teachers increasingly eschewed the staff common room, marking or completing essential intranet data in their classrooms during any free time available to them. Biggsy tried to relax but was finding it difficult to resist the urge to take himself off to his laptop. The online reports for years seven, nine, eleven and the sixth form would, he calculated, add at least fifteen hours of non-contact time to his week.

"I feel sorry for her, Andy. Holed up in that house all day on her own. A decent enough place to live in, but pretty isolated and no neighbours. I've never seen any other family or visitors coming or going. Who would with Bulmer around the place?"

"Caretakers are a special breed. Not a job I'd fancy. Anti-social hours and a solitary existence. Small wonder they have a reputation for being such cranky buggers."

"He was more than cranky yesterday. Before I arrived on the scene, he'd made some nasty racist remarks to poor little Bevan, according to Padfield, one of my tutor group."

"Don't know how he ever got the job in the first place. He couldn't do anything right. A total liability if you ask me. I remember asking him to put up a display frame on the wall outside my classroom to highlight pupils' work. I came in the next morning and he told me, 'I've put your display board up outside your room. If you want it put up straight, I'll come back later and do it again.' I went to my room and the frame was listing about ten degrees from the horizontal."

Biggsy almost choked on his coffee.

The full story of the drunken outburst painted Bulmer in the worst possible light. He was, it seemed, a hopeless case, with a malicious streak that he struggled to control. Bevan regularly played football with his classmates on the patch of tarmac next to the caretaker's house. Whenever the ball went over the six-foot high featherboard fence into Bulmer's garden, Bevan was invariably the one who was sent in to fetch it, usually through the open gate but sometimes over it. Being well into his cups, the caretaker had disgraced himself for the last time. *An almost Pinteresque series of events,* thought Biggsy. He drained his mug and stood up.

"I think I'll have a further word with young Bevan, Andy. He may need to hear some reassuring words after what he was subjected to. The boys who regularly sent him over the top will also need a chat. Catch you later."

******

Sixth Form parents evening came around all too soon. He understood the reason for having parents' evenings, but they were rarely enjoyable experiences. Increasingly, from his perspective, too many parents demonstrated an instinctive mistrust of those with the responsibility for teaching their children. In his opinion, their grievance was misplaced: it should have been directed at the curriculum planners who'd designed the national curriculum in all its educational sterility, with content overload subjugating intellectual curiosity.

No live football was being televised, so more than the usual handful of fathers would turn up. That could be a bad thing. In the main, mothers in attendance outnumbered fathers by more than two to one. Males tended to put work commitments and football loyalties before their sons. A sizeable minority of those who did come along had unrealistic expectations, testosterone-induced in Biggsy's opinion. Where a mother might ask 'What can I do to improve my son's motivation?', a father would be more likely to ask, 'Why is this school failing my son?'

This was the one evening that could prove problematical for any staff members who were under-prepared, lacking an essential piece of performance data that parents might demand. Reports with interim examination grades had been sent out in late November, and some parents might be out for blood if their sons' lacklustre grade predictions had taken them unawares. Public squabbles sometimes broke out. Toner, on patrol around the school, would be quickly on the spot to pour oil on troubled clients. And Fingleton always got to hear about any disturbances.

As he walked to the library where he and members of his department would be holding discussions with parents, accompanied by their sons, he imagined what Douglas Adams' fictional creation, Marvin the Paranoid Android, might say if presented with the challenge facing him:

"Parents? Don't talk to me about parents."

All was quiet as he was the first to arrive. He switched on the lights and checked the radiators. Good, Bulmer's replacement had remembered the heating. But nobody had rearranged the tables and chairs for the evening, so he set to it. On a table he'd placed in front of a radiator for himself, he laid out his mark book and a pile of students' literature essays on 'Mansfield Park'. He'd decided the latest piece of written work would make a good starting point for his fifteen ten-minute conversations. It was going to be a long evening if everyone turned up.

The physical work done, he sat down in position behind his table, a reassuringly sturdy protective barrier. Sarah arrived, using her shoulder bag as a ram to force a way through the spring-loaded door. Seeing her head of department, she waved a hello and looked about her.

"Hope I'm too late! Is there any chance you're the last person to leave?"

"Sorry to disappoint, and you've probably wasted ten minutes of your life by arriving early."

"Is that right? Do you know I've passed up the chance of going to my son's martial arts grading for this evening's fun fest?"

"Deep down you know that, of all places, this is where you'd rather be tonight."

Angela Davies arrived next, coffee spilling from a mug as she struggled through the doorway with a pile of A4 exercise books.

"Oh, thank heavens it's warm in here!" she exclaimed gratefully. "I just popped into the main hall where maths and science are and it's freezing."

"If we're to be putting in another three or four hours here on top of a full day's teaching, it's good to know that we're in the best place we can be," he reassured her.

******

It was just after eight o'clock. He'd been so busy, there had been no opportunity to check how well the evening had been going for everybody else. The only relaxation of pressure for him had been meeting Mr and Mrs Dixon again. A no-nonsense couple who ran a local pub, they once again expressed their heartfelt thanks for all that the school had done for their son. Unlike many parents, the Dixons were entirely supportive of St Saviour's and had every respect for the teaching staff who'd struggled with Richard's academic and behavioural difficulties over the years. Although not the model scholar, he'd become a steadier student under his form master's guidance and supervision.

Ten enjoyable minutes were spent exchanging pleasantries with them. All that was missing were a few pints on the table. They left the meeting with confirmation that their son was working to his potential and on course for a respectable pass in A-Level English Literature.

Far from feeling chilly as the evening progressed, he began to find it too warm in the library. He stood and opened a window behind him. He looked across at Andy who had a queue of three sets of parents, each couple accompanied by a son. Polite indifference or undisguised boredom registered on the faces of the students. Andy took a quick slurp of the tea that had been placed on his table by a parent who'd volunteered for catering duties that evening. He then looked at the disgruntled parents facing him and made to stand to indicate the end of the interview. The mother pushed back her chair in readiness to depart, but the smart-suited father sat tight and shook his head sadly. He looked to be too depressed to leave.

"I won't take that from you!"

Biggsy turned his head in the direction of the raised voice. An Asian father was looking sternly at Nick Devlin and pointing a finger at the teacher's chest.

"I'm not sitting here any longer! Come along, you two," he instructed his wife and embarrassed son. He pushed his chair away from him and began hauling his wife out of her seat.

"Mr Mohammed, we need to—"

Nick's attempts to restore order and continue the interview were ignored.

"You can't speak to me like that. I shall complain to the headmaster about this. Hurry up, Akmal!"

"But, Dad," his son bleated.

Nick Devlin pushed a hand through his hair and pinched the bridge of his nose with thumb and forefinger.

Embarrassed, Akmal held his arms out toward his father, who ignored the supplication. The student looked an apology at Nick and followed his parents. Mrs Mohammed, her hand in her husband's grip, turned at the door and gave one last mournful look in the direction of her son's teacher. Biggsy rose from his seat, strode across the room and managed to catch up with the parents in the corridor. He introduced himself and asked if he could be of any assistance. Studying his face with a penetrating stare, Mr Mohammed quickly adjudged that, no, this teacher was not important enough to deal with his problem.

"I only want to see the headmaster about this matter, thank you very much."

When Biggsy returned to the library, Nick was doing his best to welcome the next interviewees. About to interrupt the proceedings to offer a word or two of support to his junior colleague, Biggsy felt a hand at his elbow.

"Can I speak to you outside?" a soft voice asked.

Angela Davies inclined her head toward the door. Once outside, she provided an account of what had caused Mr Mohammed to become so agitated.

"I've finished my interviews, but I had to speak to you before I went home. I was sitting at the desk next to Nick and was about to leave because I'd seen all my parents. His meeting didn't seem to be going too well because the father was doing most of the talking and not paying much attention to anything Nick had to say. The son and mum made no input whatsoever. They seemed anxious. Then, when she did try to make a comment, her husband looked at her with an angry expression and said, 'Shut up!' He was in a filthy mood. Nick must have been upset at the way the poor woman was being treated and said, calmly and reasonably, 'You can't speak like that to your wife, Mr Mohammed.' The father became incensed at that, and you saw what happened next."

"Oh, my God! And things were going so well."

This situation had the potential to be a serious cultural collision. The expression 'Shut up!' would be troubling him once again. He felt a degree of admiration for Nick, but feared that his cautioning Mr Mohammed as he had might result in management censure. The deputy head would be sure to hear of the incident and, in all likelihood, handle the matter with the same degree of insensitivity that Angela had experienced a few weeks earlier.

"Thanks for telling me that, Angela," he said attempting a smile. "You get off home now. I've got to get back as I've a few more meetings. I'll speak to you again tomorrow if that's OK."

"Yes, I'll get along. I really hope Nick doesn't get into trouble over this. What he said was right."

"He was right, Angela. Would you do me a favour and keep this to yourself? Fingers might want to speak to you about it at some point. I only hope that, if he and his favourite deputy do pursue the matter, they see it our way."

At nine fifteen, Nick concluded his final interview. Biggsy went across the room and sat facing his despondent colleague.

"Sorry your evening was spoiled by such a rude parent, Nick. It's bad enough coping with difficult boys, but difficult parents are another ball game entirely."

"I couldn't stop myself. I had to say what I did. He was being completely unreasonable – wouldn't listen to anything from me. Akmal and his mother seemed nervous before we even got going. When Mr Mohammed humiliated his wife in front of me, I just had to speak up."

"It was brave of you to confront him, Nick. Angela heard everything. She told me about his behaviour and what was said. I asked her to keep it all to herself. If the parent's as good as his word and does talk to the head about it, you'll have my total support. It amounts to bullying of staff as well as a domestic issue nobody was probably aware of."

"That would figure because Akmal is an intelligent boy, but he has such a nervous disposition. I'd wondered if someone at school might be giving him trouble."

"Try not to dwell on the matter. Don't lose any sleep over it. Anyone who may be persuaded to look into the business will only be able to come to one conclusion: you were in the right."

"It won't be easy putting it out of my mind, but thanks for the reassurance."

******

"You'll be useless tomorrow."

He dropped into his armchair and tuned in to what remained of the late news programme. Myra, snugly wrapped in her scarlet dressing gown, handed her husband a plate. She placed a mug of tea on the coffee table. He was heartened by the sight of two slices of cheese on toast, a generous helping of pickle topping one of the slices.

"Meetings with parents should be built into the school day, not tagged on as a four-hour extra. How can you be expected to do a proper job tomorrow?"

Having become used to his wife's resentment at the unreasonable demands made of the family by his job, he attempted a winning smile. She also worried about his health. In a moment of weakness, he'd let slip that he'd cut down on his fluid intake during the school day because he couldn't risk needing to go to the loo during lessons. Big mistake. He bit into his toast, the plain slice first to get the full flavour of the extra mature cheddar.

"And how was your day, love?"

"Not quite as congested as yours thankfully. Oh, we're all up for job reviews. Cost-cutting exercise, I think. Could be out of a job after Christmas."

He turned from the image of the prime minister trying on a Manchester United shirt at Old Trafford and looked at her intently.

"Any serious chance of that, do you think?"

"It's certainly possible, but at least I'm not one of the newbies in the department. I'm not too worried, though. I'm not quite as devoted to the health service as you are to teaching. I'd find something elsewhere."

He suddenly found his cheese on toast extra tasty.

"Somewhere down south, perhaps?" he queried.

"Ah, still nurturing that little seedling, are we? I walked straight into that one, didn't I?"

"Just a thought. The world is our lobster, as the cockney wide boy once said."

"Talking of lobsters, do you fancy eating out at the weekend? I'm getting a yearning for a seafood platter at Benito's."

"I will if you can convince me you're not pregnant. You haven't had a yearning for some time now."

"As if? But have you noticed that Ellie's put on a bit of weight lately? I'll have to devise a subtle plan to find out why."

"Haven't noticed anything myself. Think you're being a little alarmist. Perhaps she's just happy in herself."

"I'm sure you're right, but I'll keep my weight-gain antennae raised for the time being. By the way, you seem to be looking a bit more washed out and peaky than usual recently. Have you lost any weight?"

"Thanks very much for the compliment. No, not that I'm aware of. Still using the same hole in my belt."

"Well, I'm going on up to bed. Don't stay down here too long. I need something to warm my feet on."

"I might watch half an hour of that Swedish detective series I recorded before I come up. Need something mindless to help me switch off before trying to sleep."

"Is that the one you were watching over the weekend where the police discovered body parts in a hotel's recycled food waste?"

"That's the one."

"Sick! Sick! Sick! These Scandinavian cop series are plumbing every depth of vomitsome violence. You're welcome to it. See you later."

"I take your point, but I'm only watching it to brush up on my Swedish. Godnatt," he muttered, as Myra pecked him on the cheek.

"You're a laugh a minute. Don't be long now."

Chapter 12

"When I arrived first thing, there was a message in my pigeonhole. The head wanted a word," Nick explained to Sarah, Andy and Biggsy in the English office.

There were two minutes to go before the morning registration buzzer. Raindrops weaved pathways down the windowpane. Steam rose from the spout of the kettle.

"He explained that he agreed personally with the sentiment expressed in my comment but, with his headteacher hat on, he thought my words were ill-advised."

"That's encouraging," said Andy. "Not what I would have expected him to say."

"You were very restrained, in my opinion," said Sarah. "I can't imagine how I would have reacted had I been in your situation. I'd probably have been arrested."

"Then he went on to say that, when Mr Mohammed spoke to him last night, it was clear that Mrs Mohammed and Akmal were both embarrassed at his complaining about me. He said that, when he'd heard my account of events, he'd phone the father back and take it from there."

"Akmal's a great kid," Andy enthused. "He'll talk his old man round. Fingers is banking on there being no need for any kind of meeting."

"Hope so," said Biggsy. "Not an easy one to deal with, but there's only one stance he can take. He knows that. It'll all blow over."

"Sorry to have stirred this up. The words came out even before I had time to think."

"Apologies are not required, Nick," reassured Sarah. "We're in total agreement on that."

The buzzer sounded. Nick hoisted his holdall on to his shoulder.

"See you at the staff meeting after school, everyone, if I don't see you before then."

Sarah picked up a pile of 'Waiting for Godot' off a shelf and followed him out of the door. Andy delayed his exit.

"Have you heard the rumours that Toner and Aimes are getting it on? Apparently, Aaron was out with the PE crowd last night celebrating Doggy's birthday and his tongue ran away with him whilst under the influence."

"That's interesting," he replied, revealing nothing.

"Seems a very strange combination to me, but there it is. See you later."

Alone in the office, Biggsy became aware of a sudden modification in his attitude toward the person he'd come to perceive merely as his arch enemy. He realised he was revising his views on staffroom gossip about colleagues. One's private life was just that and should remain so, whoever you were. In situations of this kind, some found the temptation of making women the butt of ribald comments difficult to resist. Himself included. He recalled a comment he'd made to Andy about Toner at the start of term and concluded that he'd been too open in the past with flippant comments about the deputy head. Much as he felt professionally threatened by her, he could take no pleasure now in staff-room mischief-making about her relationship with Aimes.

A romantic attachment between a senior teacher and a junior member of staff was unusual, particularly one that involved such risk-taking demonstrations of passion on the school premises after hours. Reassessing his professional anxieties, the idea came to him that he needn't be at all anxious about his position at St Saviour's, if the focus of his fears were someone so emotionally insecure herself. Top Tip No. 5: All teachers regularly feel degrees of personal insecurity in the job.

He ran over a few of his convictions about those in positions of authority, as distinct from those who were authorities in specific fields. He held to the prejudice that, in the main, organisations and institutions, including nation states, were run by sharp-suited types of dubious moral integrity. He rejected Myra's accusation that he was a congenital cynic with the argument that he was a realist. The Faustian pact was the deal awaiting every ambitious professional, and the majority signed up. Myra had tackled him directly on this point: if he felt that way about those selected for promotion within St Saviour's, why had he never expressed this opinion publicly and loudly to those needing to hear it – Fingleton, for one? Why had he chosen to adopt the posture of subservient humility in the workplace? The possibility that he was a moral coward troubled him. He knew the stock answer to those questions, of course. He'd be perceived as a 'blocker', a feather-headed pedagogue who threw himself unthinkingly before every new school initiative or educational bandwagon.

He'd sat on the fence for twenty-five years, observing and despairing. Why? He didn't want to jeopardise his role as a breadwinner. He put the security of his family and his pension before all else. He also felt that too obvious a determination to seek promotion was undignified behaviour in one claiming to be a public servant. But the burden of professional passivity was becoming too much for him to bear. He wondered if he were justified in having nurtured a special grievance against Ms Toner. Would he feel any different if he were dealing with a male? He couldn't be sure. Surely, he should allow her to be just as hell bent on promotion as any ambitious man desperately seeking a headship.

He wondered if there were any correlation between an abnormally high level of professional competitiveness and excessive sex drive. That might explain the scene he'd witnessed in the PE changing room. Another consideration was that emotional insecurity could be at the root of one's determination to be recognised as a management top dog.

Perhaps Toner was not pursuing a personal vendetta against him. He decided that, from now on, he shouldn't allow himself to be surprised or upset by her criticism of his educational practice. She was displaying behaviour that one must expect of such an ambitious workplace type, male or female. He concluded that he must develop a harder professional shell when dealing with managers generally. Toner would, of course, be included in that group.

He did up the top button of his shirt and tightened his tie in preparation for registering his form group.

******

He looked absently out of the window at the tall trees lining the far side of the school field.

"You not feeling too well, sir?" inquired Gibson, a note of genuine concern in his voice. He'd noticed his form tutor swaying slightly as he stood before the whiteboard.

"As it happens, Jermaine, I do suddenly feel a little light-headed."

He was finding it difficult distinguishing the features of individual students. As he tried to focus his gaze on the class, he experienced the sensation of looking down a tunnel. His peripheral vision had become a hazy blur, interrupted by occasional pulses of light. Looking at his laptop, he was unable to make out students' names on the register page. He sat down and closed his eyes.

His students were silent, awaiting an update.

"I just need to keep my eyes closed for a moment, everyone. The room seems to be looping the loop for me. The feeling is similar to the seasickness I got once going on a rough Channel ferry crossing."

"You've not been putting whisky on your cornflakes, have you, sir?" Bellchambers asked.

"Afraid not. This is something new to me."

Closing his eyes had the effect of increasing the nausea. He was due to be teaching after registration. His left eye began to throb. He could do nothing in this state. Anxiety turned to panic: there was no time or space for illness in his job. His temperament was not equipped to cope with being unwell. The last time he'd felt as sick as this was when he'd been on a funfair ride with Ella. He'd travelled all the way to Alton Towers on a family day out, only to throw up on The Twister, the very first ride he'd dared tackle with his young daughter. There were far too many things to get done in a school day, and he hated the thought that colleagues would be inconvenienced by him for whatever reason. But, as the chair on which he was sitting seemed to be lurching this way and that, he knew he had no choice but to get on the phone to the school office. He rose from his seat and made his shaky way to the English office. The boys looked on in silence, unsure as to whether or not they were being conned. Gill, the school secretary picked up his call at the front desk.

"Good morning!" she sang cheerily. "St Saviour's School here. Can I help you?"

"Hello, Gill. It's me, Biggsy. I'm in the English office. Sorry about this, but I'm suddenly feeling very unwell. Can you get on to whoever's organising lesson cover today to find someone to teach my first lesson? I'm hoping I'll recover soon and be able to carry on later."

"Ooh! Not like you to be ill. Hope it's nothing serious. I'll get on to it straight away."

******

He'd managed to get a doctor's appointment after suffering for two days and nights at home. Myra had been sympathy personified, doing her best to make him comfortable. Even though he'd tried to remain motionless whenever possible, he'd continued to experience reeling drunkenness whilst awake and had slept only in bouts. He'd been prepared for a longer wait to see his GP but had been squeezed in thanks to another patient's cancellation. Dr Panting was the longest-serving doctor at the health centre. Biggsy and Myra got on so well with him that they were on first name terms.

He heard a beep and looked up at the illuminated screen. His name appeared, with the instruction to go to Room 8. He rose unsteadily and did his best to avoid lurching along in an ungainly manner. The door was slightly ajar. He knocked lightly twice.

"Morning, Paul."

"Come in. Come in."

He was just about to close the door behind him, when one of the receptionists appeared. She carried a tray, in the centre of which was a cup of tea. The classic teacup and saucer pattern of red, yellow and pink roses seemed familiar. He looked enviously at the tray and its contents and twitched the corners of his mouth at the receptionist, as she apologised for interrupting.

"I am sorry, but I thought I'd bring this along between appointment slots," she said, nodding politely in his direction. "The doctor likes his mid-morning tea to keep him going."

"No problem, Sheila. Thank you so much," replied Panting.

Turning smartly on her heel, she gave the patient a full-lipstick smile and hurried off. Biggsy wondered what it must be like to be waited on at work so dutifully.

Panting's tall trim physique spoke of many years dedicated to gym exercise. A framed photograph above his desk showed him smiling broadly in the company of a group of dark-blue vested rowers. The large silver cup they were holding aloft indicated success in a highly prestigious competition. The GP hadn't changed much over the years. The patient considered his own physical transformation since he'd started teaching. He thought himself almost unrecognisable from his university days. Beside the accumulation of two stones of superfluous fat, he saw himself looking facially like a puffy version of Robert De Niro. He looked around him at the impressive working environment: silent, warm and tastefully decorated. The contrast between this workplace and his own couldn't have been more striking. No thick dust on the shelves and there were even working window blinds.

"Sorry about that. Now what can I do for our illustrious English teacher?" beamed Panting.

Biggsy sat down on the upholstered chair beside the desk, sighing as he struggled out of his jacket.

The regulation checks on chest, mouth, ears and blood pressure completed, it didn't take the doctor long to reach his diagnosis.

"You're suffering from a condition called labyrinthitis. It's a problem in your inner ear that interferes with your sense of balance. It may have been caused by an infection, but it can be brought on by acute stress. I'm not convinced of any infection at this stage. Have you been experiencing undue anxiety of any sort recently?"

"How can I put it, Paul? I'm being run ragged, as usual, along with half a million others in my profession. Nothing new there."

"Just as I thought. Just as I thought. I suppose I should have guessed as much."

"Are you telling me that teaching has made me drunk? If so, will it be permanent?"

"Strange as it may seem, it could be the case that you feel inebriated. Apart from the acute vertigo you're experiencing, you aren't displaying any other symptoms. You've no hearing loss and haven't been vomiting. You're lucky."

"I always thought I was, but today I can honestly say I don't feel lucky. I still haven't found my sea legs. Is there some medication that will stop this constant dizziness? Is it something that could come back in the future?"

"You'll quickly recover from this bout and be back to your old self, but it may return. If, as I believe, your labyrinthitis is brought on by stress, you may be prone to future attacks. I'll prescribe a course of prochlorperazine and you should start feeling fine by tomorrow. The tablets take effect quickly. I can sign you off for a few days to recover if you'd like."

"Thanks, but no. I need to be back at work. How soon can I return?"

"If you feel well enough after a good night's sleep, there's no reason why you shouldn't go back tomorrow. But, if you do, don't spend long hours in front of a computer screen. And by the way, have your eyes checked as soon as possible. Your condition may have been exacerbated by poor vision."

"How strangely ironic! Dodgy waterworks, feeling drunk and eyesight loss! I'm like a wino, despite not having had the pleasure of a single drop of the hard stuff."

"You're right. It does seem cruel."

"Never mind. By the way, I usually spend thirty hours or more a week in front of a computer screen, so I'll have a problem there."

About to take his leave, he thought of his other ailment requiring attention.

"Almost forgot, Paul. Can I request a PSA check? As I said, problems are developing with the waterworks in my old age. Peeing takes an age these days."

"Oh dear. It comes to us all. Roll up your sleeve and I'll take a few drops of your blood."

Returning home on foot, he saw a mother with a young son of pre-school age walking toward him. She was warmly wrapped in a green parka coat, hurrying along head down. The skinny-legged boy stumbled along silently and obediently at her side. Suddenly, he disengaged himself from his mother's grip and jumped into the air, one fist directed heavenward in a victory gesture.

That's the spirit, thought Biggsy.

******

"Good to see you back, sir," said Gibson. "We missed you."

"Where ya bin, sir?" Colley demanded, feigning aggression.

"Sorry, guys, but I've had a bad time of it these last few days. I seized up unexpectedly."

"We've had to put up with a right weirdo registering us while you were off," added Bellchambers, his top lip curling. "Some supply guy with turn-ups on his trousers and huge bifocals came in yesterday. He was late and complained he couldn't find our form room. He said it was bedlam in the corridors because the kids here are so noisy. Then he started spouting off about something called chaos theory. He must have been trying to get us off to sleep."

"Illuminating stuff. I think that's the longest and most succinct speech you've ever delivered."

Bellchambers smiled, as he looked around at his form mates to acknowledge the gentle applause.

"If you found the theory boring, you might read a short story by Ray Bradbury called 'A Sound of Thunder' – science fiction. It would make the concept clearer to you. I can recommend it."

"What's it about?"

"Time travellers who go back to the prehistoric period to shoot some big game. In this case, they're after a dinosaur."

"Oh yeah," Bellchambers replied, showing some interest. "Sounds like something out of 'Jurassic Park'."

"Now we're on to cloning. Amazing how one strand of thinking makes connections with so many others. There's so much order to be discovered from what may be perceived as chaos in the world. Anyway, yes, I'm with you all again. So, back to humdrum realities. Have you all finalised your university applications and got them ready to send off?"

He allowed a few seconds for general groaning.

"Don't hesitate to corner me if you need some last-minute assistance. Whatever problems you may think you have with the forms, I can sort you out."

He glanced discreetly in the direction of Gibson, looking for any signs of antagonism regarding the topic of higher education. His expression was impassive.

"It's not the forms we're worried about, it's the debt that scares us," complained Padfield. "Would you go to university, sir, if you knew you'd end up with a bill of at least thirty grand in three years' time?"

He scanned the faces before him. Most of the expressions reflected resignation to a future of huge debt, tempering any sense of excitement.

"You guys have it much tougher than I did when I was your age, I admit," he conceded. "My own daughter's in the same boat as you."

"Yeah, but you've got brains and a well-paid job and can help her," complained Padfield. "My dad's just been made redundant. And how do I know I'll be able to get a job even if I do get a degree?"

"I'm not here to force any of you to apply. I feel a duty to put a few pointers to you that may focus your thinking. First, studying is a wonderful way to spend one's time. I'm aware that you're put under a lot of pressure to think of acquiring a degree as a means to an end – a good job. But studying is genuinely rewarding and fulfilling. Second, the hard truth is that many careers and occupations you may be thinking of following in the working world require degree qualification nowadays."

He hesitated before making his final point, one that he wished he could overlook. He had the undivided attention of every member of the form. They trusted him. He had to be honest with them.

"The third point's a pretty brutal truth. A poor pass at degree level may not count for a great deal in the jobs market. A good degree will certainly enhance your chances of gainful employment. It must be said that, in the current economic climate, where there are countless applicants for each job advertised, you need a good degree to put yourselves in the running for serious consideration. I clearly remember the day I went to my university on results day, when results were posted on a noticeboard. A girl looking at the board alongside me saw her low pass grade and said aloud to nobody in particular, 'I've just realised I've wasted three years of my life.' I'll never forget that moment."

"Ouch!" exclaimed Bellchambers, with no hint of humour.

The buzzer sounded. Nobody moved for a few seconds as every student took in the import of what had been said.

"What grade did you get then, sir?" asked Colley.

"A first."

"What the hell are you doing here with a first, sir?"

"You may well ask. Seriously though, believe me when I say I'm here to be your teacher. On that bombshell, it's time you headed off for lessons."

Chairs scraped as boys got to their feet and threw rucksacks across their backs. Again, he wondered why no one ever bothered to lift his chair to prevent the din. Girls usually did, he felt sure. A thought occurred as he saw Gibson leaving the room. He called him back.

"Can I have a quick word, Jermaine? Are you having any doubts about applying? I can imagine that UCAS may not be the main priority for you after what you've been through recently."

Gibson's eyes met his and held them.

"I'm applying, sir. I know that I've got to get away, and it can't be far enough."

Biggsy was pleased by the student's renewed sense of commitment but concerned at the change in him. The form group was aware of the alteration as much as he was. He was withdrawing into himself. The ready supply of witty contributions to casual tutor-group chat had dried up. No longer the assured and carefree innocent, he was already one of life's long-term casualties.

"I'm relieved to hear you're set on going to university again, but sad when I think of the reason for your change of heart, Jermaine. Are your parents happy about you wanting to get away from London to study?"

As he spoke, he was wondering if it were 'sad' that he also wanted to get away from London.

"Mum and Dad are all for it. They think a change of scene will do me good."

So Mr and Mrs Gibson were pleased. If his daughter had suffered as Jermaine had done, he'd also be happy if she were moving out of the capital.

"Where will you apply?"

"My first choice is York – an English degree obviously."

"Good for you, Jermaine. Don't forget I'm available if you need any further help or advice."

Gibson flashed a smile, turned, and left his tutor to his thoughts.

The noise from children in the corridor outside his room didn't cause his heart to race as was normally the case immediately after morning registration. The reason was that he had a free period. He could use the welcome non-contact time to make inroads into the physical admin pile that had built up on his desk and the virtual pile on his laptop.

Before immersing himself in the daily detritus, he indulged in a few moments of reflection. Should he follow Gibson's lead and take himself and his family off to pastures new? Would Myra and Ella eventually prove to be amenable? Surely, they couldn't begrudge him looking for an easier life at his age. He'd served his time in the big city and deserved a less challenging educational environment. But the idea of 'copping out' beset him. Perhaps he'd reached a point in his life when he'd simply prefer to turn his back on all work-related pressures. Further, the possibility occurred to him that most people eventually reach a point in life when avoidance of pressures of any kind becomes habitual. Going gently into that good night does not become an option but a compulsion for many.

He was straightening a few chairs behind tables when Andy walked into the room.

"Won't keep you a minute. I was talking to Angela this morning and there's a spot of bother."

Andy screwed up his face as if in apology for being the harbinger of grim news.

"She's being targeted through social networking by some of our boys who've obviously got a crush on her. Quite a lot of online activity, apparently. Toner got to hear about it and is now involved, if you know what I mean."

"Please, no! How bad is it?"

"She says it's nothing sexually explicit but, as she told me this morning, she does find some of the comments about her embarrassing. At worst, boys' compliments move on from saying how good a teacher she is to some mention of what she wears to school."

"Not being a subscriber to any online sites myself, I assumed most teachers gave them a wide berth, Andy."

"Apparently, some of the comments she's received recently are, she admitted, unwelcome."

Angela's petite figure and outgoing personality would be bound to appeal to some of the more precocious elements at St Saviour's. She dressed fashionably and occasionally wore clothing to school that he would have advised against. He wondered if he should have spoken to her about dress code beforehand.

"She doesn't need this. How do you know that Toner's involved?"

"She got wind of what was going on and went to see her. Gave her a couple of options to think about. Suggested she consider her dress sense more carefully and think about terminating her account. Sorry, gotta rush. Angela will tell you everything when you see her."

Having destroyed Biggsy's attempts at inner peace, he hurried off.

"Don't believe this. I just don't believe it," he said aloud to the four walls.

******

"Do you believe in the devil an' demons and witches, sir?"

It was Miller's 'The Crucible' with his year ten class, and Errol Wickens wanted an answer.

Biggsy sighed. This was going to take at least ten minutes out of the lesson. But, when someone asks an interesting question, a teacher is obliged to deal with it, whatever the time constraints imposed by the National Curriculum. A difficult one to deal with, though not as contentious as the inquiry about seventy-two virgins with which he'd once had to contend.

"That is such a good question, Errol, and I don't think many in this class would have had the courage to ask it."

"No messin', sir!" exclaimed Errol, smiling broadly at the compliment.

"The answer may seem obvious to some, but not to me. If I were to say I don't believe in the devil, I could also be accused of denying that God exists. I do believe in God. Therefore, it would seem, I must believe in the devil. Good and evil are two sides of the same coin. Discussion of one, in my opinion, must include discussion of the other."

He studied the intent faces before him. Even if he'd already lost some of them with his opening statements, nobody was interrupting him. Moments like this were what made teaching such a special job.

"So that you're in no doubt about my religious beliefs, Errol, I need to add further explanation."

He realised the problematical nature of any considerations of organised religion when addressing a multi-ethnic audience. A monotheistic religion wasn't to everyone's liking. Some already had no interest in religion whatsoever. No matter – Errol had asked him about his own beliefs.

"Terminology is an issue here. We often use words without always being certain of their meaning, for ourselves and for others. I choose to use the word 'God' to describe what I see as a positive force in the universe – positive energy, say. This is more acceptable to me than imagining a man with a beard living in the clouds. I think it's possible to call upon or access this force to do good in one's life. I also think that there are negative forces in the universe that I could just as easily use to do things that are morally wrong. This force I could call the devil. But I'm not imagining a man with a pitchfork who waits for wicked souls in burning hell."

The admission that his interpretation of the Christian faith, into which he had been baptised, was unorthodox made him apprehensive. His perception of 'God' would be, to young minds, an unconventional one. He couldn't pretend otherwise with children who were hanging on his every word. However, whilst on the subject, he felt he should issue a warning.

"I think that many people gain comfort and consolation from believing in God or their gods. Ideally, this is how religion should work. However, I also believe that there are others who claim to be devoutly religious who can't cope with religion. They use their faith as a weapon against people of other faiths or even of their own. For these, their faith becomes a cancer that festers inside them. They consider themselves believers, but their belief is harmful to themselves and others around them. We get this with every religious group, which may explain why many nowadays choose to turn their backs on organised religion. The moment a person becomes convinced that theirs is the only true religion, they become potentially dangerous. We call such people religious bigots."

"Blimey, sir. I thought I'd get a simpler answer than that," laughed Errol.

Others joined in the laughter. Many sat with blank uncomprehending faces.

"Almost finished, Errol. Returning to the question, you asked about demons and witches, I think we bump into them regularly throughout our lives. They are people who have absolutely no consideration for anyone but themselves. They're not all ugly and misshapen, as they are depicted in books on the supernatural. They don't have horns or fly around on broomsticks. Many of them wear fashionable suits and drive expensive cars."

Errol leaned back in his chair and looked expansively around him. Just as Biggsy was about to continue with the lesson, the inquisitive student threw in another beauty.

"Hang on a minute, sir. So why do all the young girls in this play go on and on about the devil and demons and such? Don't see any boys taken in by all this."

This was going to take another half an hour.

******

The buzzer for morning break sounded. There would be enough time to have a word with Angela in her classroom. Her door was open. He tapped on it and walked in. His disarming smile, he hoped, would put her at ease before he got down to the business at hand.

"Hello, Biggsy," she welcomed, brightening at his appearance.

"Morning, Angela. Thought I'd catch up with you as soon as I could after hearing from Andy about the unwanted online attention you're getting."

Her face dropped. She shook her head slowly.

"Oh, you've heard about it. I'm a bit confused about it all to be honest. The first contacts just praised me for my teaching, then there were a few drawing attention to my appearance."

She closed her eyes, pursed her lips and threw her head back.

"Ms Toner came to see me at the end of school yesterday, saying she'd overheard some year ten boys talking about me. She mentioned that I'd become of interest to them online. I was stunned. I'd never imagined this sort of thing happening to me."

"It happens, I'm afraid, Angela. The students concerned will have no idea of the upset they're causing. In the unsophisticated minds of teenage boys, they may think they're being complimentary. What was Toner's take on the matter?"

"Well, although she didn't say so directly, I had the feeling she thought I'd unwittingly invited the attention from the way I dress and by being over-friendly with the children."

"Right. Friendliness not being in her professional repertoire, I can imagine how alien that quality must seem to her."

"I can't really change my teaching style."

"No, and there's no reason why you should. She may be more inclined to the view that your appearance is attracting the interest. You are closer to their age group than you are to mine, after all."

He found himself in some agreement with Toner. Great care was necessary here.

"She may just be thinking that the smart casual dress code would be preferable to the more casual style at school. Did she say as much?"

The realisation that he was advising an attractive woman on the way she dressed made him blush. He didn't even interfere when Myra tried to check their daughter's more extreme fashion accessories. On one occasion, when Ella was off on a girly night out, he'd wondered if she were intending wearing something more substantial than what looked like a large handkerchief masquerading as a skirt. But he'd not said a word. Myra, on the other hand, had had plenty of advice to offer.

"Well, she did say I should give more thought to the way I present myself at school. I felt as though she were patronising me, but I suppose it's a fair point, given the situation that's developed. I've resigned myself to going off to the high street shops at the weekend to buy something more formal in the clothing line. What do you think will happen to the boys involved?"

Relieved at hearing that Angela would voluntarily be making additions to her wardrobe, he tried to sound as relaxed as possible, as though he were playing down the significance of the issue.

"This matter may go to the year head, Dave Palmer. He'll speak to the lads concerned – may even get the parents involved, but I doubt it. There could be some form of disciplinary action, probably not. He'll have a word with you to let you know what'll happen."

"It seems so stupid that a few boys could face punishment for unacceptable behaviour that they may never have intended," she bemoaned.

She'd unknowingly become a target for teenage boys. Biggsy made the connection between Angela and Jermaine Gibson.

"Unfortunately, it's all too common nowadays with kids hooked on social networking. Before they know it, they get themselves into all kinds of trouble. Now that this has happened, be wary of signs of something irregular going on in the future."

"I'm not sure that I would know if anything 'irregular' were going on. Do you mean this is something that could keep happening throughout my career? Why me?"

"It's unlikely to be repeated. You'll put this down to experience and make the necessary adjustments."

"I suppose it will help to start with some weekend shopping."

He was feeling more uncomfortable. This was a situation calling for him to show leadership and offer cast-iron advice. But he couldn't bring himself to express open agreement with the deputy head and state categorically the importance of adopting a more conservative dress sense. The complexities of the sort of conversation that would result was something in which he did not want to get involved. He was unsure whether he was being sensible or a coward. Perhaps brave Dave would enlarge on the subject.

"Unfortunately, Angela, this situation may simply be one of the professional drawbacks of being an attractive person. Anyway, don't dwell on the matter because it will get sorted."

But he wasn't so sure. Troubled by the popularity of social networking, he feared that young female teachers in secondary schools would continue to face similar problems from adolescent admirers.

Chapter 13

He became aware of a noisy disturbance in the corridor. On investigating, he discovered Archie Matthews, the pastoral deputy head, having difficulties with a loudly argumentative year ten boy. An audience of twenty others was loitering to see what would happen. Matthews, a tall wisp of a man in his mid-fifties, was trying to propel the burly student in the direction of the withdrawal room, with little success.

"I ain't done nuffin'!" cried the offended student at the top of his voice. "Why are you pickin' on me?"

"Now come along, Roberts. You know you were insolent to Miss Greaves. You used totally unacceptable language in her classroom."

"She's always pickin' on me. She's never liked me. I'm goin' 'ome to get me dad."

He shook Matthews off with such force that the deputy head lost his balance and ended up on all fours. A loud cheer arose from the onlookers. Biggsy ran to Matthews' aid. He picked up the senior teacher's glasses that had fallen to the floor and helped him to his feet. At the same time, he turned on the pupils who were hanging around to watch the fun.

"Get off to your lessons, every single one of you!" he barked, surprising himself at the loudness of his voice. "If any one of you is within ten yards of me within the next five seconds, he'll be back at school for a three-hour Saturday morning detention."

The students made off, some whooping excitedly to prolong their fun.

"And be quiet, the lot of you!" he bawled after them.

Matthews brushed himself down and straightened his tie. He shook his head and faced his rescuer.

"Thanks for your assistance. I'm most grateful. I really can't imagine doing this for much longer. Some of our pupils are becoming totally unmanageable."

The deputy head's words were drowned out by Alan Baker, a maths teacher who taught in a classroom close by. He began bellowing at the line of boys waiting outside his room.

"You can stop here all morning," continued Baker, "if you continue to talk out of turn. When I say 'quiet', I mean quiet. It's the same every lesson with you lot."

Archie rolled his eyes and strode away from the scene of his recent embarrassment. Biggsy wondered why some teachers insisted on tormenting themselves and their students with the pointless pre-lesson drill in which Baker was engaged. Humiliating children only increased the risk of making a minority of them despise you, school and education in general. Allowing them to walk into a classroom as they arrived made life so much simpler. The idea of waiting until every pupil had arrived, and lining them up outside the classroom, was anathema to him. He had no truck with any school procedures that had the taint of military protocols. Tall and imposing, with hands on hips, Baker rocked back on his heels.

Biggsy looked away from the din in disgust. For some reason, his attention was attracted by a poster recently mounted outside his room. Looking along the corridor, he saw several of them spaced at regular intervals. The one he was studying read, 'What a great day to learn something new!' Above the text was the face of a young boy who looked as blissfully ecstatic as someone about to reach nirvana. Somebody had already defaced the poster with a doodle in black felt tip pen. A syringe had been drawn, directed into the jugular of the enraptured boy.

Wasn't me, he thought, tearing the poster off the wall.

Mathematics wasn't one of his favourite curricular areas. Lionel Jackson, the department head, rarely showed himself in a favourable light to the rest of the staff, particularly on examination results day. Fiercely competitive where GCSE and A-level grades were concerned, he couldn't resist the temptation to crow if his department came out on top, which it had narrowly done the previous summer. Although he had no problem with boys achieving academic success, Biggsy did balk at teachers using children to bolster their own reputations. Jackson's mathematics' colleagues, or underlings, were under no illusion that results were the only worthwhile measure of a teacher's success. Consequently, whether they liked it or not, they were roped in to supervise catch-up sessions at lunchtime, revision programmes at weekends, and constant reinforcement of

Jackson's infamous key points programme. And Baker was one who thrived on the lot.

Biggsy was vehemently opposed to such anti-educational strategies. When teaching became nothing more than a narrow diet of strict training regimes, the product would be teenage androids, resentful ones at that. Students should never be given an excuse not to think for themselves. Jackson and his like might boost the reputation of the school, but they were playing a key role in limiting the cognitive development of a generation of children. Such teachers seemed oblivious to the damage they were inflicting on young minds.

Lost in his thoughts, he jumped visibly as Baker roared once again.

"I can wait here all day!"

One of the boys in the line winked at Biggsy.

"Wipe those silly grins off your faces if you know what's good for you," sneered Baker. "Don't you want to move into the classroom to get on with your learning, for heaven's sake!"

Despite the proximity of their teaching rooms, the two teachers had little to do with each other. Baker's authoritarian approach, little short of bullying, made any kind of social intercourse impossible. Wondering just how long the lining-up discipline was going to last, Biggsy decided that he should return to the safety of his own classroom.

Top Tip No. 6: Antagonise children unnecessarily at your peril.

******

Ambling to the rear of the school hall, he took stock of the sight before him: eighty teenagers' backs. Each boy was bent low over an examination paper, some so low they could have been mistaken for sleeping. The rule of not looking around at other candidates was being closely observed by everyone as the exam was only half an hour in. He strolled back to the front of the hall, following a course this time between two rows of desks at the far side. As he passed Kim Buttrell, standing still and intent next to one of the two emergency exit doors, he flashed his boring-or-what! expression. She rolled her eyes, as keen to be elsewhere as he was. Policing pupils wasn't enjoyable. As assessment procedures abounded in schools, teachers spent more and more of their time as custodians of the law. He wondered if nightsticks would soon become standard issue for teachers to go with their whistles.

This was Paper 1 of the GCSE Business Studies mock. He resented the three weeks in December that were taken up with 'mocks' when he could be teaching students. Assessment tools had become the bane of his teaching life. Not only that, valuable lesson time was also lost to coaching pupils for tests. He knew what Socrates would have made of the situation:

"They are idle also who might be better employed."

He wasn't given to remembering scores of pithy quotations, but this snippet of wisdom he'd never forgotten. It was the same with poetry. His memory wasn't equipped to store whole poems, as some could, but memorable lines or phrases remained fixed. At times when he was low in spirits and a victim of self-doubt, he would recall lines of T.S.Eliot:

I should have been a pair of ragged claws

Scuttling across the floors of silent seas.

His poetic meanderings were interrupted, as he strolled once more to the rear of the hall. One student was slumped back in his seat, staring at the ceiling. Biggsy recognised Denny Lowe, not a student he taught, as one whose reputation for intractability was well known by all, and feared by some. Obstreperous but astute – a description that could apply to a sizeable minority of the boys he taught. Denny was of that ilk. His physique alone could be intimidating to the inexperienced teacher.

Well over six feet tall, he was far too big for the cramped desk at which he had to spend two hours scribbling away. His feet rested against the back legs of the chair in front of him. A little pressure would be all that was needed to shove the unwitting examinee forward. There was still an age to go before the instruction to put pens down. Biggsy inclined his body toward Lowe.

"Are you taking a breather, Denny?" he whispered.

"Finished, sir. Can't write any more."

The student continued to eye the ceiling speculatively. His deadpan tone conveyed two messages: he was bored, and nothing was going to induce him to write further. This was not going to be the easiest of situations to deal with. No candidates were allowed to leave the hall before the end of the exam. He and Kim had another thirty minutes before the arrival of two more members of staff to continue the invigilation. Sitting still and quietly for a further hour and a half doing nothing would be impossible for this character.

"Why don't you give yourself a few minutes to look over the paper again? You may find you can continue then."

"I won't, sir," replied the boy, running a hand through his straggly blond hair and throwing his head back.

"Why's that?"

"I didn't revise."

"Why not?"

"Didn't want to do Business Studies, sir. I wanted to do Economics, but they wouldn't let me."

This boy felt he'd been hard done by and wouldn't be making life easy for anyone. The situation was exceptional and required an executive decision.

"If you feel that strongly, I'll do you a deal. Remain silent, don't disturb anyone and try to write a bit more for the next thirty minutes, then I'll release you from the next hour. I'll take you with me when I finish my stint here in thirty minutes. You can come to my classroom, which will be empty, and do some revision for your English mock. What do you say?"

His back was aching from leaning forward too long. He winced and placed one hand on the desk to prop himself. Lowe offered a sympathetic grin.

"All right, sir. I'll give it a go."

"Good man. So, don't attract any attention to yourself for the next thirty minutes and I'll see you when this invigilation finishes."

Lowe nodded. Biggsy walked to the side of the hall, keeping him in view. He was relieved to see him pick up and peruse the question paper. Result. Now all he had to do was get away with it. If Toner got to hear of him extricating a student prematurely from an exam, he'd be quizzed. He believed he'd found the best way to do the deed with as little ceremony as possible.

******

A sigh of relief escaped him as he finished marking the homework of his A-Level English Literature class. He looked at his watch. Five thirty-five. An extra two hours of intense concentration at the end of a full teaching day, but at least he could go home now. He stretched his arms wide then loosened his shoulders. The school's heating system had gone off half an hour earlier. December was taking a grip. His chair scraped on the parquet floor, as he stood and stretched. He frowned at himself for being unable to stand up without making a noise. Why should he expect better from his pupils?

"Oh, sorry, sir. I didn't know anyone was still here."

The cleaner hovered in the doorway, uncertainty showing in her young face. Dowdy in jeans and a grey hoody, she clutched a bulging bin liner in one hand and a broom and dustpan in the other. Working unsociable and lonely hours, school cleaners had his sympathy. He hadn't seen this one before. He wondered if she had small children she'd rather be taking care of at home. She sighed, as she pushed a wave of mousy hair from her eyes.

"Come in. I'm just off," he said.

She busied herself with emptying the waste bin into her black bag and then started placing the pupils' chairs on the tables. Realising he'd again forgotten to ask his final class of the day to do this, he began to help her. Raised eyebrows indicated her thanks. She had no time to waste on idle chit-chat. He wondered if she would feel patronised by any effort on his part to engage her in conversation, so he remained silent. In how many more classrooms would she be required to perform this extra chore before she could sweep the floor? Extra time would surely be added to her shift. She was being performance-managed just as he was. The time allowed her per classroom would probably be just enough to empty bins, wipe over tabletops and sweep up. There'd be none for getting rid of the dust that had accumulated on shelves and window ledges.

He placed the pile of marked essays in his attaché, walked to the back of his room and locked the office door. He resisted the temptation to thank the cleaner for performing her thankless task, leaving her to complete her work with a murmured, "G'night." He suddenly felt a pang of guilt, as he recollected a detail from the earliest days of his teaching career. It was the nickname he and the rest of the staff had used when referring to one elderly woman who'd provided staff with their morning break refreshment. She really hadn't deserved to be called Tea Bag.

The musty-smelling corridor welcomed him. He turned at the sound of a door opening and shutting at one end, just in time to see a figure disappearing toward the school's back exit. Curiosity got the better of him and he slipped into a darkened classroom to investigate. Through the window, he saw Aaron Aimes. Clutching a large kit bag, he made his way across the school field to a car parked in the road at the rear school gate. The passenger door of Ms Toner's car was flung open. Aaron threw his bag in the back, climbed in, and the car began accelerating away before he'd even shut the door.

******

His favourite time of the week was Saturday morning. It was a time of refuge, a full forty-eight hours before, once again, buttoning up his collar, tightening his tie and exposing himself to the administrative jungle of new education. He looked at his drawn face in the bathroom mirror. He tried taking Michael Stipe's advice – 'Why Not Smile?' The character grimacing back at him was surely taking the piss.

He was shaving half an hour earlier than usual this Saturday morning. Myra had reminded him that their trusty odd-job man would be arriving at eight thirty sharp to start work on concealing the cracked and dusty patio at the back of the house with a stretch of decking. She had decided that home improvements were necessary. He had aesthetic reservations about decking as a garden feature, and was also concerned by horror stories he'd heard about the possibility of rats infesting the spaces created beneath one's feet. He imagined himself relaxing on the decking with coffee and ginger nuts, and a family of rats immediately beneath him waiting with outstretched paws for crumbs to drop through the gaps in the planks.

The doorbell rang as he was pulling on his jeans.

"Can you get that, love? It'll be Kevin," instructed Myra from the shower cubicle.

Still in his pyjamas and barefoot, he hurried downstairs. He remembered that his house keys were still in his jacket on the hallway coat stand. Rummaging in the pockets, he called aloud in the direction of the front door.

"Sorry, Kevin. Haven't unlocked yet. Just looking for the door keys."

Fragments of grit on the carpet embedded themselves in his feet. The keys now in his hand, he fumbled with the Yale and mortise locks. When he eventually swung the door open, Kevin Donovan's huge frame greeted him.

"Morning, Biggsy, old pal. How ya doin'?"

One of Myra's friends had put her on to Kevin. He was a godsend. She no longer needed to ask her husband to do jobs around the house for which he had little time. Kevin could turn his hand to any home improvement work, from plumbing to plastering. Biggsy experienced an uncomfortable sense of guilt whenever her handyman was on the premises, doing work he could do himself.

"Not so bad, Kevin. You know. Thanks for helping us out at the weekend like this. Can I get you a tea or coffee?"

"Don't touch the stuff, mate. I'll have a soft drink later if that's OK."

"Sorry, forgot about that. But if you don't drink tea or coffee, how do you manage to start your day?"

A look of utter resignation spread across Kevin's full-bearded face.

"Ah, sometimes I wonder that meself," he replied softly, looking heavenward.

Biggsy laughed aloud at the Irishman's gentle humour. Kevin was a one-off, a philosopher and a master craftsman.

"How's the schoolteacherin' goin'? I wouldn't be doin' your job for a king's ransom."

"I don't think we need to pursue that line of conversation, Kevin. Let's just say, it's not getting any easier."

"Ah, like that is it? Well, I'll be headin' out back if that's OK with you. Thankfully, it's not rainin', so I should be able to make good progress. I'll use the alley at the end of your garden for access to me truck, so I won't be treadin' muddy boots through the house."

"Thanks, Kevin. If there's anything you need, don't hesitate to ask."

There goes a man who seems to be happy in his work, he thought. *Oh, to be one's own boss.*

"Morning, Dad. You're up with the lark," Ella said as she appeared, drawing her dressing gown tightly around her. "Cold, isn't it?"

"You're always cold. The heating's kicking in all right. Got anything on for the day?"

"Not really. Might be on for a girly night with friends in Kingston. I've come to a big decision, though."

"Oh, and I haven't even given you my Christmas present list yet."

"No, something really important. Prepare yourself. I want to be a teacher."

He looked hard at his daughter. Of all the career openings she could have gone for, this was the one he'd advised her against on countless occasions.

"I know you're not keen, but I really want to be a primary school teacher. I did give serious consideration to your suggestion of crocodile wrestling, but I've decided I want to work with children."

She looked at her father, tilting her head to one side.

A sympathetic smile was all he could manage for the moment. Yes, the ideal of thirty hours a week working with children would be a wonderful calling. But there was the additional thirty hours plus each week completing paperwork. He'd told his daughter one needed real physical and emotional stamina to stick with teaching any longer than five years. These requirements had recently become hot news in the media. The demands of the job could not be imagined. But he'd gone over this ground several times with her already. She'd had first-hand experience of the effect teaching had had on him. But it was Saturday morning. He didn't have the energy to warn her off yet again. Hope and good intentions had sustained him in the job for almost three decades. Ella might be of the same mould.

"You're right, love. Working with children is great. If you do eventually take up a teaching career, don't let the rest of the job kill your spirit." He gave her a hug and kissed her on the forehead. "Does your mum know about this?"

"No, I thought I'd get the difficult bit over first. Once I've got through my English degree at uni, I'll get straight on to a PGCE course. There's nothing else I want to do."

He was pleased at her assumption of gaining a degree. She wasn't being arrogant: her diligence deserved academic success. For her, there had never been the distractions of alcohol, drugs and a preoccupation with 'hoody' music. At the other end of the musical spectrum, bland pappy pop had never had any interest for her. They'd once enjoyed an entertaining five minutes deciding on words that should be banned from popular music lyrics. The handwritten list, including all the old chestnuts, such as 'forever', 'always', 'endless', 'heartbreak', 'wherever' and even 'love', was still attached to the fridge door with a magnet. He believed that one of the main benefits of a stable home life was the increased likelihood of producing well-balanced offspring. Padfield was right.

They were interrupted by the appearance of Myra, in dressing gown and slippers and her hair tightly wrapped in a luminous orange towel.

"Aha! Caught you both. And what are you two plotting then?"

******

"You got a minute, mate?"

Dave Wheelhouse needed a chat. He approached Biggsy, as they were exiting the main hall. Mr Fingleton had called a staff meeting to 'discuss' outbreaks of unruly behaviour by a sizeable number of boys from years ten and eleven at a local bus stop after school. Excitement levels amongst the boys were rising as the term drew to a close. Discussion of this matter had involved the headteacher outlining the most pragmatic solution that he could devise to a weary audience unable to muster much resistance. Biggsy was looking forward to returning to the English office as soon as possible to get to grips with loose ends before going home. He'd heard the expressions 'zero tolerance', 'staff patrols' and 'increased vigilance', but had only a hazy recollection of what had been 'agreed'.

He was tired. He tried to smile as he turned to his colleague, but his expression remained passive.

"Can you spare a few minutes in private?" asked Dave.

"If it's that important, of course. Your office?"

"Yes. This is something that may concern you directly in the future."

Catching the urgency in Dave's tone, he began running through any sixth-form matters that might have a direct bearing on him. All that he could come up with was the possibility of a problem with his students' university applications. Other than that, nothing. Dave's troubled demeanour suggested something far more serious.

"The autumn term's a killer, but this one seems to have been the toughest yet," Biggsy said in an attempt to lighten the atmosphere between the two men, as they walked together.

"Humph," replied Dave.

The sixth form office was a mess. All manner of papers and documents littered every surface. Dave heaved a pile of lever arch files off a seat and invited his guest to sit down. He sat at his desk and raised his hands in a gesture of helplessness.

"Look at this lot. I can never seem to make much headway with anything other than the most pressing paperwork. I suppose it's no different for you?"

"It's the same for most of us now, I think."

Making a conscious effort to compose himself, Dave inhaled deeply before continuing.

"I'm looking to retire as you know, but I've agreed to hang on until the end of the spring term. The head talked me into staying on for another term to make sure there were no problems with university applications. Actually, UCAS is one of the reasons I wanted out."

"But that's one of your strengths. It's always been thanks to you that the school has been able to boast excellent higher education take-up."

"Let's just say that I've had a re-think. I've come to the conclusion that many of the students I've encouraged to pursue degree study would have been better suited to an alternative route, anything other than spending three years acquiring a mediocre degree pass that's of questionable value to anyone. I know university has been the accepted destination for kids after sixth form, but I've lost my conviction that it's the only route for as many of our boys as can manage it."

"But what else is there?" Biggsy queried, keenly aware of the limited educational alternatives. "There aren't many apprenticeships around in the current economic climate. More and more young people are having to get used to working for nothing as interns."

"My position is that it's nothing to do with me that the commercial world, society, or whatever, is unable to present viable alternatives for which many of our students would be better suited. I've become ideologically opposed to the idea of higher-education grooming. I also don't want to be part of a system that loads undergraduates with debt. I no longer wish to coax, cajole, persuade or force children to apply for university places."

Dave's eyes widened and his jaw set. He leaned forward, elbows resting on his desk, and lowered his head. A few loose sheets dropped to the floor. This was a Dave Wheelhouse Biggsy had never seen before. He wondered if he were witnessing a case of professional burnout. Dave's words had struck a chord in him, but he struggled to comprehend such a radical change of heart.

Then came the bombshell.

"Just between you and me, I've heard that you're being lined up to take over as head of sixth. I thought you ought to know."

"Me! Where did that come from?"

Completely taken aback, his professional world began to spin off its axis.

"You know management. Something gets leaked to test the water, and what happens after that is anybody's guess. But I'm pretty sure you're in the frame."

"You've got to be joking!"

"Not at all. You're the ideal candidate in so many respects. A word of warning, though, just in case you are approached and give the offer serious consideration. Don't let them talk you into taking this on, even as a temporary filler for a term, as well as doing your head of English job. I wouldn't put that past them. This job is full on, just like everybody else's."

"If you're right, I have to say I'm amazed. I've been thinking lately they'd like to see the back of me."

"Can't imagine why you should be of that opinion. You're an asset to the school. The kids respect you, and the staff too."

Biggsy, like most teachers, was unaccustomed to praise. Wheelhouse's words had thrown him. Personal objectivity regarding matters of professional competence eluded the modest.

"I don't know what to say."

"Nothing to say yet. You don't know anything, do you?"

"I've got to get off home, Dave. Thanks for the tip off, but I need to give my brain time to catch up with what you're telling me. I never could have foreseen anything like this."

"Another word to the wise," Dave said, indicating his desktop with an arm flourish. "Take a really good look at this lot before you leave. They've made head of sixth form a one-man job at St Saviour's, and it just keeps coming at you. I don't know how I've stuck it as long as I have. Forewarned is forearmed."

Biggsy fiddled absent-mindedly with the catch of his attaché before standing up and turning to the door. Grasping the handle, he looked back at Wheelhouse.

"They're going to find it really difficult replacing you, Dave, whoever takes the job on."

******

"Ah, Mr Biggs. May I have a quick word?"

The address took him by surprise. This was a first. Instead of communicating with him exclusively by email, Ms Toner had intercepted him, as he was making his way outside for playground duty. Her deep, brown eyes fixed him. There was no warmth in them. He guessed immediately the reason for her according him such special treatment.

"I carried out a student check at the end of the Business Studies mock and discovered an absentee, Denny Lowe. I found out that you had taken him from the hall a full hour early."

She stopped talking and gave him an enquiring look. He waited for her to ask a question. It struck him that she was adopting the same tone she'd employ with a pupil. He decided to fill the space between them with a few words.

"Denny had stopped writing and insisted that was it with the exam. In my professional opinion, he was going to be wasting his time if he stayed in the hall any longer. I offered him the opportunity to do something worthwhile with his time, revising for his English mock under my supervision."

He found himself excited by the tension between them. He had no intention of being browbeaten or being made to seem irresponsible.

"But that wasn't a decision you had the responsibility to make. No candidate is allowed to leave an examination room early. That's the school rule regarding public and mock examinations."

Toner was on sure ground with her argument. She narrowed her eyes, but he found her accusing gaze ridiculous.

"Denny can be a difficult client and I didn't want him getting into trouble by attracting attention to himself and possibly disturbing those around him. The invigilators following on after Kim and me would have had a difficult time with him for a full hour."

"But that would have been for them to deal with, following examination protocols."

"I took the action I did in order to do a good turn to the rest of the students taking the exam, and to Denny. School protocols are necessary guidelines, but they are not absolutes, in my opinion."

He was enjoying the argument. It involved a clash of two imperatives in which there could be no 'mediation', as Toner might have said. He returned a look as penetrating as that of his accuser. He was prepared to stand his ground for as long as necessary, but the deputy head was losing her patience.

There was also the matter of his absence from playground duty to consider. The deputy head's next statement presented him with the opportunity to make an exit.

"If that's your final word on the matter, I will have to consult with the management team."

He had to admit that he liked that idea. He smiled. The irony that she could, unwittingly, be doing him a great favour warmed him. A formal complaint about him to management could result in any potential offer of the head of sixth form post not being made. End of problem. Now would be a good time to conclude this meeting, but he must retain a polite demeanour. Rudeness would not assist his case in this instance.

"As you think best, Ms Toner. I'd better get out to the playground."

Pursing his lips and nodding slightly, he left her pouting in annoyance. He didn't feel in the least admonished.

Chapter 14

"I've got to stop watching the news."

Myra switched the television off as he tottered into the front room and dropped his case to the floor. Loosening his tie, he sat himself down beside his wife on the sofa and looked at the blank screen.

"Why's that, love? Somebody upset you again?"

"What do you mean 'again'?" she asked, glaring in her husband's direction. "No, I just find it so irritating watching these men performing in the Commons, all pumped up with their own self-importance and testosterone."

"They can't help having testosterone," he reasoned.

"I could bloody well help them, the whole shambolic lot of them."

He had no doubt that she could.

"They should take a lesson from the women MPs. No fuss, no fireworks. Women just make their points reasonably and sensibly. And does any man pay the slightest attention to what they say? Do they…!"

He leaned across to his wife and gave her a kiss on the cheek. "You can't seriously be rubbishing the majority of our nation's political overlords."

"Overlords! Warlords! Whatever they are!" she sniffed. "They're all megalomaniacs."

"Sure you're not being a little extreme here? Some of them are quite reasonable people working for the good of society."

"If you believe that… They really are getting worse than ever, and the women are too timid. Piped music ought to be belted out in the Commons whenever a woman gets up to speak, something rousing to get them geed up. Say, 'The Ride of the Valkyries'. That'd stir women MPs up and make the men sit up and take notice."

He chuckled at Myra's faux-strident views. He enjoyed the nonsense conversations that had become a feature of their married life.

"So, what should be played when men take centre stage?"

"Oh, Barber's 'Adagio for Strings', Chopin's 'Funeral March'. Something of that ilk to take some of the wind out of their sails."

She checked herself, pulled her cardigan tightly around her and stood up. "So how was your day?"

"Oh yes. I'll just come in again." He walked back into the hall, hung up his jacket and returned. "Hello, love." He kissed her again. "All well with you?"

"I've had a funny kind of day, as it happens. You remember the jobs review I told you about at work? Seems that I may be in line for a mini-promotion," she said with a knowing look.

"What's a mini-promotion when it's at home?"

"It's a sideways move to another medical department, but the job would carry a little more responsibility and more money."

He considered the complementary nature of their workplace fortunes.

"Thank goodness someone in the health service has their head screwed on."

"Good, isn't it? The same hours and a smaller department. Got to be a winner. Anything staggering to report from the chalk face today?"

"Not really. Same old," he replied, deciding to give this day over completely to his wife's success. In the silence that followed their sparring, he switched the television back on and flicked through the channels. Wall-to-wall advertisements greeted him.

A dark-brown voice offered reassuring words from their thirty-seven-inch screen: "Did you know that, for only forty-nine ninety-nine a month, you can ensure absolute security for you and your family?"

He frowned at the use of the word 'absolute', another example of the hyperbole running riot in the media world, and pressed the remote's power button.

"Do you think anybody is fool enough to pay any attention to any of these adverts?" he groaned, placing maximum stress on each utterance of the word 'any'.

It occurred to him that he had just contracted a dose of whatever his wife had succumbed to from their television set. The speed with which television could move from entertainment to irritant was staggering.

******

Living so close to school, a fifteen-minute drive at most, he was the first to arrive at the site on the odd occasion, sometimes getting in before the head in his stately silver Jag. There had been times when they had pulled into the empty car park together, as was the case on this particular day.

He tried to delay getting out of the car after a smile and a wave of the hand in Fingleton's direction. Talking directly with the head on any school-related subject, particularly the hot topic of head of sixth form, was the lowest item on his to-do list. However, as he leaned sideways to retrieve exercise books from the back seat, he heard a light tap on his window. Turning, he saw Fingleton smiling and rotating his right hand in a wind-your-window-down gesture. He did as instructed.

"Good morning, Mr Biggs. I hope you and the family are all well."

He nodded and was about to return some pleasantry, but the head continued.

"How opportune that we should arrive together. Would you be able to spare a few minutes in my office before you start your day? I'll try not to detain you too long."

His spirits fell. A discussion about Wheelhouse's replacement or a grilling about the Denny Lowe incident surely awaited him. His gratitude to Dave for broaching the head of sixth form matter was tempered by the fact that he'd not discussed it with Myra the previous evening.

"That's no trouble, Mr Fingleton," he heard himself reply.

"Splendid. I'll leave my office door open for you. Just walk straight in and make yourself comfortable. I'll see you in a moment."

The contrast between the head's coldness toward him when they'd spoken about Dixon and the amiable manner he'd just encountered couldn't have been more marked.

His first stop was the English office, where he deposited his attaché and bagful of exercise books, before making his way in some trepidation to the head's lair. As he entered, he heard a lavatory flush. *This must be important,* he thought, *to bring on a bowel movement.* Fingleton appeared a minute later from a door behind his desk. He finished drying his hands with a paper hand towel which he threw into a bin.

"Well, I'll get straight to the point. There is a matter about which I should very much appreciate your input before I proceed. You may know that Mr Wheelhouse will be retiring this academic year. He's done a sterling job for the school but has decided that a more relaxed lifestyle would suit him."

He beamed at Biggsy, perhaps imagining the prospect of a life free of cares for himself at some time in the not-so-distant future.

"He will be staying on until the end of the spring term. That leaves us with the matter of finding a suitable replacement. One of Mr Wheelhouse's many strengths is his ability to form good working relationships with young adults. I consider that a key consideration, when searching for a replacement, is that the appointee must possess the same quality. The ability to guide young men towards fulfilling their optimum intellectual development is taken as read, of course."

Biggsy could see which way the wind was blowing. He searched for the word that best summed up his state of mind at this precise moment and found it. Bollocks.

******

"So, what did you tell him?"

Myra placed two mugs on the worktop, popped a tea bag from the caddy into each, flicked the kettle switch and turned to face her husband. He yanked his tie off completely, sat on a bar stool and took a deep breath.

"I explained that his offer had come as a surprise, that I'd never envisaged myself in a pastoral role, and that I'd need some time to consider. He was OK about that. I asked if I could give him my decision before the end of term."

"You've got a few weeks then. Is it a promotion?"

"He said that if I took the job, he'd see to it that I'd be on the senior leadership team as an assistant head by the start of the next academic year. He also said that I should keep the business under my hat."

"For a term, then, there'd be no extra money. Still, the offer's encouraging, bearing in mind that you thought the school wanted rid of you three months ago." She gave her husband a mischievous look, as she lifted the boiling kettle and filled the mugs. "You'd be on the management scale."

"He must be desperate. I'm not a manager. And what makes him think I'd be able to do the head of sixth job? He's never seen how I get on with sixth formers."

"Toner has, though. Don't I remember you telling me on the first day back that you saw her watching you through the window of your classroom door?"

"Possible, I suppose."

"You realise what this offer means, don't you?"

"What's that?"

"There was never any school policy to get rid of you. You imagined it. Toner may be a management bully, but she's not part of a conspiracy to force you out of St Saviour's."

Myra gave her husband some time for the words to sink in. He didn't respond.

"I've told you before; you've nothing to worry about as far as your place at the school is concerned."

Anxious to relieve his discomfort, she brought the conversation back to practicalities.

"Will it be Andy doing your job if you take this promotion?"

"Best not to jump the gun here. I'm still trying to get my head around all of this coming out of the blue. But, yes, Andy would seem to be the heir apparent."

"So, there wouldn't be too much disruption to the department."

"Not really, but I'm anxious about Sarah Clifton being passed over for head of sixth form. She's had her eye on it. She could also do the English job. She's ambitious and highly professional. Then again, she might welcome a promotion to second in English."

"Really? Was the head aware of her interest?"

"Not as far as I know. She's been waiting for the post to be advertised. Looks as though Fingleton's angling for the person he wants before putting the job out officially. Still struggling to believe that he wants me."

"That's what sickens me about the way business works these days. Most people who sweat over an application for a post and put themselves through the torture of an interview haven't got a hope in hell of being appointed. Everything's already sewn up."

"Can't disagree with that. Education employment practice is getting just as underhand as anywhere else these days. Wonder if I should tell him I'm not interested?"

"No. You can't do that. Things happen for a reason. Everybody's time comes for advancement – a slice of luck. This happens to be yours, and you haven't even pushed yourself forward."

"But there must be opportunities in other schools, down south, say," he asserted, hoping to keep alive his hopes of a quieter life elsewhere. "Do we really want to prolong our stay in Greater London, Myra?"

She shook her head and fixed her gaze on the floor tiles.

"I've told you already how I stand on that idea of yours. I can't recall expressing any inclination to go off in search of premature old age."

He gagged, as he swallowed a mouthful of tea, then coughed and laughed simultaneously. Myra's sense of humour was as sharp as a tack.

"If I were to accept this promotion, we could be committed to staying here for the next ten years or so."

"Besides being your doting wife, my love, I've a circle of friends to which I'm very much attached. I enjoy my social life at present and would prefer not to have to start again."

"So, you'd be happy with the prospect of ending your days in the smoke?" he questioned. "I thought we might enjoy the freedom of the wide open after three decades of suburban claustrophobia. The thing is, London's becoming a dangerous place to live. The Gibsons will confirm that. There's a part of me that definitely wants out."

"Don't worry. You can come back and visit me as often as you like. I'll still be here."

"Seriously, Myra, can't you see that moving away would be better for all of us? I'm just not happy with the local knifestyle here. Ella won't be needing London when she's off at university."

She frowned and looked directly at her husband.

"There are far too many advantages on our doorstep that outweigh the possible risks occupying your imagination. Friends, hospitals, theatres, cinemas, transport links, to name just a few. There's too much we'd be giving up."

He tried to think of the number of friends he'd miss. He couldn't think of any. He was a family man who'd never had a circle of close friends. Myra was gregarious, many of her friendships having endured since childhood. He was an isolate who occasionally tagged along at social events she'd organised. He'd be giving up no social circle if they left the capital. Where he foresaw freedom, she envisaged stagnation.

"I'll take that as a no then, love."

"I'll tell you what you can take, and that's a look at the recycling box you made out the back. I've seen mouse droppings in it."

He'd used an old door he'd found in the shed, together with a selection of wood off-cuts and lengths of larch lap, to make the box as a summer DIY project four months ago. He was proud of the results of his efforts. The fact that small rodents had found a place of refuge for the winter didn't trouble him unduly.

"They've got in there for the winter. You can't begrudge them a bit of shelter. Poor little buggers!"

"What are you on about – little! Jenny next door's got 'em in the house. She's seen two and she says they're huge. I don't want the horrible shits in here," squealed Myra, wide-eyed.

"That bears out what I've been saying. London's not safe. Even the mice here are ripped."

"If it came to a choice between fighting off ripped mice and death by seaside bungalow, there would be only one choice. But I'm not keen on either, so get rid of the perishers."

Always the last word, thought Biggsy.

******

A roast potato bounced off Fingleton's shoulder onto the table and plopped into the cranberry sauce.

"I should be grateful if Mr Barker would keep the PE department in order," Mr Fingleton said in a raised tone, without looking up from his meal.

Archie Matthews, sitting alongside the head, picked the potato out of the sauceboat and wrapped it in a serviette. Barker, his acolytes seated either side of him, stifled a smirk by pushing a forkful of turkey into his mouth.

"High jinks have started early this year, headmaster," Archie murmured.

"The sooner I'm off home the better. Eat up, Archie."

The final day of term had arrived. There had been no lessons during the morning, only form periods and two assemblies for the handing out of student honours. The last of the pupils had left the school premises soon after one o'clock.

As was the custom, teachers were enjoying the staff Christmas dinner, the final event of the school year. They were in playful mood. Seated in festive rows at the aluminium-dining hall tables, the seventy adults were being waited on by canteen staff uncharacteristically aglow with seasonal cheer. A staff collection, taken at the end of the meal and divided amongst the half dozen ladies, would provide them with a welcome Christmas bonus. Sixth-form students had had that privilege in recent years, but the management team had decided to discontinue the tradition. Students had seen rather more of relaxed teacher behaviour the previous year than the head had thought good for them.

Lubricated by the wine Fingleton had provided out of his own pocket, the teachers were well into their first course. Biggsy had come to school by train. After a few glasses of red with the meal and more drinks afterwards at the local, he suspected that he might need to walk home later to sober himself up a little before bed. He was impressed with the meal, the canteen team having gone to the trouble of preparing his favourite tasty extras of pigs in blankets and chestnut stuffing.

Since informing Fingleton that he would be interested in applying for the head of sixth form post, he'd been in a number of quandaries. He couldn't trust that news of his being earmarked for the job wouldn't be made common knowledge by management. At some point, therefore, he'd have to share the information with his department prior to the advertisement appearing. Then there was Sarah's position. Her disappointment at being overlooked would require sympathetic handling. But the major issue was his fear of becoming a manager, an enforcer of top-down policy. Brushing aside reservations he shared with Dave about maintaining high numbers of university placements was only one problem area. There would be many more. In the eyes of many on the staff, he would be perceived as becoming 'one of them'. But, as Myra had explained to him, management needed to have some pockets of sanity. His elevation might play a part in toning down some of its more extreme policy-making ventures.

"Can't complain about this year's offering. These sprouts are superb."

Andy, sitting to his right and well into demolishing a huge main course, had interrupted his thoughts.

"Don't overdo it with them," Biggsy advised. "Remember you don't want to be embarrassing yourself in company later."

"The company I'll be keeping at the Rose and Crown tonight will be too far gone to notice any sprout-induced alimentary tract trauma."

Sarah, Beth and Bridget, sitting opposite, exchanged amused looks. Hazel Frears, loosening up after draining her first glass of wine, laughed aloud.

"Let's hear it for fibre!" grinned Sarah.

"You'll definitely hear it, Sarah," Andy confirmed.

The nearby pub on the London Road was the evening destination for those wishing to continue their end-of-term celebrations with colleagues. The saloon and lounge bars became very crowded if there were more than thirty customers on the premises. The place would be heaving when fifty teachers turned up. None of the managers ever ran the risk of putting in an appearance.

As fast as empty dinner plates were collected, bowls of Christmas pudding and jugs of hot custard appeared. The canteen staff had no intention of staying any later on the site than was necessary. The dessert course over, the noisy entrance of a familiar figure signalled a collective cheer from the diners. Mischief was afoot. A red-clad figure entered the dining hall, wheeling an office trolley stacked with Christmas presents. An even louder cheer resounded, as Dave Wheelhouse adjusted his stick-on beard and moustache and waved a greeting.

"Ho! Ho! Ho!" he bellowed. "I've got lots of lovely Chrissy presents here for all the teachers who've been good throughout the year."

He pushed the trolley into the middle of the dining hall and surveyed the mound of gifts.

"This should be fun," said Andy, pushing away his empty bowl. "Secret Santa usually has a few surprises up his sleeve."

A maximum of five pounds per gift was the general rule, but some spent a lot more. Christmas was, after all, a time for giving. Biggsy remembered the year he'd received a bottle of malt.

"What a lot of lovely pressies Santa has to give out this year!" announced Dave. "You must all have been very good girls and boys."

His audience roared its approval. Expressions of amusement and pretended concern appeared on the faces of the deserving 'girls and boys'. Dave began his rounds, receiving hugs and kisses from the female recipients of his offerings and handshakes from the men.

He approached the English Department's table and began handing out presents. Sarah took her neatly-wrapped package and chose to shake Dave's hand, a gesture that elicited cries of disapproval. Waving away the playful protests, she pulled away the wrapping to reveal a tin of Fortnum and Mason clotted cream cookies.

"Now that's such a thoughtful gift. I wonder who went to the time and trouble to buy me those?"

"You may never know, Sarah," said Andy, holding up for examination a Disney silk tie depicting Tigger in all his luminescent glory. "Just what the doctor ordered."

"I'll swap you," said Biggsy, passing him a Boots gift pack of after shave and antiperspirant.

"What's worse – smelling like a ponce or looking a twat? I think I'll keep the tie. Hey! Look at this. Something's going down."

His concentration was fixed on the top table. With a wave of his arm, he directed his colleagues to follow his gaze. Toner was motionless, a look of disgust fixed on her face as she looked down at an object on the table. A length of shiny silver plastic lay amongst the torn paper before her. She hastily covered it with the Christmas wrapping, but not before curious eyes had seen the gift she'd received.

"Oh, my God!" blurted Hazel. "It looked like a sex toy."

"If it is, somebody's got a sick sense of humour," added Beth.

Sniggers and guffaws could be heard over the excited chatter. There were one or two serious expressions from those seated close to the deputy head but, for most, the joyous mood was heightened. A hoot of laughter echoed through the hall. Toner inclined her head toward Mr Fingleton, uttered a few words, pushed her chair back and left the hall. Her gift was left on the table. A look of bewilderment on the headmaster's face, he turned to confer with Archie Matthews.

Biggsy looked at those around him, trying to gauge the reactions of his department to what had taken place. Andy put a hand across his mouth to wipe away a smile. There was movement to his right. Aaron Aimes, looking uncomfortable, was beginning to rise from his seat, but Barker stretched out an arm and pulled him down.

"Somebody should feel ashamed of himself," said Sarah. "I'm assuming it is a man who's responsible. You just can't do that."

Biggsy shook his head, sharing her disapproval. Whatever his personal thoughts about Toner, he couldn't have subjected her to a stunt amounting to sexual aggression. He was unable to join in the general hilarity at her expense. The overwhelming sense of fatigue he'd experienced before the meal returned. The idea of carrying on drinking at the pub suddenly had no appeal. He decided to make his apologies.

"Tell you what, guys, I'm feeling I'd rather duck out of the pub after this. That was unpleasant. I ought to get off home."

"You sure, mate?" Andy questioned. "That was just a bit of fun. Nothing serious. Quickly forgotten."

"Fatigue's got the better of me, and I'm not really in the mood now. There'll only be one topic of conversation tonight, and I don't want to be involved. I'll just get home and watch a bit of tunnelvision."

"Very good," Sarah complimented. "Perhaps I'll do the same. It's been a tough term. Sorry, guys, but you all go on and enjoy yourselves."

"Oh, you spoilsports!" chided Bridget. "Would it change your minds if the first round was on me?"

"A magnanimous offer, Bridget, but I think I'll give it a miss. You all go on and let your hair down," replied her head of department.

"I've got to prepare for my parents coming over Christmas, so I'll duck out, too," added Sarah.

As the meal drew to a close, the prospect of relaxing at the Rose and Crown was now uppermost in the minds of serious revellers. Groups began to move off to the staff room to gather belongings before making their way to the pub. Biggsy didn't want to hang around. He followed his team out of the dining hall.

Andy came to his side.

"Toner didn't seem very grateful for her gift from Santa this year," he murmured, in a satisfied tone.

"Can't believe what I witnessed there. Good job students no longer wait at table."

"Yes, I took that into consideration."

"How do you mean, Andy?"

"Well, I wouldn't have gone to all that trouble if there'd been kids around."

He looked Andy in the eye, waiting for his second in department to check himself and say that he'd been joking. But Andy stared back, anticipating a sly smile or ripple of laughter from his line manager.

Biggsy tried counting to ten but only reached four.

"That was a bit extreme, Andy. I'd rather you hadn't done it. Even more, I wish you hadn't told me."

"She deserved it, mate. She's been getting away with murder in this place. When I pulled Toner's name out of the hat, I knew what I had to do. She had payback coming."

"But that was beyond payback, Andy."

"You sure we're talking about the same person, mate? You've complained about her as much as anyone else."

"True. But…that was…"

He could be about to do irreparable damage to what he'd believed could never be anything but a trusted relationship. Before he continued, he checked that no one was within earshot.

"I couldn't have done that. I wish you hadn't."

"Good job you didn't then. She'll get over it and, who knows, she might be a better person for it."

A few glasses of wine seemed to be having an adverse effect on Andy's professionalism. He held his grin, in anticipation that it would be returned.

"If I were you, I wouldn't share this with anyone else, Andy."

"Absolutely. I only told you because I know you loathe her."

Biggsy could say no more. He'd need to think this through. For now, he would make a swift exit and get home to Myra. She'd see it right.

"I'm making a move, Andy. I don't want to get talked round to going to the pub. You and Mags have a good Christmas. Enjoy yourselves."

"OK, mate. Love to Myra. Have a good one."

He watched Andy, as he made his way to the staff kitchen area where a few more bottles of wine awaited those determined to embrace the holiday mood. An animated Doggy Barker raised a glass in welcome. The possibility of alcohol loosening Andy's tongue was a concern. His special delivery must remain a secret.

"Bye, Biggsy! Love to all the family," called Sarah. The rest of the English department gathered round her blew him kisses and waved madly. He forced an expression of childish glee, waved back and took his leave. As he passed the head's office, he noticed the red 'Engaged' light illuminated.

A bracing wind hit him as he opened the main door. Having excused himself from a five-hour drinking epic, he hurried down the hill for the bus home.

******

Chapter 15

"Fukkem!"

The front door slammed behind him. He was the first home. Myra wouldn't be in for half an hour and Ella's movements were unpredictable. He switched on the central heating and made himself a cup of tea. An evening at home now seemed a far more attractive prospect than the one he had planned.

Strong gusts whipping up outside howled and moaned around the house. How could anyone think that an anonymous gift of a vibrator to a female staff member would be an intelligent person's idea of fun! Worse than that, he despaired of Andy's stated conviction that his line manager would enjoy such a stunt. His open contempt for Toner had been responsible, to some degree, for Andy's actions. Nobody deserved the humiliation to which he'd unwittingly been party. But, then again, perhaps she did. To those members of staff who'd been amused by the incident, she most certainly did. The flowing alcohol hadn't helped. He recalled his advice to Dixon when listening to music on his headphones.

He'd reached the end of an exhausting term and found himself in a state of physical fatigue and emotional wretchedness.

He switched on the lights of the Christmas tree he and Ella had decorated. The cardboard fairy she'd made as a child looked down at him benevolently. He flicked the switch of the security light in the back garden and surveyed his plot from the kitchen window. The wind buffeted the branches of the rowan ash. Leaves blew across the decking Kevin had constructed.

He raised his mug to his lips. It wasn't often he was in the house on his own. In his present mood, the reclining armchair and hot tea were preferable to propping himself at a bar and drinking multiple beers. He enjoyed an occasional social drink but, the embarrassing conclusion to the school meal apart, the lethargy he was experiencing would have made him poor drinking company.

Work, family, money and sport, the staple constituents of adult conversation, did not hold his attention long. Stock opinions expressed on stock topics. He kidded himself that he was a listener, rather than a talker. The truth was otherwise. Attentiveness to others in relaxed settings required a serious mental effort on his part, and he was certain it showed. Did politeness show through the attempt at total concentration? Talk, he believed, mostly involved people making reassuring noises to each other. The substance of everyday chat was generally immaterial.

The exception, of course, was conversation with children. Their guilelessness and honesty had sustained him throughout his career. Spontaneous and ingenuous, children made for far more engaging company than adults. The dark arts of social camouflage were, as yet, unknown to most of them. Few teachers shared his belief that providing opportunities for children to think aloud was the exciting part of his job. Most just wanted to find effective ways of shutting them up.

Sixth formers readily took up his 'ninety-nine per cent of everything is crap' challenge. He would pick any topic, from sitcoms to politics, and assert that most of what was on offer was rubbish. He then left it to the students to counter this claim. The result: genuinely exciting interaction. He'd found himself totally out on a limb when he'd included 'Friends' on the crap list in a chat about sitcoms. The torrent of scorn that had assailed him had been truly memorable. The assertion that 'The Royle Family' and 'Porridge' were examples of vastly superior entertainment had prompted total incomprehension.

"But nothing happens in 'The Royle Family'," sneered one brave youth.

"You're absolutely right," he'd responded. "That's what life is like on a daily basis for many people throughout their lives. Have you ever heard of the Theatre of the Absurd?"

On that theme, the whole term appeared to have taken a turn for the absurd. His belief that Toner was the only thing between himself and a quiet professional life had been blown out of the water. He would have to deal with the prospect of an unexpected pastoral move, with potential for promotion, and the likelihood of a changed dynamic in his relationship with Andy. Were he to take up the head of sixth form post, he would be required to recommend a replacement head of English. Andy was no longer the automatic replacement.

The front door banged.

"Anybody home?" called Ella.

"Only me," he answered.

Ella appeared in the doorway, rearranging her windswept hair.

"I thought you were out on the booze tonight, Dad, on your St Saviour's Christmas bender?"

"I should be, but I wasn't in the mood for a mad end to the term."

"Ooh, you old Scrooge. You should have gone."

"I'm not taking any lessons from that old wife-abuser, Dickens, on how I should celebrate the festive season," he quipped.

"A wife abuser! What do you mean?"

"Oh, you're asking what the Dickens I mean," Biggsy grinned. "A-Level Lit. students aren't ready for that information yet, so best sit on it for a few years."

"Don't know what you're on about, Dad. But, really, you should have gone along."

"I know, but some stupid things happened at work today and my Christmas spirit evaporated. I'd rather be with you and Mum here this evening."

"That's nice, Dad. Do you fancy another cuppa while I make one for myself?"

"All night long, Ella."

A key turned in the lock of the front door and it flew open. Myra staggered in with two plastic carrier bags. She groaned, as she pushed the door to with her backside. She managed to place one bag on the hall floor, but the handle of the other snapped and the contents tumbled out. Ignoring the devastation she had created over the engineered-wood flooring, she kicked off her shoes, pulled off her parka jacket, threw it over the bottom bannister post and hobbled to the lounge.

"I can hear the kettle, chaps. I'll have a redbush too. Someone pick that up," she said in a whisper.

Biggsy and Ella exchanged looks of playful concern as Myra walked past them into the lounge and spread herself over the sofa.

"TLC alert," he announced.

They followed her, expressions of concern tempered by the idea that this could be Mum's way of having a little fun. But she wasn't play acting. Her face was pale, and her top lip showed beads of perspiration.

"You feeling OK, love?"

"Not good at all. I'm coming down with something. Think it's the office flu. Can't believe I managed the shopping. What are you doing here, anyway? Thought it was your late-night shindig with the staff?"

"Didn't feel up to it. The dinner was a bit of a downer."

He suddenly hoped that the tiredness he was feeling wasn't an omen of illness for him too. Myra stood up, went to the mirror over the fireplace, stuck out her tongue and studied it.

"Looks as though we're in for a rough Christmas," she concluded in a mournful monotone. "It may be off altogether if I don't pick up."

"Look, you go and lie down upstairs, Mum, and I'll bring you a cup of tea after I've put the shopping away," volunteered Ella.

"I'll do just that. Help yourselves to any of the food I've bought. Nothing for me."

This is it, thought Biggsy, *the third disaster of the day: vibrator, Andy, flu.*

He decided it was Dylan time. He switched on the hi-fi, dug out a CD from the rack, slipped it into the tray and turned up the volume. The mellow guitar intro of 'Not Dark Yet' had the intended soothing effect. At such times as this, he was both persuaded and consoled by The Jester's philosophy: we are all in it up to our necks in the cosmic joke of The Creation.

Next term could bloody well wait.

******

But it couldn't.

As he shaved, he made some mental calculations. He had sixty GCSE and twenty-four A-level mock examination papers to mark over the Christmas break. At half an hour a paper, that amounted to forty-two hours of work he'd have to find over the 'holiday' period. With twelve days left before returning to work, that meant three and a half hours of marking per day, including Christmas Day. He'd have to make a start that afternoon.

The doorbell rang. He wondered whether he should answer it in his pyjamas. It could only be the postman this early at nine o'clock. Him or somebody wanting to re-lay his drive. He wiped away foam from his half-shaved face and hurried downstairs.

His surprise couldn't have been greater when he opened the door and saw his father-in-law on the doorstep. He rarely went anywhere without Annie.

"My God, son, you look a mess out of civvies. Nobody else up and about yet, then?"

"Wasn't expecting it to be you, Russell, and this early in the day. We had a rough night. Myra's still in bed with a Christmas bug. I've left her to sleep on. Ella's not up yet, either. Anyway, come on in."

"I will, but I won't stop long. I'm off to the health centre for my annual check. Myra can't be too bad. She's a tough one."

"I hope she's over the worst. She's having a tough time. I was up at the centre recently for a prostate check. Came back all clear, but it takes an age for me to pee."

"You're not alone there, my lad. But we suffer in silence like good soldiers."

"Anyway, it's Myra I'm worried about at the minute. She needs to rest if she's going to be fit and able for Christmas."

"Ah, now that's what I've come about. We're coming to yours on the day, so I wondered if you could look after the present I've bought for Annie, so that she can open it here? I don't want it left at home in case she finds it."

Biggsy was impressed that his father-in-law was going to such lengths with the gift to his wife. Perhaps he had a romantic side that nobody in the family knew about.

"No problem, Russell. Where is it?"

"It's in the car. The shop assistant put it in the boot when I bought it yesterday. It's a bit delicate and I'd appreciate a hand getting it out."

"I'll have to go upstairs and throw on some clothes, then. Just wait in the kitchen for a few minutes. Sure you don't want a cup of tea?"

Russell was sure he didn't. Two minutes after Biggsy had made his way upstairs, he reappeared in jeans and a fleece.

"Right, let's do this thing, Russell. Sounds as though you've gone to a lot of trouble to surprise Annie."

"Too true. It cost a packet."

They went outside, and Russell clicked the boot lid open.

"There it is," he said proudly, pointing at a large box. "A coffee machine. Top of the range. Four hundred pounds it cost."

"A coffee machine!" exclaimed Biggsy. "I didn't know you drank a lot of coffee."

"Oh, I love one mid-morning. Annie's getting quite the taste for it too."

Biggsy scratched his head, smiled, and managed to keep his thoughts to himself. He shifted the box in the boot to get the best purchase before lifting it out and carrying it indoors.

"Thanks, son. Glad to get shot of that for the time being. You couldn't do me a favour and wrap it, could you? It's a bit of a tricky one with my arthritic fingers. Well, I'd better get myself off to see the doc. Give my love to the girls."

******

Christmas Day had gone well for him so far. Myra had been delighted with the gold necklace and large bottle of perfume. She'd been especially pleased that he'd remembered to buy eau de parfum, as opposed to eau de toilette. Besides the gift of a voucher toward a new suit from Standish and Son and a novel he'd asked for, she'd promised him a night of passion he'd never forget. He immediately began trying to remember where he'd put his libido over the past few weeks. Wherever it was, it needed reactivating.

Ella had wanted cash as usual, her argument being that she could buy bargains of her choice in the Boxing Day sales. Thus, there could be no chance of her being disappointed with a present she didn't want. Children were more hard-nosed when it came to receiving these days, he decided. She didn't ask her parents if they wanted cash. The idea would never have occurred to her. Nevertheless, they appreciated the thought she'd put into her gifts: a critical work on Thomas Hardy for him, and a cream silk blouse for Myra.

It was ten thirty, and each member of the family was in a separate room of the house. Ella had stated an intention to shower, but she'd already spent an hour in the lounge messaging friends. Sitting in her pink fluffy dressing gown on the sofa, legs tucked under her, she'd be on her mobile for another hour at least. Sipping her second coffee of the day, she kept half an eye on a TV romcom she'd recorded.

Wrestling with a six-pound turkey in the kitchen, Myra was now fighting fit. She was extra pleased this Christmas morning on two counts. First, the five-day flu from which she'd been suffering had caused a loss of appetite, and she'd lost four pounds in weight. Second, she was officially celebrating her promotion at the hospital. Showered and dressed, and in the best of moods, she wanted all preparations for the meal to be completed before her parents arrived at midday.

Biggsy, also washed and dressed, had sneaked up to the office. His plan was to make full use of the next ninety minutes by marking three GCSE mock exam papers. His only fear was that Myra would ask for his help down below. If she simply called for him up the stairs, no one need ever know how his private festive celebrations were going. If she came searching for him and discovered him hard at it with the red pen, there could be all hell to pay. It was a risk he had to take.

An hour into his task and oblivious to any extraneous sounds, he was taken by surprise, as the office door was slowly pushed open.

"You little sod! I thought it was too quiet. What the hell do you think you're doing? It's Christmas Day for heaven's sake!"

Remonstration was pointless. He couldn't have felt any more guilty if he'd been caught letting down Fingleton's tyres.

"Sorry, love. I just came in here to check emails and suddenly found the pen in my hand. Picking up an exam paper was pure reflex over which I had no control."

"Well, I hate to spoil your Christmas, but I need the table laid up downstairs. Pronto! They'll be here in half an hour."

She'd taken it well. He surmised that she'd become so accustomed to his anti-social aberrations that she now took his obsessive-compulsive marking disorder in her stride.

"Come on down and give me a hand – now! And I want to see some Christmas spirit. Forget Saint Saviour's and concentrate on Saint Nick for half an hour."

He followed her dutifully down the stairs.

******

"This stuff is incredible!" exclaimed Biggsy.

Russell had his weaknesses, but alcohol was not one of them. He'd brought round a bottle of Drambuie to aid digestion and relaxation after the Christmas dinner. Annie, Myra and Ella weren't keen on the taste and were sticking to the white wine. But his son-in-law, who'd never tried it before, was struggling off the sofa to fetch a refill.

"It is a tasty drop," enthused Russell. "I used to drink nothing but malt, but I've lost the taste for it in my old age. I can manage the occasional nip of this on special occasions."

The family meal over, everyone had retired to the lounge to raise their glasses to Her Majesty. Forgetting to remove his paper hat in the company of the queen, Biggsy tried to focus on her as she summarised the nation's year. Austerity was biting, but she seemed in good spirits, much like himself.

Annie and Russell had pride of place, an armchair each, whilst the rest squeezed up together on the sofa. Ella was close to falling asleep, the exertion of focusing for most of the morning on her phone beginning to take its toll. Myra's full concentration was on the television screen.

"That woman's stamina is amazing. I can't imagine what her life must be like," she declared.

"I agree," concurred Annie, raising her glass respectfully. "She's an example to the nation."

"Really amazing," said Biggsy, studying the label of the bottle. "It says here that it's been around since 1745. I'd never even heard of it."

A radiance suffused his body, and a warm fug filled his head. He hadn't felt this relaxed in an age.

He was unaware that he'd wobbled, as he topped up his glass, but Russell noticed.

"You'll have to take care with that, my boy. It's got a bit of a kick. You want to make sure you see the evening out."

"Just one more to set me up for the big film, Russell. I don't need to bother about whether this is shaken or stirred. In fact, it's so good it should be available on prescription."

He laughed too long and alone at his joke.

"That would certainly go down well with me," agreed his father-in-law. "Can't see any chance of it happening the way the economy's going, though."

"Yep, it's not good. I thought education was supposed to be ring-fenced against this new austerity programme. Our departmental capitation for buying textbooks was cut this year. I'm having to ask boys to bring a roll of sticky tape to school to do repairs on the tatty copies we can't afford to throw out."

"That's scandalous," said Annie. "Did any parents complain about having to send their sons to school with sticky tape?"

Biggsy turned to her, eyes pressed shut and grinning.

"Only joking about the tape, Annie. I have to do repairs of that sort. Good old dogsbody, that's me."

"Oh, you are a wag, love," added Myra, without smiling. "Come and sit yourself down before you fall down."

"That was the tastiest Christmas dinner you've ever cooked, bar none," he complimented, sinking into the spot beside his wife.

"Let me put that drink on the table beside you, dearest, before you spill it."

******

"I'm telling you I haven't peed since yesterday evening."

Biggsy looked without enthusiasm at the Boxing Day meal Myra had prepared. They were eating alone, Ella having disappeared to the sales with her loot. His lower abdomen had swelled and was causing him discomfort.

"In that case, you're not drinking enough water. You overdid it yesterday with the booze. Can't believe how much of that Drambuie you drank. It's supposed to be a liqueur, sipped slowly, not downed like a shot."

"Yes, sorry about that. I did rather embarrass myself this year. I understand my snoring interrupted everyone's enjoyment of the film."

"I apologised to Mum and Dad when they left. Fortunately, Dad seemed to think he was partly to blame for introducing you to a spirit that you'd no experience of. I haven't seen you in such a state for years."

"Was I that bad?"

"We managed to get to the end of the film, thanks to me jabbing you in the ribs every time you started sawing logs."

"Hey, that may explain why I've got this pain down below. You may have ruptured my spleen."

"Don't be so soft. Any pain you're suffering is of your own making."

"Perhaps I was subconsciously making up for the fact that I didn't go on the staff bender when we broke up."

"I think it was more a case of you just being unconsciously out of your head. And what happened to the night of passion I was looking forward to? That went down the pan."

"I'm truly sorry about that, love, but I really do wish that something else would go down the pan."

Myra poured a glass of water and held it before him.

"Drink all of that now," she ordered. "Hopefully, it will activate your bladder and flush everything through. Then we can reschedule what I'd planned for last night."

He pursed his lips, took the glass and did as he was told.

******

"Hello, Mum. We're still at the hospital."

Myra watched her husband squirming in discomfort, as he lay on the bed in a small curtained-off section of a side ward.

"Yes, we're still in casualty," she continued. "He's been unable to urinate for over twenty-four hours now, poor thing. We were three hours in the waiting room and now we're waiting in a cubicle for a doctor."

Standing had become difficult for Biggsy. Lying down was the best way to get some relief from the pressure on his bladder. He was worried, despite his recent negative PSA result. Prostate problems were serious, and he knew he was in a serious condition.

"I hate hospitals," he said. "It's not just the smell. You go in to be treated for one problem and come out with half a dozen more."

"No, we've no idea yet exactly what may have set this off. He blames his job. Says he never drank enough fluid because he couldn't leave classes for loo breaks. Anyway, Mum, I'll get back to you as soon as we've any news. I hope we get seen before midnight, but I can't see anything happening quickly on Boxing Night."

"I can't wait until midnight. My bladder'll burst before then."

"Ella's on her way. I managed to get hold of her eventually. She was out with girlfriends celebrating their success at the sales. Bye then for now, Mum. I won't ring if we're not seen before twelve. You'll be in bed."

"You shouldn't have made me drink that extra glass of water."

"OK, then. I will ring after midnight if you're going to be waiting up, anyway. Bye, Mum."

**TO BE CONTINUED
IN 'CLASS CONFLICT'**